Intel® Internet Exchange Architecture and Applications

A Practical Guide to IXP2XXX Network Processors

Bill Carlson

Publisher: Rich Bowles
Managing Editor: David B. Spencer
Copyeditor: Lynn Putnam
Text Design & Composition: Marianne Phelps
Graphic Art: Donna Lawless (illustrations), Ted Cyrek (cover)

Printed in the United States of America

    10 9 8 7 6 5 4 3 2 1

First Printing, May 2003

To my wonderful wife Lily, my daughter Lauren, and my son CW

Contents

Chapter 4   **Intel® IXA Microarchitecture 81**

Foreword

Today, there is a tremendous opportunity for flexible system platforms that provide telecommunication and data communication vendors with the capability for high performance cell and packet processing. The current economic challenges are causing a very careful inspection of communications industry core competencies. As very deep submicron ASIC design gets more costly and time-consuming, it is attractive to the communication industry to seek alternative means of providing rich services with higher capability. With the advent of the IXP2400 and IXP2800 family of Intel network processors, the promise of network processors is ready to be fulfilled.

Intel is delivering the second generation of the Intel® Internet Exchange Architecture (Intel® IXA), which provides all the hardware and software building blocks to enable high performance communication services. Intel IXA has paid careful attention to developing a software framework that communication vendors can employ to preserve software investments for current and future Intel network processors. The flexible combination of the IXP2XXX network processors and the software framework enables a tremendous range of applications, such as IPv4/IPv6 Forwarding, Diffserv, and MPLS capabilities for Packet Over Sonet (POS), Ethernet, and ATM. Additional software framework applications include: Radio Network Controller (RNC) apps, TCP termination, IPSec Tunneling, and SCTP.

The key to this flexibility and performance is the innovation incorporated in the IXP2XXX family of network processors. This book guides you through the hardware constructs of the IXP2XXX product line, as well as the two major software paradigms available to unleash these hardware capabilities: Pool of Threads programming or Hyper Task Chaining (HTC).

I have had the pleasure of working with the author of this book for the last several years. Bill is a field specialist responsible for IXP2XXX product line customers in the western United States. He has introduced me to many of his customers, and through his active engagements with his customers, he provides a user-focused approach to explaining the hows and whys of the new network processor family. Bill brings to this explanation a clear, precise style that comes from his friendly and engaging personality. I truly believe readers will find this book both insightful and useful.

Software and hardware developers using the IXP2XXX network processors will find the organization of this book engaging. Starting with fundamentals of data plane processing, the external architecture, and the internal micro-architecture, the book builds a clear picture of how a designer employs coherent parallel processing. Bill then moves on to describe a software producer or consumer model that is enabled with hardware-managed rings and lists. Then, once all the fundamental hardware constructs are understood, Bill describes the programming models. Then, he explains the portability framework for software investment preservation, and finally, performance considerations.

I am pleased to introduce this book to you and am satisfied that Bill has expended the effort to provide a rich explanation of the network processors, so that users and researchers of network processing can optimize their IXP2XXX product line experience.

Matthew Adiletta

Intel Fellow and Director of Communication Processor Architecture, Intel

Preface

Working as an Intel Field Application Engineer (FAE) Specialist for Network Processors for the past 5 years, it's been my privilege to talk to scores of customers and developers in the western United States about Intel's network processor products. During this time, many developers have expressed their desire to better understand the architectural foundation of these network processors through "deep dive" technical training. Developers want to know the details of the network architecture before they actually code their application software or make a decision to use the network processor in the first place. During the summer of 2002, several architects, technical marketing engineers, and FAE-Specialists trained dozens of development engineers at one of our larger customers. The actual decision to use IXP2XXX network processors was made by a smaller group of this customer's system architects, and they wanted the rest of their engineering organizations to "get up to speed" on the network processor architecture before they began developing products with it. At another customer site, we presented the IXP2XXX network processor architecture to the Chief Technology Officer, the Vice President of Engineering, and other engineering managers. Before deciding which network processor to use, they wanted to understand the architectural details, and then follow up with training on the software development tools and software applications. They wanted the architecture training so they wouldn't have to wade through hundreds of pages of documentation contained in a dozen user manuals.

This book is the result of those training sessions and many other customer requests for a foundational architectural understanding of the IXP2XXX product line of network processors. Much of the material in this book came from the material we've used for on-site customer training. Additionally, the book includes newer information that hasn't yet been published, especially information on performance estimation techniques and software programming models. Many developers already have this architectural knowledge and are past this stage of their learning. For them, this book probably duplicates what they already know. They might be already to jump in and start programming, and they only need to know how to get started with coding real-life applications. For these developers, the *IXP2400/IXP2800 Programming* book by Erik J. Johnson and Aaron R. Kunze offers valuable programming and practical insights for software developers targeting these new network processors.

Questions Answered by Each Chapter

As I mentioned earlier, this book combines the answers to a number of customers' questions. The following summary tells you the questions answered in each chapter. Use it for guidance to the chapters that are most appropriate for your own unique needs.

Chapter 1, "Introduction to the Architecture," gives you the basic concepts and poses the basic problem of packet processing.

Chapter 2, "Packet Processing Basics," answers the question "What does a network processor do?" with an examination of overall systems architecture and a description of the differences between the management, control, and data plane. The chapter gives you some basic descriptions of data plane processing and could help those who are new to these concepts. Experienced networking development engineers probably want to skip this chapter.

Chapter 3, "External Architecture," answers the question "What does a system based on IXP2XXX network processors look like?" The chapter traces the external architecture of the IXP2400, IXP2800 and the IXP2850 network processors, and describes the various buses and external interfaces, such as memory, PCI, and the Media and Switch Fabric (MSF) unit. Special emphasis is placed on the MSF interface, as this is the primary packet data interface through the network processor. Several common system configurations are discussed, which illustrates the various ways to architect different Intel IXA-based systems.

Chapter 4, "Internal Architecture," answers the question "What exactly do the IXP2XXX network processors look like on the inside?" It describes the internal blocks of the IXP2400, IXP2800, and IXP2850 network processors at a functional level and each of the internal buses, to give a solid understanding of how these functional units interoperate. This chapter gives special emphasis to the chassis, microengines, and internal operation of the Media and Switch Fabric (MSF) because these functional units directly touch packets during data plane processing.

Chapter 5, "Parallel Processing," answers the question: "What is multiprocessing and multithreading and how are these techniques used to maximize performance?" The network processors in the IXP2XXX product line have solved the critical serial stream-processing problem that is common in parallel processing architectures. This chapter describes the problem and shows you techniques to cope with it.

Chapter 6, "Managing Data Structures," answers the question "How can I hit line speed in rich processing applications when complex memory operations are required?" Because these network processors use a store-and-forward architecture, having a very efficient mechanism to buffer packets and data structures in external memory is critical. This chapter explains how that mechanism works.

Chapter 7, "Mapping Tasks to Microengines," answers the question: "How are applications mapped to Intel IXA?" The chapter explains two programming models and when they should be used. The Pool of Threads model is most suitable for applications where maximum flexibility, intuitive programming techniques are needed for moderate line rate systems. Hyper Task Chaining offers potential for the highest performance systems with predictable processing stages.

Chapter 8, "Performance Considerations," answers the question "How is network processor performance calculated?" Through an examination of the major internal resources of the network processors, you explore resource budgeting and ways to calculate performance headroom.

Naming Conventions

This book is full of unavoidable acronyms and new technical names. Please see the Glossary for help whenever you need it.

It is always difficult to deal with lots of related but different processors. Throughout this book, you will find the phrases "IXP2XXX family of processors" or "IXP2XXX network processors" used for general references to the IXP2400, IXP2800, and IXP2850 network processors.

Acknowledgements

Writing this book on Intel's newest network processors has been a real privilege. It has been a rewarding experience to express the design innovation and creativity of the hardware and software architects in Intel's Network Processor Division. As such, this book is about the work of many, many Intel architects and engineers. In a sense, I am just telling their story. Much of the material in this book came from the architecture team that defined the Intel® Internet Exchange Architecture. Because so many were involved on such a large and complex architectural development project, it is nearly impossible to name every contributor. However, a few deserve special acknowledgement.

Throughout this book, many concepts, ideas, and materials came from Matthew Adiletta, Intel Fellow and Director of the Intel IXA Hardware Architecture. Referencing each of Matthew's specific contributions would require several pages. Suffice it to say, the Intel IXA hardware architecture is his brainchild and his influence is felt through every page of this book. Alok Kumar, software architect, gave me much assistance with the section in Chapter 1 on the IXA Portability Framework and with Chapter 7 on programming models. Much of this information hasn't been documented before and I deeply appreciate the time Alok spent helping me to understand these difficult concepts. Our Technical Marketing Engineers (TMEs) contributed much of the material in Chapters 4 and 6, specifically the material on the Media and Switch Fabric Interface and SRAM Q_Array unit that came from training material that our TME organization painstakingly produced.

I also want to thank the editor of Intel Press, David Spencer, for his help and guidance throughout this past year while getting this book to print. David's editorial support and help was invaluable and very much appreciated. I also want to thank Jack Johnson, FAE-Specialist, who technically reviewed every page and paragraph of the manuscript. This book was also reviewed by a team of Intel Architects to whom I owe much thanks.

Of course, this book would not have been possible without the Intel Internet Exchange Architecture existing in the first place. Matthew Adiletta led the hardware architecture team, including Mark Rosenbluth, Debra Bernstein, Gilbert Wolrich, and Hugh Wilkinson. Raj Yavatkar, Director of Intel IXA Software Architecture, led the software architecture team, including Don Hooper, Uday Naik, Larry Huston, Duke Tallam, Travis Schluessler, Prashant Chandra, and Adrian Georgescu.

Finally, I want to thank my friend Matthew Adiletta for inspiring this book. His enthusiasm, dedication, and technical achievements are felt throughout Intel's Network Processing Group, and he has been a role model for all of us.

Chapter 1

Introduction to the Architecture

With the introduction of second generation network processors, developers are demanding greater capabilities than they received from earlier versions. The new processors run more sophisticated applications, such as advanced quality-of-service (QoS), which performs such tasks as policing, multi-protocol conversion, and content-aware packet inspection and classification.

Developers are considering sophisticated and innovative uses for network processors, such as video distribution, iSCSI storage gateways, virtual private network (VPN) edge servers and other secure content processing applications. At the same time, data rates continue to climb past OC-12 or gigabit rates to OC-48 towards 10-gigabit ethernet. Developers also require network processors to scale from the low end to these higher data rates. Scalability is critical. Developers want to use a single common architecture across multiple platforms of varying line rates. Maintaining software portability is also a critical concern so developers can preserve their large software investment. In summary, the four critical metrics developers require of a network processor are:

- Flexibility
- High Performance
- Scalability
- Software Portability

To address these requirements, Intel developed the IXP2XXX product line and the Intel® IXA Software Portability Framework. Together, these are the Intel® Internet Exchange Architecture (Intel® IXA).

What is the Intel® Internet Exchange Architecture?

The IXP2XXX product line of network processors and the Intel IXA Portability Framework are the two key components of the Intel® IXA, as shown in Figure 1.1. For those wanting additional insight and understanding of IXP2XXX network processors, refer to the paper "The Next Generation of Intel IXP Network Processors" (Adiletta et al. 2002).

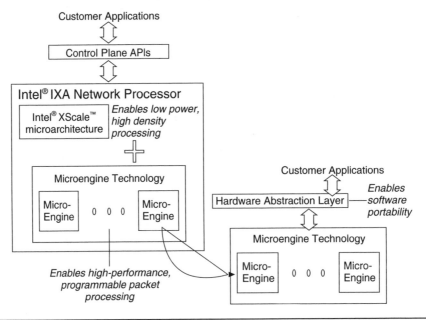

Figure 1.1   The Intel® IXA Model

Intel IXA protects a developer's software investment by maintaining architectural consistency from one processor generation to the next. The key components in this definition are:

- Microengines handle the bulk of packet processing tasks by executing software algorithms, assisted by special-purpose hardware acceleration. These microengines handle the "fast-path" or data plane packet processing.

- The Intel® XScale™ microarchitecture processor runs a real-time operating system (RTOS) and controls the overall functionality of the network processor. The Intel XScale processor interfaces to the rest of the chassis or system. The Intel XScale core executes lower level control applications, such as signaling stacks and communicating with other processors in the system. These functions are commonly called the *Control Plane*.

■ The Intel® IXA Portability Framework allows data plane software written for the Intel XScale core and microengines to be reusable and portable among the various IXP2XXX network processors. This software framework consists of modular Intel XScale technology and microengine building blocks supported by a hardware abstraction layer (HAL) along with industry standard APIs. These APIs allow signaling stacks from various suppliers to be ported to Intel IXA with a minimum time and effort.

The architecture meets the requirements of the developer in the following ways:

■ *Flexibility*. Intel IXA is completely programmable, its software accelerated by several low-level hardware functions. Using multiple software programmable microengines and external memory, processors in the IXP2XXX family can perform a variety of flexible protocol processing functions. In addition, the flexible architecture supports two different software paradigms. The choice of which to use depends on your end application. If your application requires an intuitive run-to-completion model, use the *Pool of Threads* model. When you want to extract every last bit of performance for the most demanding applications, use the *Hyper Task Chaining* model. Intel IXA allows you to choose the software architecture that best fits your needs.

■ *Software Portability*. Intel IXA uses the Microengine HAL and the Intel IXA Portability Framework to achieve software portability. Software abstractions enable you to port software from one processor in the IXP2XXX product line to another. Having a portable software API enables rapid code migration with minimal effort.

■ *High Performance*. Intel IXA can handle complex functions even at OC-192 data rates. The modern processor's compliance with Moore's law is enabling higher and higher clock rates. The IXP2800 processor reaches 1.4-gigahertz clock rates using a standard, high volume 0.13 micron manufacturing process. With advanced 90-nanometer lithography, frequencies reaching 2.0 gigahertz will be realized, enabling the IXP2XXX product line to process faster line rates, such as OC-768, or to lower overall systems cost through functional integration, such as Media Access

Controllers (MACs). As clock rates continually increase, memory latencies will have a greater adverse effect on performance. Intel IXA addresses these negative effects with special hardware and software functionality.

◼ *Scalable*. Intel IXA scales to meet customer requirements from OC-3 to OC-192 bit-rates and beyond. Scalability is more than just dialing up the clock rate, however. As clock rates increase, their relation to external memory latencies becomes a critical system-level performance concern. Thus, scalability must be addressed with a thorough architectural approach. Intel's new Microengine Version 2 (MEv2) and internal architecture provide scalability from the lowest to the highest bit rates with specially built Intel IXA hardware to address the harmful effects of memory latencies.

Why the IXP2XXX Network Processors?

You might wonder why Intel introduced this new family of processors when the IXP1200 processor has become a leading network processor. Very simply, developers required additional functionality from a network processor. Secondarily, increasing data rates caused a significant mismatch with the memory latencies of even the fastest memory technologies currently available. The IXP1200 processor had several architectural characteristics that minimized the effects of memory latencies, such as multithreading and an advanced SRAM controller, but the processor needed extensions to enable a software-based packet processing paradigm that could scale past 10 gigabits per second. Where the IXP1200 family of processors was effective to OC12 and gigabit rates, the new network processors in the IXP2XXX product line are designed for the advanced packet processing requirements at 10+ gigabits per second.

With today's general-purpose microprocessors exceeding 3.0 gigahertz, (such as the Intel® Pentium® 4 processor), it may appear that increasing the frequency of the network processor is the best way to increase its performance. But just cranking up the clock rate on the IXP2XXX network processors isn't enough to solve the highest speed packet-processing problems. The IXP2800 processor, with 16 microengines running at 1.4 GHz, provides throughput that exceeds 22,400 MIPS. However, this capacity alone isn't sufficient for the advanced packet processing applications required at bit rates exceeding OC-48. A processor must clear the common technical hurdle of high-speed packet processing, known as the *serial stream-processing (SSP) problem*, which can seriously degrade performance if not directly addressed. The SSP problem is common with parallel processing architectures. Intel IXA provides the solution to this critical problem in the hardware with associated software programming techniques. The solution to the SSP problem must overcome two challenges, as follows:

■ *The Challenge of Dependence.* When interdependent, related streams of packets are associated with common data structures, a lock contention problem occurs. A lock contention problem occurs when two or more processes simultaneously want to update common data structures. One process is forced to wait until the previous process has completed. This *serialization* cripples performance because it removes the performance benefits of parallel processing.

■ *The Challenge of Independence.* When independent and non-related packets are associated with common data structures, the serialization problem previously described can occur. This causes performance degradation when multiple processes concurrently access a common data structure.

First generation network processors used parallel processing and pipelining to achieve their performance advantages over traditional RISC processors. These network processors relied on the fact that, statistically, the majority of network packets are unrelated to each other. However, these first generation processors overestimated the unrelated nature of the packets. They either ignored or minimized the significant amount of inter-packet or inter-process dependencies for some of the most complex processing tasks. As a result, performance levels did not meet the expectations of many network designers, whether the network processor was fully software programmable or used a more fixed-function design. At OC-12 and gigabit-per-second line rates, such performance issues are manageable. At the higher OC-48 and OC-192 rates, these conditions can become completely unacceptable. The IXP2XXX network processors solve very challenging serial stream processing problems at these high line rates.

What is the IXP2XXX Product Line?

As the first three processors in the second generation of Intel IXA, the IXP2400, IXP2800, and IXP2850 processors meet the need for richer packet-processing requirements. The IXP2400 processor targets line rates from OC-3 to OC-12 and the IXP2800 processor targets line rates from OC-12 to OC-192. The IXP2850 processor is similar to the IXP2800 processor, and it has integrated crypto capabilities. All members of the IXP2XXX network processor family share the same fundamental processing paradigm. By processing packets entirely in software that is supported by low-level hardware acceleration, these network processors achieve maximum flexibility. The same IXP2XXX network processor can be the hardware platform for a high end IPSec-enabled VPN or layer 3, diffserv-enabled router.

Customer-specific software algorithms offer more flexibility than fixed-function hardware-based processors. Many developers want to use their own traffic-shaping algorithms or tailor their congestion management functionality. Developers also need to use industry standard interfaces between the network processor and widely available third-party components such as framers, MACs, coprocessors and switch fabrics. So, the IXP2XXX network processors can be programmed to adapt to these different algorithms and interfaces.

Figure 1.2 illustrates the internal architecture of the IXP2800 processor. The IXP2400 and the IXP2850 processors are variations of this architecture.

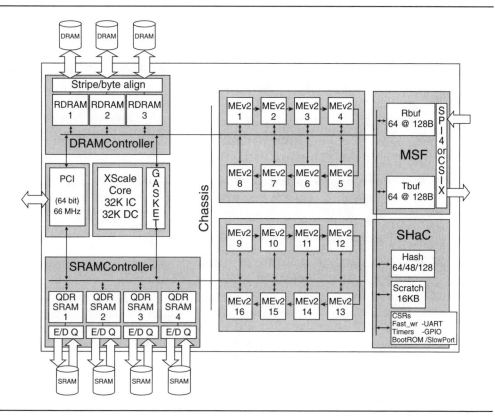

Figure 1.2   IXP2800 Internal Architecture

Microengines

The microengines are based on the latest MEv2 architecture. The micro-engines process the packets at line rate; as such, this processing is often called the fast path or data plane. The microengines are *multithreaded*, which means that they can manage multiple tasks simultaneously. While each MEv2 has only one execution unit, they can manage up to eight tasks or contexts simultaneously. While the microengine is processing one task, the other seven tasks are asleep waiting for memory or I/O accesses to complete. The IXP2850 and the IXP2800 processors have 16 MEv2 microengines. The IXP2400 processor has eight.

Because the microengines perform fast-path processing, they need to operate at the highest speed possible with hardware acceleration for specific functions. The MEv2 runs up to 1.4 gigahertz on the IXP2800 and the IXP2850 processors and up to 600 megahertz on the IXP2400 processor. The MEv2 architecture enhances the MEv1 architecture that was used on the IXP1200 by adding additional instruction and data memory space as well as several hardware acceleration units, such as:

■ Content Addressable Memory (CAM) to quickly determine inter-thread dependencies.

■ Next Neighbor registers allow for fast and low latency data and message passing from one microengine to its next neighbor.

■ Generalized Thread Signals (GTS) enables much easier inter-process communication.

■ Cyclic Redundancy Check (CRC) generator for error protection for ATM, Ethernet, and other layer 2 protocols.

■ Global and local timers for packet time stamping and general use.

■ Pseudo Random Number generator to enable congestion avoidance algorithms such as Random Early Detection (RED).

■ Reflector reads and writes for direct MEv2 to MEv2 communication.

Intel® XScale™ Microarchitecture Core

The Intel XScale core typically manages the control plane of the network processor where it processes exception packets, chip configuration and control, as well as managing route table entries and running signaling stacks. Because the type of packet processing the Intel XScale core performs is typically out of the primary data path, it is often called the "slow path." However, in several protocols, such as terminating TCP/IP, setting up Network Address Translation (NAT), and IPSec connections, the Intel XScale core needs to process the initial packet of a flow or connection as quickly as possible to enable subsequent packets in that flow to be processed by the microengines at line rate. As such, the Intel XScale core needs to run at the highest clock rate possible; its frequency is 600 megahertz on the IXP2400 processor and 700 megahertz on the IXP28X0 processor.

Media and Switch Fabric Interface

The Media and Switch Fabric (MSF) interface is the primary interface for transferring network packets. The MSF connects to MACs and framers with industry standard interfaces such as UTOPIA and SPI-3 (for the IXP2400 processor) and SPI-4.2 (for the IXP2800 processor and IXP2850 processor). The MSF also interfaces to switch fabrics, either with traditional SPI interfaces or with the CSIX interface standardized by the Network Processing Forum.

Because the MSF is in between the MACs and framers and the microengines, which handle the bulk of the packet processing, the MSF needs to buffer the packets effectively as they enter and leave the chip. This buffering is required because of small variations in processing rates and packet arrival rates. To accommodate the difference, the RBUF buffers packets that are received from the network and the TBUF buffers packets prior to transmitting them. Because you can configure the IXP2XXX family of network processors for a variety of system architectures, the buffer memory of the MSF needs to be partitioned so that it can separate the UTOPIA or SPI network traffic from the CSIX switch fabric data and control information. This partitioning is critical to maintain line rate performance without dropping packets.

SRAM Interface

The SRAM interface is used for tables, buffer descriptors, free buffer lists and for interfacing to coprocessors such as Ternary Content Addressable Memories (TCAMs) and classification coprocessors. Typically, a programmer (or Intel's microC compiler) uses SRAM to store variables and packet state information. Therefore, the SRAM interface needs to have the highest bandwidth possible as well as the lowest latency. The bandwidth must be as high as possible to support dozens of microengine threads (a total of 128 threads in the IXP28X0 processor) as well as to support higher end applications where multiple SRAM accesses per packet are needed to maintain complex state data structures. The SRAM unit uses the latest Quad Data Rate (QDR) SRAM technology to achieve these high bandwidth requirements. The IXP28X0 processor supports four channels of QDR SRAM while the IXP2400 processor supports two channels.

The SRAM unit also needs to have the lowest latency possible from the simplest to the more complex tasks. Very often, memory locations need to be incremented or decremented, values added or subtracted to/from them, or swapped with register values. Other more complex functions such as managing linked lists and ring buffers need to be handled both simply and with the lowest latency possible. As such, the SRAM unit of the IXP2XXX family of network processors has a sophisticated memory controller that implements these functions atomically with minimal latency and microengine interaction. These functions include:

■ Automated ring buffer management

■ Automated linked list buffer management

■ Atomic bit manipulation, including set, clear, swap, increment or decrement, and add or subtract

DRAM Interface

DRAM is the initial storage area for packets while they are being processed. DRAM also stores large data structures such as route tables and flow descriptors. The requirements for DRAM are very different than for SRAM. While both DRAM and SRAM need to support the highest bandwidth possible given a particular line rate, DRAM doesn't require as low latency as SRAM does. However, systems typically require much more DRAM storage than SRAM. The IXP2400 processor uses a single channel of DDR DRAM, offering 19.2 gigabits per second of bandwidth, while the IXP28X0 processor utilizes three channels of Rambus (RDR) memory offering 50 gigabits per second of bandwidth. All three processors support up to 2 gigabytes of storage.

SHaC Unit

The SHaC (Scratch, Hash, and CSRs) is sort of a catch-all functional block. This block contains the 16-kilobyte scratch memory, the hash unit, and the CSR register block. The scratch memory is often used for internal microengine-to-microengine communication and local data storage. Like the SRAM unit, it supports automated ring buffers for simplified inter-process communication. The hash unit supports 48-bit, 64-bit, and 128-bit hash calculations. The CSR register block stores the bulk of the chip wide control and status registers. The SHaC unit enables the reflector read and write operations so microengines can send messages directly to each other.

PCI Interface

The PCI version 2.2 interface is used for modest speed interfaces to control plane processors, management processors, other IXP network processors, and to standard PCI Ethernet NICs for data, control, and debug applications. While the PCI interface isn't as fast as the MSF interface for transferring data, it does have a direct interface to the microengines so packet data can be transferred very quickly across the PCI interface. All three members of the IXP2XXX family utilize the same 64-bit wide data path and 66-megahertz data transfer rate.

Chassis

The chassis forms the internal highway for the internal functional units of IXP2XXX network processors. The chassis has multiple full duplex, unidirectional data buses and arbitration units to take advantage of the full benefits of parallel processing.

What is the Intel® IXA Portability Framework?

The network processors in the IXP2XXX product line are targeted at a wide range of applications with varying packet-processing and throughput requirements. The programmability and flexibility of the IXP2XXX product line makes them suitable for applications ranging from voice over IP to mobile IPv6 with data rates spanning OC-3 to OC-192. In this kind of an environment, the software development investment by equipment manufacturers becomes increasingly significant. Preserving this investment and leveraging it across multiple projects is a key consideration when choosing a network processor.

The Intel IXA Portability Framework provides the associated software infrastructure to help you develop modular, reusable software building blocks for these processors. Developers use the Intel IXA Portability Framework primarily to develop data plane software and to help them interface their applications with code running on the control plane. This section explains how the Intel IXA Portability Framework helps accelerate software development and improves code reuse across applications.

Figure 1.3 shows all the elements of the Intel IXA Portability Framework:

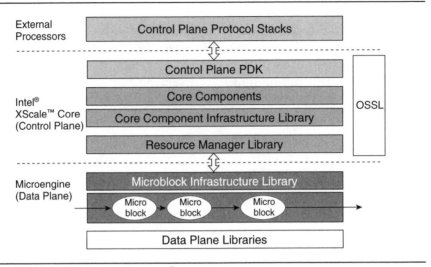

Figure 1.3   Elements of the Intel® IXA Portability Framework

Data Plane Software Structure

Intel IXA Portability Framework for the microengines consists of the programming model and associated support API's and libraries. In this programming model, the developer divides the fast-path processing of the application into high-level logical components called microblocks.

In this programming model, microblocks must be written in a way that makes each microblock independent of others. By providing clean boundaries between these blocks, it is possible to modify, add, or remove microblocks without affecting the behavior of the other blocks. This modularization improves reusability and allows developers to combine microblocks in different ways to create a meaningful application. The net benefit is that the task of writing fast-path code is simplified and time to market is shortened.

A microblock has an associated slow-path component on the Intel XScale Core. The application is typically written so that that the microblock will process most common cases and exception cases are passed to the Intel XScale component for further processing.

Figure 1.4 represents the data plane portion of a sample diffserv application written using microblocks.

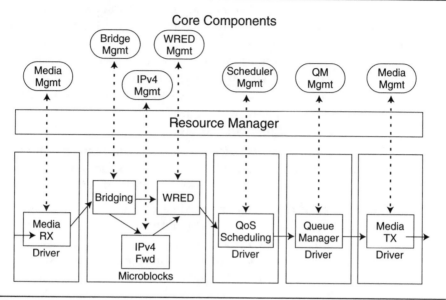

Figure 1.4 Representation of Data Plane

In the lower portion of the diagram are the fast-path building blocks, which are either packet-processing microblocks or hardware-specific driver microblocks. A dispatch loop combines packet-processing microblocks running on the same microengine thread. In the upper portion of the diagram, are the Intel XScale Core Components, which interface with control plane software via the Control Plane PDK.

The Intel XScale core components are written using the Resource Manager APIs and the Core Component Infrastructure (CCI) Library. The Resource Manager and the CCI provide a library and support infrastructure that allows the microblock and the Intel XScale core component to work together.

The following subsections provide a brief overview of each component of the Intel IXA.

Microblock

The fast-path processing on the microengines is divided into logical networking functions called *microblocks*. Each microblock is an assembly language macro or a C function that is written using the underlying low-level data plane libraries. Unlike a low-level function such as `ipv4_checksum()`, a microblock is coarse-grained; it has state and associated data structures that typically are shared with the Intel XScale Core. Examples of microblocks include IPv4 forwarding, Ethernet layer 2 filtering, 5-Tuple Classification, MPLS label insertion.

The two types of microblocks are:

- *Packet Processing Microblocks* perform high-level protocol specific functions on a packet such as IPv4 forwarding, IPv6 forwarding, Bridging, Network Address Translation (NAT), and so on.

- *Driver Microblocks* are hardware or media specific code blocks, which future versions of the network processor might implement in hardware. Two examples include Receive/Transmit blocks that interact closely with the MSF interface on the IXP2XXX processor, and the Queue Manager microblock that manages the queuing hardware (Q-Array).

Dispatch Loop and Microblock Infrastructure Library

A dispatch loop combines microblocks running in a single microengine thread into a microblock group, which is instantiated on one or more threads on multiple microengines and implements the data flow between the microblocks. Typically, driver blocks are not combined with other blocks on the same thread of execution. They usually run on a separate microengine thread (or threads), so that a dispatch loop is not needed.

The dispatch loop provides infrastructure for microblocks to efficiently access commonly used fields in the packet descriptor and header. It also provides a mechanism to send and receive packets between other dispatch loops and the Intel XScale core. You implement the dispatch loop using support libraries called the Microblock Infrastructure Library, which provides APIs to access the cached packet descriptor. Figure 1.5 is an example of dispatch for ipv4 and diffserv packet processing.

```
// include header files
#include "dispatch.h"    // generic dispatch loop
structures
#include "dl_pos.h"      // pos specific dispatch loop
variables
#include "IPFwd.h"       // IP LPM forwarding block
#include "Meter.h"       // Metering block
#include "WRED.h"        // WRED block

extern DL_PosRx dl;      // instantiate dispatch loop
control structure

void main()
{
    DL_Source_Init();    // initialize DL_Source block
    IPFwd_Init();        // initialize the Ipv4 Forwarding
block
    Meter_Init();        // initialize the meter block
    WRED_Init();         // initialize the WRED block
    DL_Sink_Init();      // initialize DL_MESink block

// Run the dispatch loop

    while(TRUE) {

        // Get a packet from the scratch ring.
        DL_Source();
        // call the IP forwarding block
        IPFwd();
        // call the metering block
        Meter();
        // call the WRED block
        WRED()
        // pass block to another microengine
        DL_Sink();
    }    // end dispatch loop while
}        // end main
```

Figure 1.5   Sample Dispatch

Data Plane Libraries

The data plane libraries contain low-level macros or micro C functions that are used to write microblocks or any other microengine code. These libraries promote maximal reuse of microblocks that are built with them. The libraries routines are optimized for high performance and minimal use of code space. Some examples of the functionality that these libraries provide include hardware specific functions such as CAM, local memory, and critical sections, as well as protocol header parsing functions for protocols such as IPv4, IPv6, and utility functions for hash table lookup or CRC.

Intel® XScale™ Core Component

The Intel XScale core component implements the configuration, management, and exception-processing code for the microblock. A core component may manage more than one microblock. In the extreme case, a single core component might manage all the microblocks.

Two ways to implement a core component are through the Core Component Infrastructure Library and through the Resource Manager API. The CCI specifies the design of the core component and the mechanisms used for configuration and packet or message processing when you use that method. Implementing the core component as a software entity that uses the Resource Manager API leaves the design of this entity entirely to the developer, including the decisions of whether it is a shared library, driver, thread, process, and of how it processes packets and messages.

Resource Manager

The Resource Manager is a software component on the Intel XScale core that provides an API for the following:

- Hardware initialization, configuration, and resource management
- Communication between the microblocks and their associated core components

The Resource Manager API simplifies the task of hardware initialization, configuration, and resource sharing. It also isolates the developer from the details of the microengine to Intel XScale core communication.

Operating System Services Library

The Operating System Services Library (OSSL) provides an operating system abstraction layer for all code running on the Intel XScale core. It is used by the Resource Manager, CCI, and other code on the Intel XScale core to enhance their portability across multiple operating systems. To ensure portability of their code to different operating systems, application developers writing Intel XScale code should also use this library instead of directly using APIs that are specific to any particular operating system.

Control Plane PDK

The Intel IXA Portability Framework package contains a Control Plane Product Development Kit (CP-PDK) that supports industry standards and enables data plane software to interface with the control plane.

Typical External System Architecture

As Figure 1.6 illustrates, Intel IXA allows for an ingress/egress configuration for a typical line card configuration. In this configuration, two IXP2XXX network processors are used, with the IXP2400 processor shown in this illustration. The ingress IXP2400 processor processes data from the network to the switch fabric. Data arrives from the Ethernet LAN (or SONET ring or whatever link layer it is connected to) via a MAC or framer, which interfaces to the IXP2400 processor via the MSF configured as either a SPI-3 or UTOPIA3 physical device interface. After the microengines finish processing the data, the packet is transmitted out to the switch fabric via a Fabric Interface Controller (FIC) chip. In this configuration, the MSF is configured as a CSIX physical interface to connect the FIC to the IXP2400 processor. The Egress IXP2400 processor processes data it receives from the switch fabric and then transmits it back to the network.

Besides the primary SPI, UTOPIA, and CSIX data path buses controlled by the MSF, the network processor has other buses. To communicate flow control information between processors, a dedicated C-Bus transmits flow control information from the egress processor to the ingress processor. The PCI 2.2 bus is used to interface to an optional control plane processor, Ethernet NICs (for debug or data), or PCI coprocessors such as encryption processors to the IXP2400 processor. Many applications require hardware accelerated algorithm coprocessor chips to supplement the software routines that are being processed internally by the microengines. To facilitate this, the IXP2400 processor enables these coprocessors to connect to the network processor via the QDR SRAM bus.

While the ingress/egress model is a common implementation, other configurations are possible. For cost and space limited designs, a single IXP2XXX network processor can be used. For performance-optimized designs, two or more IXP2XXX network processors can be chained together to extend the amount of processing resources available.

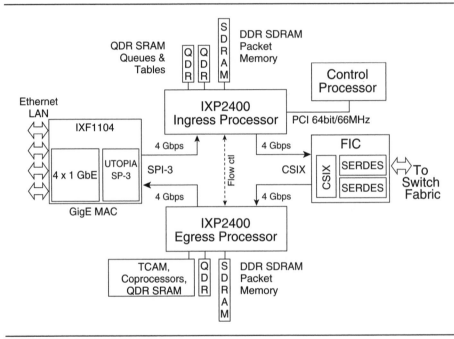

Figure 1.6   Typical Ingress/Egress Architecture

Typical Data Flow through IXP2XXX Network Processors

To fully understand Intel IXA, it is helpful to have a general understanding of how packets are processed by the various processing, I/O, and memory units. Figure 1.7 shows the general data flow through IXP2XXX network processors and the various processing steps performed when the processor receives a packet before it is eventually transmitted. In this example, the ingress path (as illustrated in Figure 1.6) is followed, with

IPv6 packets being received from the network via a quad Ethernet MAC and then being transmitted out to the switch fabric via the MSF configured as a CSIX interface. This processing follows a logical flow from receive to transmit (left to right) as packets are processed from one stage to another. Each stage is a modular building block that is configured by a Dispatch Loop that tells each module which stage is before and after it and where important data structures are located. The various data structures used in memory tend to be scattered throughout and may obscure the fact that packets are being processing in a linear fashion, from one stage to another.

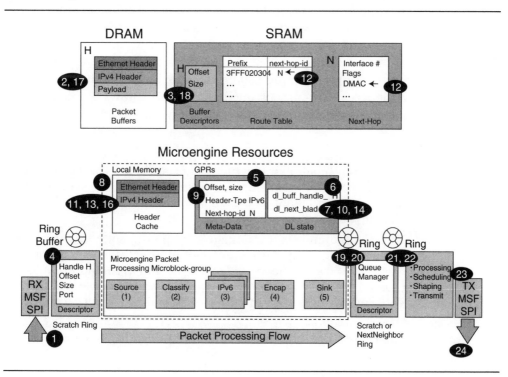

Figure 1.7   Packet Flow Through IXP2XXX Network Processors

The numbered steps below correspond to the numbered callouts in the Figure 1.7.

Receive Processing

1. The MSF receives the packet from the Ethernet MAC configured with a SPI-3 interface and buffers it into the MSF's receive buffer (RBUF).

2. A microengine (ME) that is assigned to the receive block is notified that a new packet has arrived. The ME reads the packet from the MSF, reassembles it, and then buffers the Ethernet header, the IP header, and payload to DRAM.

3. The same ME stores in SRAM a data structure (called a *handle*) that describes where the packet is buffered in DRAM.

4. This ME also puts the packet handle on a ring buffer in chip scratch memory where other microengines can get the packet for the subsequent packet-processing stage.

After a packet has been received from the network or fabric with its handle in a ring buffer, it is ready to be processed. The packet processing stage is composed of several blocks. The source and sink blocks are general processing elements that receive packets from a source and then sink them to a destination. The intermediary blocks (classify, forward, and encapsulation) rely on the source and sink blocks so they can be designed as independent processing blocks. This allows for a modular building block approach for software development.

Source Block

5. The source block extracts the packet metadata (packet location, packet type, and next hop ID) from the packet header information located in DRAM, and then stores it into the ME's local General Purpose Registers (GPRs).

6. This block then sets the Dispatch Loop (DL) state in local GPRs. The Dispatch Loop is a core part of the Intel IXA Portability Framework as it allows independent software modules to be chained together in an orderly way. Software modules rely on DL state information and inter-process signaling to get to the next stage.

7. The DL sets the next block for the classification stage (stage 2).

Classification Block

8. The classification stage gets signaled where it will store the MAC and IP headers from memory into the ME's local memory.

9. The IP header is read from local memory where it is determined that the packet is an IPv6 type. The packets metadata (stored in GPRs) is then updated with this information.

10. The DL sets the next block state to IPv6 (stage 3).

IPv6 Processing Stage

11. The IPv6 processing stage gets signaled. Its first task is to read the destination address from the header cache, which was previously stored in local memory.

12. The route table in SRAM is searched for the next hop address.

13. The IPv6 header that is stored in the header cache is updated with the new next hop address. This address is also stored in the next hop address data structure in SRAM.

14. The DL sets the next block state to the encapsulation block (stage 4).

Encapsulation Stage

15. The destination MAC address from the next hop address data structure is read from SRAM.

16. The packets Ethernet header (stored in the header cache in local memory) is modified with the next hop Ethernet address.

17. The modified headers are written back from local memory to DRAM. At this point, all the IPv6 forwarding is complete, with the updated header now in external memory.

Sink

18. The metadata from local memory is flushed back to SRAM.

19. A message is sent to the queue manager to send the packet to a transmit queue. This message is done through a ring buffer located in either on-chip scratch memory or through next neighbor registers.

Queue Manager

20. The queue manager (QM) receives enqueue requests from the receive processing stage and dequeue requests from the transmit processing stage. Enqueue operations append a packet on the end of the appropriate transmit queue. The transmit queue is configured as a linked list in SRAM. Among other data, the message contains the packet handle to indicate where the packet is stored and what queue number the packet is to be added to.

21. The dequeue function receives requests from the transmit scheduler stage to remove a packet from a transmit queue so it can be scheduled for transmission.

Transmit Processing

22. The transmit scheduler receives a packet handle from the QM and then schedules it for transmission.

23. The transmit ME sends the packet to the MSF where it is buffered in the TBUF prior to transmission. Prior to transmission, the ME checks flow control status from the egress processor.

24. The MSF transmits the packet out to the fabric via the CSIX interface.

During the life of this IPv6 packet as it traveled through the IXP2XXX network processor, critical elements of Intel IXA were exercised, including:

■ A processor in the IXP2XXX product line was used in one of several hardware configurations particular to the application.

■ The Intel IXA Portability Framework allowed modular and portable packet processing building blocks.

■ Multi-threading, parallel processing techniques were used to increase performance.

■ Ring buffer controllers were used to isolate processing stages, allowing independent building block development.

■ Linked list controllers were used to buffer packets in memory to achieve line rate performance.

■ Software techniques, such as Pool of Threads or Hyper Task Chaining, used to map applications to microengines.

■ The Media and Switch Fabric interface was used to automatically transmit and receive packets to/from MACs, framers, switch fabrics, and the processor.

■ Generalized Thread Signaling (GTS) was used by one stage to signal another.

If you have questions on Intel IXA in general or these concepts in particular, then read on, for this book is for you!

Chapter 2

Packet Processing Basics

Developing a network processor based system involves teams of many different professionals. System architects, software and hardware engineers, as well as marketing and sales personnel are all involved at some level in the project. Those closest to the network processor design are the system architects and design engineers. Others, like support engineers, managers, and those on the peripheral of the development, often need to better understand the inner functions of the network processor development. The goal of this chapter is to give these individuals a basic overview of the functions that a network processor performs as well as a system understanding of the context in which the IXP2XXX processors operate. Experienced system architects and design engineers may want to skip this chapter and move right to Chapter 3.

You can have almost as many data plane processing tasks as you have individual systems. With such a large variety of applications, it is close to impossible to narrowly define a fixed set of tasks that a network processor performs. However, you can identify enough common functions to describe the tasks that most applications demand of a network processor. In this Chapter, nine of these common tasks are summarized.

Typical Hardware Platform

Figure 2.1 shows the five basic subsystems in a typical hardware platform consisting of the following components:

- Switch Fabric
- Management and Control Processors
- I/O Blade
- Service Blade
- Trunk Blade

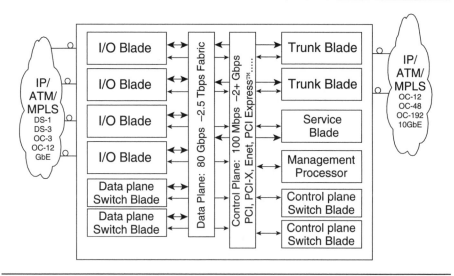

Figure 2.1   Typical Hardware Architecture

Switch Fabric

The switch fabric is the central mechanism for transferring data and control information from one blade to another. Each blade in the system connects to the fabric via a bus, and all the blades in the system are aggregated in a central switch controller, or blade. In a mesh topology, each blade may send data directly to any other blade in the system, without having to go to a central fabric. The requirements differ widely for control and data fabrics. The data plane fabric is optimized for speed, for congestion management, and for the unique packet and cell types that the system processes. Because of its central role in the architecture, the switch fabric is often proprietary and unique to the platform manufacturer. However, several semiconductor companies are developing high performance, high functionality switch fabric solutions for developers needing off-the-shelf solutions.

The control fabric differs from the data plane fabric because control information requires lower bandwidth than data and packets, which typically don't traverse this bus. To ease the difficulty of system design, developers usually base the control bus on industry standard buses, such as PCI, PCI-X, PCI Express, or Ethernet. Sometimes the control fabric is replaced by passing specially encapsulated control information within the data fabric. In this case, each blade must distinguish between control information and data in the fabric, so that a blade can switch the information appropriately.

Management and Control Processors

The management processor and the control processor share system administration functions. The management processor controls overall operation of the box. When IT administrators control the unit and gather statistics, they communicate with the management processor. Management processors belong to the well-known groups of general purpose processors—for example, the Intel® Pentium® processor, Motorola PowerPC[†], and MIP[†]s. Typically, they run WindRiver Systems VXWorks[†] real time RTOS, QNX[†], OSE[†], Microsoft embedded Windows[†] NT[†], or embedded Linux. Whereas the management processor controls and manages the system as a whole, the control processor regulates specific subsystems within the box. The control processor configures individual I/O and trunk cards, processes exception cases or low level system failures, updates route table entries, and performs other similar tasks.

Here's an example of the division of labor. When a system administrator instructs a DSLAM to add a new user, the administrator communicates first with the management processor, sending the user's physical port number and quality-of-service level. The management processor then assigns the new user a VC number and IP address when the new user is logged on. Next, the management processor instructs the control processor on the I/O and trunk blades to add the new route table entry so the IP forwarder can determine the next hop address. The control processor runs a signaling protocol, such as OSPF or RIP, to learn what this route table entry should be by communicating with other routers on the network using standard protocols. Once the control processor determines this next-hop address, it becomes part of the forwarding table stored on the I/O and trunk card where forwarding decisions are actually made.

Notice that the control and management processors typically don't process individual packets or cells. In some system designs of just a few years ago, the control processor would handle both data and control plane processing. Since then, data rates have increased, and this main processor became overburdened with dataplane, packet modification tasks. The requirements of high performance systems demand that data plane traffic be offloaded to network processors while control and management applications run on standard microprocessors.

By separating the I/O blades and trunk blades via a switch fabric interface, a platform can be customized to the unique requirements of the customer. For example, a particular customer can customize a server with the appropriate blades to aggregate multiple ATM DS-3 links, terminate ATM to add IP services, and then switch the IP frames out to the network via a Gigabit Ethernet blade. IXP2XXX network processors promote such customization through its modular hardware architecture using a switch fabric as the interconnect method.

I/O Blade

The I/O blade, also called a line card, interfaces the system to the users, whereas the trunk blade interfaces the system to the network. Because the I/O blade is on the user side of the box, it typically attaches to a wide variety of lower speed, data link layer media types. Examples of link layer interfaces are fast Ethernet, gigabit Ethernet, SONET, T1/E1, etc. ATM and POS (PPP) layer 2 packets are often carried over the SONET interface. On the other side of the blade is the interface to the switch fabric. I/O blades interface with these lower speed, link layer media types and perform a series of tasks on the packets before forwarding the packets either to the trunk blade or another I/O blade via the fabric. This lower layer of processing is often called *fast path processing* or data plane processing. The specific data plane processing tasks are described later in this chapter.

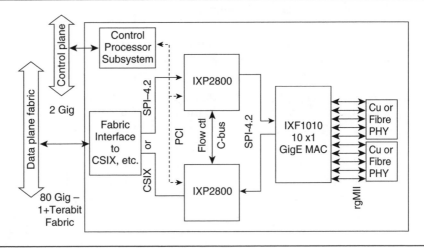

Figure 2. 2   Typical I/O Blade Using the IXP2800 Processor

Trunk Blade

The trunk blade performs functions similar to the I/O blade, except that its media interface attaches to the network, which offers higher bandwidth than the interface that attaches users. The data rate on the truck blade is an order of magnitude greater than a link on the user side. Even though the trunk blade operates at much higher speed, the aggregate performance of all the line cards is likely to be much greater than the much faster trunk blade. For a system that has 10 line cards, each with 10 1-gigabit/second Ethernet ports, the aggregate throughput can reach 100 gigabits/second. If the trunk blade is a 10 gigabit/sec Ethernet port—a very fast uplink—the trunk becomes oversubscribed by 10 times its capacity if all the line card ports were to forward their traffic to the trunk blade. To handle this situation, the system's quality-of-service (QoS) features monitor traffic flow to all of the ports. If any port gets congested, the flow control messages are sent to the other ports to tell them to stop transmitting to the congested ports.

A Standards-based Software Architecture

As with most software architectures, systems based on a network processor follow a layered approach. The Network Processor Forum (NPF and the Internet Engineering Task Force (IETF) have defined standardized APIs to facilitate system design. While most platforms have existing software architecture, it is important to have a basic understanding of the general NPF software architecture. This NPF architecture implemented with the Intel microblock modular building blocks is illustrated in Figure 2.3. While nearly all currently available systems depend on proprietary software architectures to perform these functions, it is anticipated that developers will use standardized APIs for their next generation platforms.

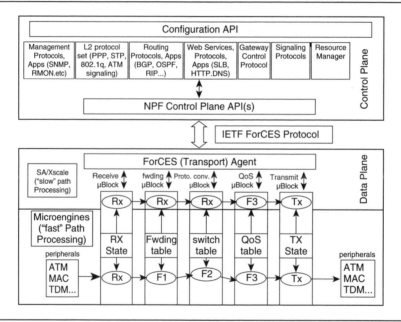

Figure 2.3 Typical Software Architecture Using Standardized APIs

The four different layers of this standardized control plane occupy the highest level in the software architecture.

- Configuration API
- Signaling Protocol Stacks
- NPF Control Plane APIs
- FoRCES messaging protocol

The Configuration API is the higher interface to the system's management processor, isolating the system-specific nature of the control plane to give the management processor a well-understood API. The signaling protocol stack layer runs a variety of management, layer2, routing, Web services, gateway, and generic signaling protocols, along with a systems resource manager.

With a modular architecture, these protocols need to communicate with various data plane blades using common and well-understood APIs. The Network Processor Forum (NPF) is the standards body that defines the control plane/data plane API. The NPF also develops other standards, such as co-processor and switch fabric hardware interfaces, among others. Several types of APIs are used, generally grouping around classification, direction, modification, and traffic management. Within each group, several APIs are unique to their function. For example, under the Classification stage, an API can be "Add Route," or under Traffic Management, it can be "Add VC n with VBR shaping parameters y". While the NPF defines a set of control plane API calls, the control plane requires a communications channel to send and receive these messages to the various data plane blades within a system.

The NPF has standardized on the ForCES messaging protocol for control and data plane messaging. The *ForCES-Forwarding and Control Element Separation* standard is defined by a special IETF working group that has standardized on this protocol for control plane and data plane communication. ForCES is an important standard because it provides signaling stack software with a common communications interface to data plane processors. The NPF APIs and FoRCES messaging protocol standards allow signaling stack developers to have a single software base that communicates with various data plane blades, so that the developer spends far less time on control plane customization for every instantiation of the data plane blades. This time savings significantly reduces engineering development time and shortens the cycle for introducing new products to market. To allow inter-processor communication, ForCES has a transport agent on the control plane and a corresponding transport agent on the data plane blade. These transport agents take higher level messages and transport them across the actual control plane hardware interface, such as PCI, PCI-Express, in-band messaging, or they use combined data plane and control plane communications methods. Having a transport agent that is unique to the individual hardware architecture of the platform allows the signaling stack messaging interface to remain unchanged as hardware systems evolve.

In the data plane, packets are received, processed, and then transmitted out. Because the packets must be processed as quickly as they arrive, this processing layer is often called the "fast path." A system has several stages of fast-path processing. Packets enter the fast path via the Receive (RX) stage and exit through the transmit stage. The intermediary stages are often called *forwarding, enqueueing* or *dequeueing*, or *transmit* stages, as shown in Figure 2.3, and described in the next section. Each of these data plane stages has a slow path component associated with it. This slow path component configures the particular processing stage and communicates with the control processor accepting control requests and status updates. Because the requirements of each stage are different, having a separate slow path component is a logical approach.

Data Plane Processing Stages

A line card application has several data plane processing stages. The example designs that Intel ships with the Software Development Kit (SDK) include several applications that demonstrate the features and performance of IXP2XXX network processor systems. Developers can follow this basic application or develop their own data plane software. Others mix and match their code with Intel's. What follows is a series of nine processing stages that are used in Intel's OC-48 and OC-192 Packet-over-SONET example design. Some designs may have more stages, others less. These nine stages can be put into three general groups:

- The Receive Processing stage has six steps:
  - Packet Receive
  - Packet Reassembly
  - Classify
  - Forward
  - Metering and Statistics
  - Congestion Avoidance
- Enqueueing and Dequeueing
- Transmit Processing has the last two steps:
  - Transmit (TX) Scheduling
  - Transmit (TX) Data

Typically, receive processing is a monolithic operation due to the close inter-relationships between reading, classifying, and forwarding a packet. Enqueueing and dequeueing tends to be monolithic because it is a fixed function, taking packets from the receive process and putting them into a transmit queue and vice versa. Transmit processing is more modular as the scheduling process and actual transmission of data are often decoupled from each other.

Data plane applications come in many variations because of equipment manufacturers' unique and varied platform requirements. Thus, a narrow definition of data plane processing that fits every application is difficult. By tracing the three common processing stages as a series of steps, you can derive useful principles.

Figure 2.4 shows these nine basic stages. Packets, cells, or frames enter the data plane on various link layer protocols and leave on different ports, protocols, and rates. In this illustration, packets are received from the outside world over the network or from within the box itself via the switch fabric. In this context, the network-to-fabric direction is called the *ingress path* and the fabric-to-network path the *egress path*. The ingress path is usually where the most difficult packet processing occurs because that is where forwarding, protocol conversion, congestion avoidance algorithms, etc. are performed. The egress path has simpler packet-processing steps, although transmit processing may utilize more sophisticated traffic management functions. This illustration shows the ingress path.

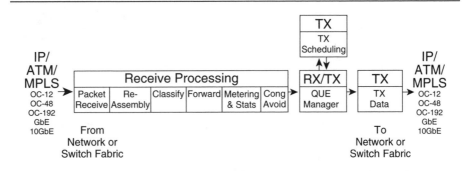

Figure 2.4   Typical Data Plane Processing Stages

The following descriptions show the functions of these data plane tasks with minimal reference to a specific hardware or software implementation. However, because the IXP2XXX processor assumes a certain processing flow, the example requires some description of implementation-specific details. The general data flow within the IXP2XXX network processor is illustrated in Figure 2.5. You can find the specifics of the internal microarchitecture in Chapter 4.

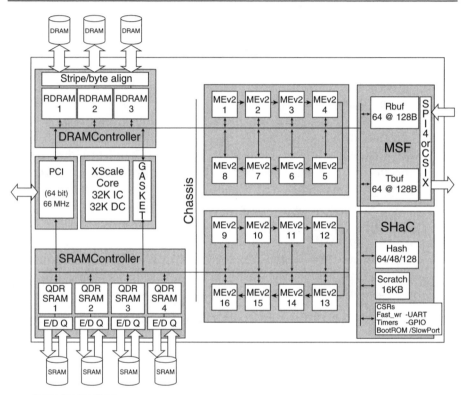

Basic Packet Flow

1. Packets arrive from the MAC or framer through the UTOPIA, SPI or CSIX interface where the Media and Switch Fabric (MSF) unit buffers the packet into one of several RBUF buffers.

2. The MSF sends a status word that describes this newly arrived packet to a free microengine that is available to process the packet.

3. The microengine reads the status word, determines if packet is the Start of Packet (SOP) or End of Packet (EOP). If SOP, then it reads the header into a local register.

4. The packet payload data is reassembled and "DMAed" to a buffer in DRAM. The buffer is obtained from a buffer freelist in SRAM.

5. The microengine classifies the packet with the header information. A lookup table is searched in SRAM for a pointer to a flow descriptor, which resides in DRAM.

6. With the flow descriptor information, the microengine processes the packet. It modifies the packet header, if needed, and determines which transmit queue to put the packet in.

7. The packet is enqueued to the appropriate transmit queue. The packet is still in DRAM, while the actual transmit queue is in SRAM. The packet descriptor is actually enqueued, not the packet itself.

8. A transmit scheduling algorithm, such as Round Robin or Weighted Fair Queuing, is used to schedule packets.

9. A transmit fill operation dequeues the packets and sends the packet to the MSF unit where it is buffered into one of several TBUF buffers.

10. The MSF hardware takes the packet from a TBUF buffer and sends it to the MAC or framer where it is ultimately transmitted out.

Figure 2.5   Basic Packet Flow Through the IXP2800 Processor

Packet Reception

This initial stage reads data from either the network, via a MAC or framer, or from the switch fabric. Once read, the data is buffered. In the IXP2XXX network processors, the packets arrive on a POS, UTOPIA, or CSIX hardware interface. MACs and framers segment complete packets into smaller packets called *m-packets*. The reason for this segmentation is that the packets arrive from the MAC or framer interleaved with other packets. Because of this interleaving, the packets get segmented. For example, a large frame is segmented into many of these smaller m-packets. These buffers are located in the IXP2XXX processor's Media and Switch Fabric interface. Multi-port MACs and framers also need to segment larger packets into smaller ones so each port can be serviced in a timely manner, thus avoiding FIFO overruns and underruns.

When multi-port MACs and framers segment the packets into smaller chunks, these m-packets get interleaved with other packets from other ports in the MAC or framer. For example, all 4 ports of the IXF1104 Quad Gigabit Ethernet MAC share a single SPI-3 interface. As packets are transmitted between the network processor and the MAC, the m-packets from the other ports are interleaved, as illustrated in Figure 2.6.

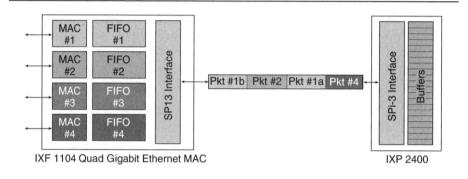

OM16014

Packets from IXF1104 quad Ethernet MAC are interleaved when they are transferred to the IXP2XXX processor.

Figure 2.6   Interleaved Packets

Reassembly

As the m-packets are received by the IXP2XXX network processor and internally buffered, they must be processed as complete packets and not as segmented m-packets. Therefore, they are reassembled then stored in DRAM to free up the internal RBUF buffers. The reassembly data is stored locally as a packet descriptor in the microengine where it can be readily accessed. (For applications with a large number of ports, reassembly data is stored in external memory). This packet descriptor has information about where the packet is stored in DRAM, the port number it was received on, the packet length, amount of buffer space left, etc. A brief description of the buffer pointer is illustrated in Figure 2.7.

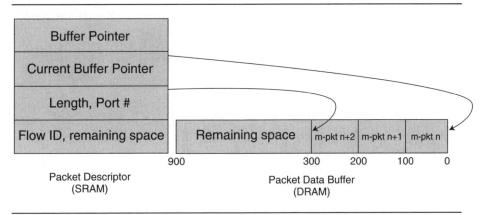

Figure 2.7   Packet Descriptor Used During Reassembly

As m-packets are received from the IXP2XXX MSF unit, they are added to the buffer that belongs to that packet. The individual m-packets are thus concatenated together in one large buffer to form the complete packet. During the reassembly process, the packet buffer remains constant, but the length, current buffer, and remaining space field change with every new packet that gets added.

Reassembly operates on packets that were segmented by the framer or MAC for transmission across a chip-to-chip interface such as the SPI, POS-PHY, or UTOPIA interface. This type of reassembly is primarily for link layer packets like Ethernet and Point-to-Point Protocol—or PPP, for Packet over SONET link layer interfaces. ATM reassembly is a different matter all together. ATM reassembly is a more sophisticated process that follows a whole set of rules that are defined by the ATM forum.

Classification

Classification is the stage where a packet is inspected to determine the action to be taken on that packet. Thus, subsequent actions on a packet depend totally on the initial classification. Classification steps can be as simple as inspecting a single address or field within a packet, or they can be complex, using multiple fields to classify the packet. A simple example of classification would be packet-forwarding, where the next hop of the packet needs to be determined. The hardware extracts the IP address from the packet header and searches a long list or table of other IP addresses to find a match. When a match is found, an associated descriptor is used to determine the next hop address for that particular packet. The table look-up entry can be a simple statement, such as:

> If IP_addr=100.222.198.237 then look up packet descriptor Pkt_desc_442

This packet descriptor would contain the next hop address plus other system-defined parameters. Figure 2.8 shows the connection made through the route table.

IP Address	Pointer		Policy Descriptor
100.100.454.222	200		Desc_flow_100
100.100.454.222	192		Desc_flow_983
100.101.989.231	983		Desc_flow_343
104.100.540.121	343		Desc_flow_769
100.222.198.237	398		Desc_flow_442
103.000.321.870	302		Desc_flow_320
100.111.453.111	103		Desc_flow_310
100.991.119.203	193		Desc_flow_989

Figure 2.8   Route Table

When searching through a large table with hundreds of thousands of entries, a simple linear search, sequentially examining each address one by one, would take an excessive amount of time, especially for a 32-bit address. So, more sophisticated methods are used to find the next hop address.

The Longest Prefix Match (LPM) method is one of the most common. This algorithm searches for the prefix of the address instead of the entire address. A subset or prefix of the entire address is likely to be sufficient because a TCP/IP destination address—your computer—is usually contained in a network subnet. This subnet may contain hundreds or thousands of other users. If a TCP/IP client outside your subnet wants to address your computer, the router that is between that source and the client only needs to look for the subnet address (not your complete address) to determine whether further classification is needed. If a subnet match is found, a 5-tuple classification is performed to determine the exact flow ID so the packet can be properly forwarded to its destination. Because a router can receive many packets on its input ports that are not intended for the subnet that it manages, it does this first level, simpler LPM search so the more sophisticated and resource intensive 5-tuple lookup doesn't have to be performed on all the incoming packets including those that aren't meant for the subnet in the first place.

Instead of searching the entire 32-bit address, the LPM search looks for a subset of that address—the first 16 bits for example—to determine whether a match is possible and if that subset of address is sufficient to determine the match. If not, the LPM search looks for the next set of 4 bits. If a match is found, the search is terminated. If not, then the next 4 bits are searched, and the process continues until a match is found. This particular search is called a 16:4:4:4:4 search and it is described in Figure 2.9.

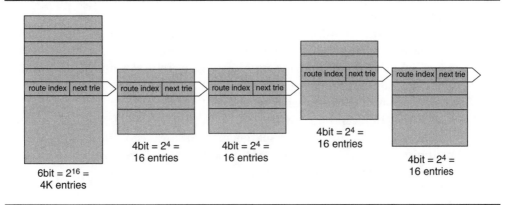

Figure 2.9   Longest Prefix Match Search

A more sophisticated classification process is to perform a quintuple, or 5-tuple, search on the TCP/IP packet. The five fields in the 5-tuple are the IP source address, IP destination address, TCP source port number, TCP destination port number, and protocol ID. These five fields in TCP/IP header are then combined together and searched in memory to find what flow a packet belongs too. In the longest prefix match algorithm, the destination address is used to search for the next hop address. However, merely examining the destination IP address does not describe the flow the packet belongs to. Most packet processing tasks, such as congestion avoidance algorithms, QoS policing, and traffic management functions, need to know the complete source, destination, and protocol type of the TCP/IP packet to determine the flow to which the packet belongs so these algorithms can be properly applied. Defining a packet by the entire 5-tuple provides QoS and other processing functions with the complete flow information they need to function. Searching through five

long bit fields in memory, however, is complex. Using software algorithms is labor intensive, consuming valuable compute and bus bandwidth
resources.

To determine the flow identification, 5-tuple searches are often performed in special co-processor ICs called ternary content addressable memories, or TCAMs. A content addressable memory (CAM) is a special kind of memory that works just the opposite of regular memories. A regular memory device first receives an address then retrieves the data at that address location for a read operation. It is easy to search for the data because a simple address decoder using combinational logic is used to find the memory location where the data is stored.

A CAM, on the other hand, is first given the data, then it searches for the address where that data is stored. CAMs employ sophisticated search algorithms that examine large memory spaces to find a match. A TCAM is a special variant of a standard CAM. A TCAM allows special "don't care" bits in the address field being searched. For instance, the bit values 0, 1, and X can be searched so they don't have to provide an exact match. This allows an address to be searched for in a range of addresses. Range matching is difficult to implement in software so hardware coprocessors are often used for the fastest systems.

Forwarding

After a packet is classified, it must be forwarded to the destination address. This actual forwarding step is quite simple. A new link layer address, such as a 48-bit Ethernet destination address that was found during the classification stage, may be all that the network processor needs to direct the packet to the proper output port. Finding the destination port number is not the only required function during forwarding. The forwarding algorithm must do a series of checks on the packet to determine whether or not it is valid. These checks are defined by the IETF in RFC 1812 and are listed below:

- If total Length < header length specified, then send exception.
- If header checksum fails, then drop packet.
- If source address = 0, then drop packet.
- If source address = limited broadcast address, then drop packet.
- If source address = loopback address, then drop packet.
- If source address = multicast address, then drop packet.

- If source address = class E address, then drop packet.
- If source address = directed broadcast address, then drop packet.
- If destination address = 0, then drop packet.
- If destination address = loopback packet, then drop packet.
- If destination address = class E address, then drop packet.
- If destination address = multicast address, then drop packet.

After passing these RFC 1812 checks, the packet is sent to the metering and statistics stage.

Metering and Statistics

Once a packet has passed the RFC1812 checks during the forwarding stage, the packet is metered. Metering is a critical part of the software processing flow as it prevents packets from entering the system if they violate their policy flow parameters. Metering is very similar to a traffic cop who gives tickets to motorists when they violate traffic laws. When a car goes faster than the speed limit the driver is given a ticket. A key difference between Internet traffic and automobile traffic is that Internet traffic metering can apply a different set of rules or policies for different packet flows. With automobile traffic, the vehicle code applies to all drivers equally, to rich and poor alike!

The most common traffic policies that govern a packet flow ensure that a particular packet does not exceed a maximum bit rate and a maximum burst rate. A burst is simply a large number of packets that are transmitted in a short period of time. If a burst falls within a certain time duration, it may pass. If too many packets are transmitted during a burst interval, the packet will fail. A similarity between an automobile and internet traffic is that the traffic cop does apply some real time judgment when deciding if a law was broken or not. For example, if the speed limit is 55 MPH and you are temporarily speeding at 65 MPH—such as when getting on the freeway, dodging another car, or some other temporary situation—an understanding traffic cop might take the situation into account, giving you a break and not issuing a ticket. On the other hand, if you were constantly exceeding the speed limit, the cop would most likely pull you over and give you a ticket. The same is true for network traffic. Packets from a particular flow can arrive in bursts and have short time periods where they can exceed a pre-specified bit rate.

The metering algorithm that is used in the Packet-Over-SONET example design contained in the Intel IXA Software Development Kit (SDK) is called a Single rate TriColor Marker (SrTCM), which is based on RFC2697. The SrTCM meters traffic flow according to three traffic parameters: Committed Information Rate (CIR), Committed Burst Size (CBS), and Excessive Burst Size (EBS). The SrTCM assigns a color (green, yellow, or red) to a packet according to how the algorithm marks it using the CIR, CBS, and EBS parameters. A packet is marked green if it doesn't exceed the CBS. A packet is marked yellow if it does exceed the CBS but not the EBS. It is marked red if it exceeds all parameters. Based on the color, packets are either passed or dropped or further evaluated if QoS algorithms are being applied to the packets to ensure fairness.

Besides metering, a line card keeps statistics on a packet flow. Based on the application, many different types of statistics can be gathered. The POS example designs that are included with the SDK are based on RFC2863. This RFC states that 64-bit counters are used when bit rates exceed 650 megabits per second for a rollover rate of 468 years. The Intel implementation uses 63-bit counters with a rollover rate of 234 years. The packet has two sets of characteristics, one for the network interface (MACs and framers via the SPI or UTOPIA interface) and one for the switch fabric (CSIX interface).

For the network interface, statistics are gathered for every port interface and every flow. The flow statistics are:

■ Received byte count

■ Received packet count

The port statistics are:

■ Received byte count

■ Received packet count

■ Time from previous packet

For the Switch fabric interface, the statistics are:

■ Received byte count

■ Received cFrame (CSIX frames) count

■ Time from previous packet

Congestion Management

Metering is the method to police traffic to ensure that packets that violate the rules for their flow are properly dealt with. Rule-violating packets may be flagged to be dealt with later, that is, given a yellow color, or they are simply dropped. However, in some situations packets must be dropped even if they don't violate any rules or policies and are perfectly legal. These situations occur when a router simply runs out of memory to buffer the incoming packets. The router becomes congested and packets have to be dropped.

The role of congestion avoidance is to intelligently and gracefully discard packets. An example of non-intelligent packet dropping is to simply drop packets as soon as memory fills up. If packet buffer memory is 100-percent full, any packet that arrives is simply dropped. Obviously, this way to drop packets is not very intelligent and graceful. For instance, some packets are very high priority and just can't be discarded due to their Service Level Agreement (SLA). As such, a packet's flow should be known to determine the priority. Also, making a decision to drop a packet as soon as memory is filled is not very intelligent; waiting until the last minute doesn't allow any flexibility in the system. Making the drop decision when there is a sizable portion of memory still available gives the system some flexibility so it can avoid a hard drop decision. Some packets that were previously metered and marked yellow may be allowed to pass if the buffer can provide enough space, whereas they may be dropped if buffer space is limited and the number of green packets is large.

When making a decision to drop a packet based on a congested situation, a router must know how the end-point clients handle the dropped packets. For example, when it sends a TCP frame, the TCP protocol segments that frame into several smaller IP packets, with the packet's size determined by the Maximum Transmission Unit (MTU). The resulting TCP/IP packets are transmitted by the source client, passed through the network with the receiving TCP client reassembling the packets into a complete frame. During a particular time frame, called the TCP window, the transmitting client expects to receive an acknowledgement that the destination client actually received the packet. If the transmitting client doesn't see this acknowledgement, it is flagged as being dropped by the network. When a packet is dropped, the transmitting client retransmits.

How the routers discard packets must take into account how the endpoints deal with those dropped packets. For instance, suppose a router suddenly becomes congested and then receives a burst of packets from hundreds of different clients. Then, the router drops the packets all at the same time. The transmitting TCP clients detect that their packets were dropped because they haven't received an acknowledgement that they were received at their destination. Assuming that the hundreds of TCP sources retransmit at the same time, the router that dropped the packets in the first place will again drop those same packets all at the same time, creating a negative cycle of packet flows oscillating between heavy traffic and light traffic. Right after the packets are dropped, the network traffic lightens, but the traffic suddenly becomes very heavy when the originating clients retransmit. This traffic oscillation negatively affects overall end station TCP performance.

To solve these problems, network routers use an algorithm called Random Early Detection (RED) and Weighted Random Early Detection (WRED) to gracefully decide which packets to drop and which to retain in the system. They make their drop decisions based on several criteria for the individual flows, including:

- *Randomness*. To avoid the oscillation problem, packets are randomly dropped with a probability that is based on a flows average queue depth. By randomly dropping packets, end stations do not detect dropped packets and retransmit them all at the same. Packets are dropped randomly so that retransmission of packets is spread out in time, smoothing out traffic. This distribution of the load can happen only if a certain randomness is applied to the dropping decision. This randomness is very similar to the way 802.3 Ethernet networks detect collisions and retransmit packets so they don't all retransmit at the same time.

- *Priority*. WRED applies a weighting factor to the dropping decision so that higher priority packets are kept and lower priority packets are dropped. Making this priority decision is based on the DSCP field in the IP header.

- *SrTCM coloring*. Optionally, RED and WRED may look at the color that a packet was previously marked to determine if the packet should be dropped or not.

To implement RED and WRED, the algorithm continuously monitors the average queue depth for each of the transmit queues. Based on the average Q depth, a probability is chosen to decide what packets get discarded or not. Figure 2.10 shows the probability of discard versus the average queue depth graphically. As the average queue depth increases, the discard probability also increases.

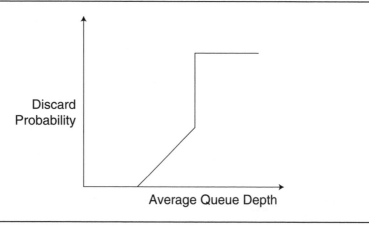

Figure 2.10   Discard Probability Versus Average Queue Depth

Enqueue and Dequeue

During the receive processing stage, a frame is reassembled from several smaller segments, classified, then forwarded. Assuming it passes through the metering and congestion avoidance stages without being dropped, the packet is ready to be sent to the transmitting stage. The enqueue and dequeue task is the gateway between the receive processing stages and the transmit processing stages. Between these stages, you have the data structure called the transmit queues. These queues hold all the packets for each of the flows, and they are organized according to a transmit schedule, which is described in the next section. Figure 2.11 illustrates a set of transmit queues along with the schedule.

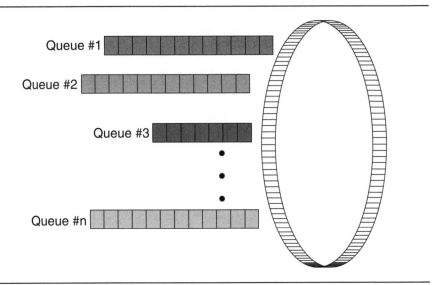

Figure 2.11 Transmit Queues

When the receive process adds a packet to a queue, it is called *en-queueing*. Removal of a packet from a queue by a transmit process is called *dequeueing*. Packets are enqueued to the tail of a queue and dequeued from the head. When a packet is enqueued (EnQ) or dequeued (DeQ), the packet data itself is not processed, rather a *packet descriptor* is added to the queue or removed from it. A packet descriptor has several fields associated with it, including a pointer to the actual packet data buffer in memory, the number of buffers for a packet, whether the buffer is the starting buffer for the packet, called start of packet (SOP), or the end buffer of packet (EOP).

Because packets are entering the EnQ/DeQ task at line rate from the receive stages and also leaving at line rate to the transmit stages, the EnQ/DeQ tasks have to operate at twice the packet rate of the system. For an OC-192 POS application, the system processes close to 30 million packets per second. The EnQ/DeQ function, therefore, must process 60 million packets per second to keep up with line rate conditions. For this reason, EnQ/DeQ performance is quoted as a critical metric for network processors.

Transmit Scheduling

A system requires traffic scheduling because of the limited available bandwidth on an output port versus the bandwidth that is required to meet the service level agreements (SLAs) for the supported flows in a system. These SLAs determine the priority of flows, a maximum allowable bit rate, maximum allowable burst size, etc. A system's output port is oftentimes oversubscribed so system administrators can give a user as much bandwidth as possible. Because statistical probability indicates that many of the flows seldom require the fully allotted bandwidth dictated by their SLA, system administrators oversubscribe the output port so a flow can use as much of the available bandwidth, similar to the way that airlines overbook flights to be sure that they fill every available seat. Because statistically some travelers cancel or reschedule flights at the last minute, the airlines want to make sure those seats are used to maximize their revenue. For networking traffic, the amount of over-subscription varies tremendously from system to system, but a 100:1 ratio would be considered reasonable for access systems such as those for DSL or cable.

To learn more about these concepts, refer to *Inside the Internet's Resource Reservation Protocol* (Durham and Yavatkar 1999).

The role of traffic scheduling is to manage this transmit bandwidth as effectively and fairly as possible. During periods of high activity, the scheduler needs to prevent some flows from being starved for bandwidth if others take more than their share. The scheduler needs to give some flows higher priority and others lower based on their SLA. Some flows absolutely require guaranteed bandwidth (for example, real time traffic such as video) so end-to-end performance doesn't suffer.

Figure 2.11 illustrates transmit queues and their schedule. The schedule is represented as a ring or wheel divided into slots of time. During each time slot, one or more packets are transmitted. The transmit scheduler traverses the ring from slot to slot, from beginning to end, in a big loop. Thus, one trip around the ring represents the maximum supported bandwidth of the output port. The system's scheduling algorithm determines how these slots are serviced. Many types of packet scheduling algorithms are possible, but here are four examples:

Simple Priority

In a simple priority based schedule, the transmit queues have priorities from highest to lowest based on their SLAs. The highest priority queues that have packets are serviced first, followed by the lowest priority queues. In a simple priority schedule, the scheduler steps through the wheel every time slot with the highest priority queues being checked first for packets. If no packets are ready to send from the high priority queues, the scheduler examines the next lower priority queues and so on. While simple to implement, a simple priority scheduler can easily starve the lower priority queues in favor of the higher priority queues. A simple priority schedule is then inherently unfair.

Round Robin

The round robin (RR) schedule solves the unfairness characteristic of the simple priority mechanism by assigning equal priority to each of the queues. Each time slot of the wheel is used to service each queue in order. While ensuring fairness to the queues to prevent a queue starvation problem, a round robin schedule does not prioritize among flows. While all flows are treated equally, you have no discrimination among high priority flows, such as real time video, and low priority flows, such as Web surfing or e-mail.

Weighted Round Robin

The weighted round robin (WRR) scheduling mechanism prioritizes queues while ensuring that low priority queues are serviced and starvation is prevented. The WRR mechanism weights each queue according to its priority. The highest priority queues are serviced more often than the lower priority ones, but the latter still have a chance at the output port bandwidth. A problem with the WRR scheduling mechanism, however, is that the system needs to know the exact packet size ahead of time to properly schedule the output ports bandwidth. This requirement can lead to complexity in the scheduling process for variable length packets.

Deficit Round Robin

Deficit round robin (DRR) scheduling allows for variable size packets. With DRR, the scheduler keeps track of the sum of the packet sizes that are transmitted so that no packets are transmitted that exceed a maximum number of bytes during their time slot. Each queue has a quantum number assigned to it as a unit of measure to count the number of bytes that are transmitted. DRR also assigns a flow-specific parameter, called a *deficit* (sometimes called a credit), which is set to 0 initially.

Each time it visits a queue, the scheduler transmits the packet only if the packet size is less than or equal to the assigned quantum number of bytes. If the packet is larger than quantum bytes, the packet is not transmitted and the quantum number for that flow is added to that flow's deficit. The deficit number grows if packets are larger than the current deficit number. The deficit number shrinks if packets are smaller than the deficit number and as they are taken off the queue and transmitted. DRR prioritizes flows by assigning a larger quantum number to the higher priority flows and smaller quantum numbers to the lower priority flows. This assignment method allows more bytes to be transmitted for the high priority flows than for the low priority flows. By using this deficit- or credit-based scheduling method, DRR allows variable sized packets to be processed while continuing fairness for both high and low priority queues.

Transmit Fill

The transmit fill operation is the opposite of the initial packet reception. During transmit fill, a scheduled packet is removed from a transmit queue and sent out to the appropriate MAC port for transmission.

Packet Buffering

Buffering packets prior to actually transmitting them is an important system characteristic. When queues are flow controlled in a heavily loaded system, the queues grow, consuming memory space. If many queues are flow controlled for an excessive time, memory can rapidly run out and the congestion avoidance algorithms may start dropping packets. The ability to buffer as much data as possible is then a mechanism to prevent dropped packets. This mechanism is one of the advantages of the Intel IXA store and forward architecture in that it buffers these packets in external memory whose size can be based on the particular application at hand. This mechanism is in contrast with other implementations that buffer the packets internally.

While packet buffering is a simple concept, its implementation has important systems implications. For example, suppose that four I/O cards are receiving 5 gigabits/second of Ethernet traffic for a total of 20 gigabits/second. Let's also assume that all of the traffic for a short period of time has the same destination I/O blade that can only handle 10 gigabits/second of traffic. In this case, that transmit link is temporarily oversubscribed by 10 gigabits/second. To detect a congested system, the I/O blades receive flow control messages from the central switch fabric, indicating the output port that is currently blocked. To prevent dropped packets, the data plane must temporarily buffer the incoming data until the congestion condition is removed. To do so would require a significant amount of external memory for a short period of time. Thus, describing buffering memory requirements versus time is a critical system parameter.

When packets are buffered, the packet buffer descriptors are located in SRAM whereas the actual packet is stored in DRAM. To understand the memory requirements needed to buffer this data, you need to make some assumptions, most significantly the amount of buffering time. In this example, 100 microseconds is a reasonable worst-case example. With the following parameters, the amount of SRAM and SDRAM can be calculated:

- 100 microseconds of total buffering is required

- Incoming data rate = 5 gigabits/second

- Buffers are obtained from a chained, linked list free buffer pool

- Buffers come in two sizes: 128 bytes and 512 bytes

- Each buffer descriptor is 8 bytes

- 60 percent of packets are 64 bytes, 20 percent are 576 bytes, and 20 percent are 1500 bytes

Figure 2.12 shows a total of 654,000 buffers required to buffer the above data stream for 100 microseconds.

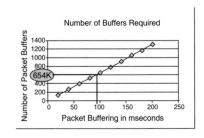

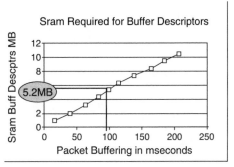

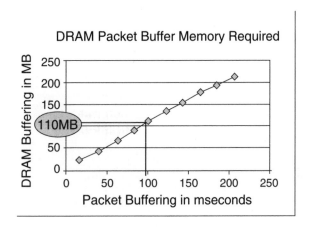

Figure 2.12   Packet Buffering

Based on the number of descriptors, you can calculate the total amount of SRAM memory. In this example, 5.2 megabytes of SRAM is used to buffer the stream for 100 microseconds. You can also determine the amount of DRAM. The graph shows that 110 megabytes is required in this situation.

Chapter 3

External Architecture

The external architecture defines how the IXP2XXX network processors interface to the outside world, which includes MACs, framers, switch fabrics, memory systems, and other IXP2XXX processors. The architecture implements industry standard interfaces to promote faster development time through a wide variety of standard, off-the-shelf components.

This chapter provides you with a general overview of the external hardware systems architecture of the network processor family. Several sample systems in this chapter show you different ways to configure these processors for specific applications. Because the Media and Switch Fabric (MSF) interface is the primary data path interface where packets are transferred through the network processor, we will look at this interface in greater detail. With the MSF description and the basic system configurations, you will better understand the internal architecture described in Chapter 4.

External Architecture Overview

The Intel IXP2400 and IXP28X0 processors follow an ingress/egress processing model, in which a receive processor operates on the ingress traffic and a second transmit processor handles the egress traffic. The only difference between the ingress and egress processors is the software that runs them. Many other system implementations are possible, such as using single and multiple processors for ingress-egress operations. Figure 3.1 illustrates the external interfaces for the IXP28X0 network processor. For additional information about the IXP2XXX processors, see "The Next Generation of Intel IXP Network Processors" (Adiletta et al. 2002).

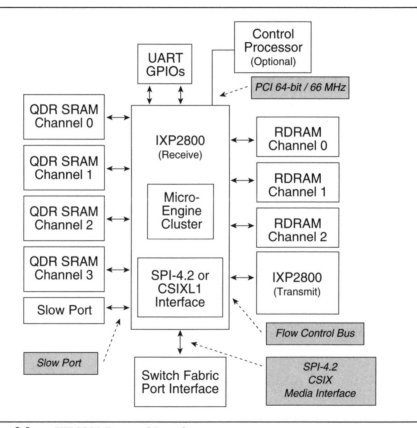

Figure 3.1   IXP2800 External Interfaces

Figure 3.2 illustrates the external interfaces for the IXP2400 network processor.

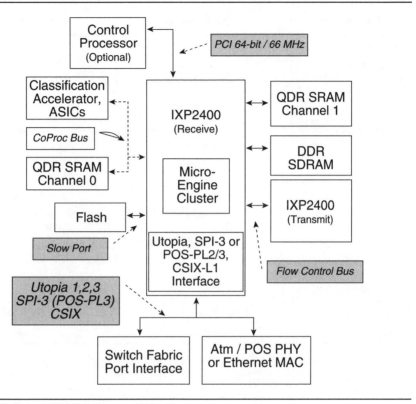

Figure 3.2   IXP2400 External Interfaces

The key differences between the two processors are shown in Table 3.1.

Table 3.1   Feature Comparison between IXP2800 and IXP2400 Processors

Characteristics	IXP28X0 Processor	IXP2400 Processor
Maximum Frequency	1.4 GHz	600 MHz
DRAM Memory	3 channels RDRAM PC600/PC800/PC1066 MHz Total 50 Gb/s Up to 2 GB	1 channel DDR DRAM 19.2 Gb/s at 150 MHz Up to 2 GB
SRAM Memory	4 channels QDR or coprocessor 16 Gb/s per channel at 250 MHz	2 channels QDR or coprocessor 16 Gb/s per channel at 200 MHz
Media Interface	Separate 16-bit Tx & Rx configurable to SPI-4.2 or CSIX_L2 16 Gb/s at 500 MHz	Channelized and Separate 8, 16, or 32-bit Tx & Rx configurable to POS-PHY, SPI-3, UTOPIA1/2/3, or CSIX_L1 4.0 Gb/s at 125 MHz
Microengines (MEv2)	16	8
Performance	Dual-chip, full duplex OC-192	Dual-chip, full duplex OC-48
Power	-21W -26W Typical	-13W Typical

System Configurations

The IXP2XXX processors can be configured for different operating modes, based on the developer's unique system requirements. Whether it's a high line rate line card with a switch fabric, a centralized control processor application, or a specialized line control card requiring extensive packet processing, Intel IXA network processors can be configured to meet these varying system requirements. The three basic configurations are:

■ Dual Ingress/Egress

■ Single Ingress/Egress

■ Chaining

With the high OC-48 and OC-192 data rates that these systems are expected to process, packet processing functions must be defined for a given line rate. Each of the three basic configurations has a common base of software functionality; they differ only in the total system bandwidth. Characteristics of ingress processing are:

- Media receive and reassembly
- Classification and forwarding
- Metering and statistics
- Congestion avoidance
- Queue management
- Transmit scheduling to fabric
- Transmit to Switch Fabric (CSIX or SPI)

Characteristics of egress processing are:

- Receive from switch fabric (CSIX or SPI)
- Congestion management
- Metering and statistics
- Queue management
- Traffic scheduling to network (QoS, TM 4.1 etc.)
- Transmit to media to network

IXP2800 Dual Ingress/Egress Configuration

The IXP2800 processor's external system follows very closely the I/O blade configuration shown in Figure 3.3. This implementation is called the *dual ingress/egress configuration* because the network processor is in the middle of the wire, providing full-duplex bandwidth to both sides. Figure 3.3 illustrates an intelligent line card Ethernet application, with 10x1Gigabit Ethernet interfaces going to the network through the IXF1010 MAC. Other implementations, such as OC-192 ATM and POS, are possible with industry standard SPI-4.2 MACs and framers.

The other side of the IXP2800 processor interfaces to the fabric through a fabric interface chip (FIC). Functioning as a thin gasket, the FIC interfaces the CSIX or SPI-4.2 bus to a SERDES that is unique to the particular fabric being used for the system. For this full-duplex line card, the media interface is full duplex and the fabric interface also is full duplex. In this configuration, the media interface transfers 10 gigabits/second full duplex (20 gigabits/second total for full duplex 10GigE) and the fabric interface supporting 15 gigabits/second full duplex (10 gigabits/second for data, 5 gigabits/second for fabric overhead; 30 gigabits/second total). Thus, the total bandwidth for a full duplex, 10-gigabit/second line card is 50 gigabits/second (2x10 Gb/s for the MACs and 2x15 Gb/s for the fabric).

This configuration also supports system wide flow control through the CSIX interface. CSIX allows for Virtual Output Queue (VOQ) flow control messaging (described later in this chapter). These messages are received by the egress processor. However, because the ingress processor is the one actually transmitting packets to the fabric, flow control messages must be processed by this processor. To allow for this situation, IXP2XXX network processors allow the egress processor to receive the flow control messages from the fabric and then automatically (via hardware) transmit them to the ingress processor via the Cbus. The transmit scheduler software of the ingress processor reads this message which prevents sending packets to the congested ports. This Cbus flow control bus is illustrated in Figure 3.3.

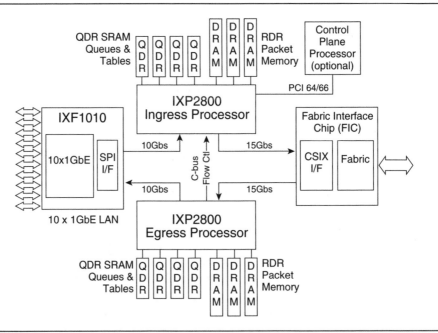

Figure 3.3 IXP2800 Dual Ingress/Egress Configuration

The Dual Ingress/Egress configuration can also be used in a network appliance, a "pizza-box" system, or other systems that don't use a switch fabric for inter-blade communication and data transfer. Figure 3.4 shows such a configuration in which protocol conversion between two networks is done on the same board instead of a fabric based chassis configuration as shown in Figure 3.3.

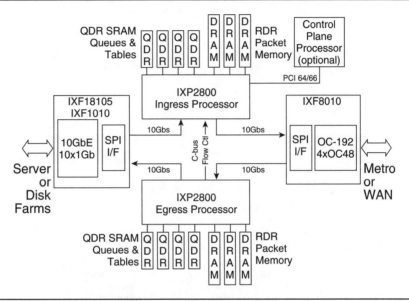

Figure 3.4   Gigabit Ethernet LAN to SONET WAN (or metro) System Using Dual Ingress/Egress Architecture

In this system, the Ingress IXP2800 network processor receives Ethernet packets from a server or disk farm, processes the packet, then schedules and transmits the packet out the WAN via a SONET ring. The egress architecture performs a similar function, but going from SONET to Ethernet.

IXP2400 Dual Ingress/Egress Architecture

The system architecture for the IXP2400 processor is similar to that of the IXP2800 processor. Both processors follow an ingress/egress software flow for intelligent line card applications where a fabric is used to communicate to multiple blades. This architecture performs the set of ingress and egress tasks as shown in Figure 3.5.

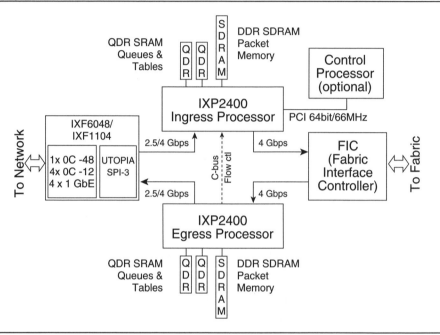

Figure 3.5   IXP2400 Dual Ingress/Egress Architecture

In this diagram, the IXP2400 ingress processor can receive data from the network via several interfaces, such as POS or ATM with an IXF6048 framer, or from an Ethernet Network, such as the IXF1104 Quad Gigabit Ethernet MAC. The IXF6048 is a SPI-3 framer that can be configured as either a single OC-48 framer or four OC-12 SONET framers. Because the IXF6048 handles OC-48 bit rates, the interface to the IXP2400 processor is 2.5 gigabits/second full duplex. The IXF1104 framer can provide the interface to Ethernet networks. Like the IXF6048, it also has a UTOPIA3 or SPI-3 Interface. However, since it contains 4-gigabit Ethernet MACs, the interface to the network processor can operate at 4.256 gigabits/second full duplex (32 bits x 133 Megahertz).

The IXP2400 processor also can be used in appliance or control card applications where all protocol conversion is performed in a single board, as shown in Figure 3.6. In this dual ingress/egress architecture, the ingress process receives data from several Ethernet LANs via the IXF1104 then transmits the data to a SONET ring via the IXF6048. The egress processor performs a similar, but symmetric function in the reverse direction.

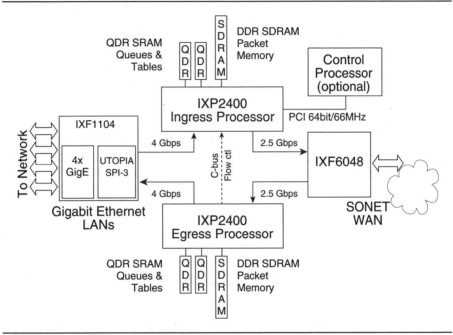

Figure 3.6   IXP2400 Dual Ingress/Egress Appliance Configuration

While these appliance or control card functions do not interface to switching fabrics, the tasks they perform are similar, even for transmission processing. While switch fabric traffic scheduling and transmission are particular to fabric and internal system requirements, these tasks are similar when interfacing directly to the network. Scheduling algorithms can be very similar, often times consuming an equivalent amount of system resources. An exception is ATM TM4.1 traffic shaping, which has very stringent requirements for cell scheduling and consumes more SRAM and computing resources than the round robin or priority-based scheduling mechanisms that are more common for IP networks or switch fabric systems.

IXP2800 Single Ingress/Egress Configuration

For many system implementations, very rich packet processing is required at OC-48 data rates. These applications can use a single IXP2800 processor, as shown in Figure 3.7.

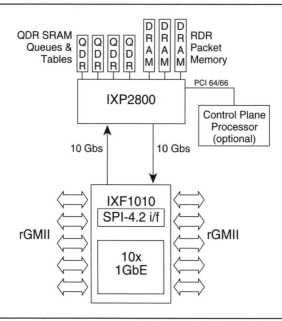

Figure 3.7   IXP2800 Single Ingress/Egress Configuration

In the single ingress/egress processing mode, the system bandwidth is half that of the dual mode because no fabric is supported. In this mode, the equivalent packet processing functions of the in-line mode is achieved with one IXP2800 processor because the bandwidth is now 20 gigabits/second for full duplex 10 Gigabit Ethernet links rather than 50 gigabits/second.

While the previous example illustrated a 10x1 Gigabit Ethernet application, other configurations are also possible when interfacing OC-48 class MACS and framers through SPI-3 interfaces. Figure 3.8 illustrates a dual OC-48 Packet-Over-SONET line card. A blade of this type can be a trunk card that receives IP frames from other blades in the system then encapsulates these frames using Point-to-Point Protocol (PPP) over a SONET backbone. In this typical application, the card interfaces to a switching fabric through the CSIX interface, with dual OC-48 SONET framers interfacing to the backbone WAN infrastructure. A SPI-4.2 to SPI-3 gasket chip enables the IXP2800 processor, with its SPI-4.2 bus, to interface to SPI-3 peripherals, such as the IXF6048 SONET framer.

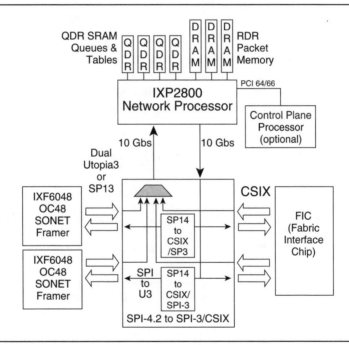

Figure 3.8   Dual OC-48 SONET Line Card Utilizing Single Ingress/Egress Architecture

IXP2400 Single Ingress/Egress Model

The IXP2400 processor can also operate in a single ingress/egress configuration as shown in Figure 3.9. In this example, the IXP2400 processor interfaces either to the Ethernet network via the IXF1104 or to the SONET network through the IXF6048. This single ingress/egress configuration combines the receive software flow from the ingress and egress directions into one data flow. Thus, each stage in the processing must identify whether the data comes from the ingress or egress direction then jump to the appropriate section in the program.

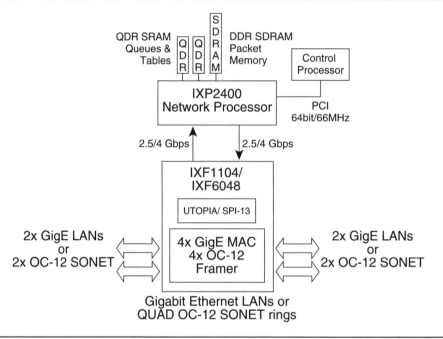

Figure 3.9   IXP2400 Single Ingress/Egress Configuration

The configuration in Figure 3.9 allows a single IXP2400 processor to be used in a full duplex manner when the MAC or framer is used to split the ingress and egress paths. This configuration is optimal for systems where the ingress and egress networks use the same type of link layer interface (e.g., Ethernet or SONET, but different interfaces may be needed for the network interface and fabric interfaces. For example, Ethernet may be required for the network interface and ATM for the trunk interface. To support this, the MSF unit on the IXP2400 can be channelized to support 8, 16, and 32-bit PHYs. Because each physical channel is point-to-point, only one physical device (PHY) is supported for each channel. Thus, each channel supports MPHY mode of 32 ports in 32-bit mode or 31 ports in 16 bit mode. SPHY can be supported in 8-, 16-, or 32-bit mode. Thus, multiple, physical chips can be attached to the IXP2400 processor. This ability is advantageous in lower line rate, full-duplex applications (such as OC-12 and 1 Gigabit Ethernet) where only a single IXP2400 processor is needed. Figure 3.10 shows a typical application, showing the IXP2400 processor configured with two 16-bit, MPHY SPI-3 interfaces.

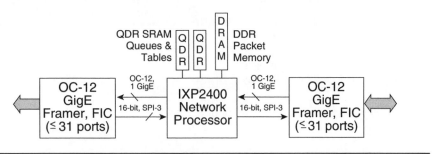

Figure 3.10 IXP2400 Single-chip, Full-duplex in 16-bit, MPHY SPI-3 Mode

Chaining Configuration

Many applications require extensive processing of each packet, exceeding the upper limits of typical single processor applications. Examples are multi-stage classification and protocol conversion where a packet undergoes several transformations. In these applications, a chaining configuration might be more appropriate, as shown in Figure 3.11. The chaining configuration for the IXP2400 processor is similar, although most applications would use the IXP2800 because it offers higher performance processing (1.4 gigahertz vs. 600 megahertz) and twice the number of microengines.

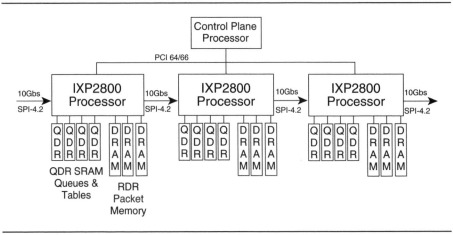

Figure 3.11   IXP2800 Chaining Model

A Complete IXP2XXX System

The complex, multi-service platforms that are typically found in edge routers use a multi-blade system, in which each line card performs protocol processing specifically for the data link layer to which that card is connected, as illustrated in Figure 3.12. The line card then encapsulates the packets in a format that is unique to the platform for internal communication and processing. For example, ATM cells arriving on one slot are received and assembled in complete AAL5 frames, and then they are classified. Once identified as belonging to a specific connection, forwarding information is attached to the packet, identifying the next hop intended for these frames. Any protocol conversion is done at this time, and then the frame is encapsulated in a frame format particular to the platform's switch fabric before the frame is scheduled and transmitted to the fabric. The fabric forwards it to the appropriate slot. Figure 3.12 shows this system.

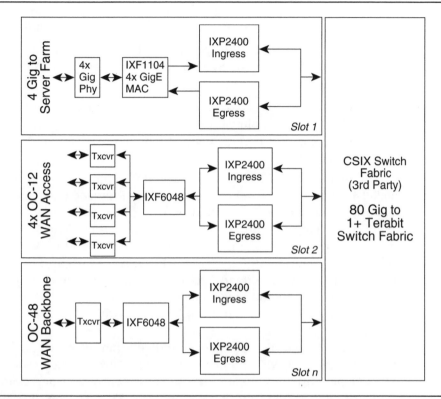

Figure 3.12   Complete System Based on the IXP2400 Processor

IXP2XXX External Interfaces

The IXP2XXX family of network processors provides industry standard buses to interface to common, off-the-shelf components. While PCI, SRAM, and DRAM interfaces are commonly understood, the MSF's SPI-3, SPI-4, and CSIX interfaces may be new to many designers. As such, we will spend a bit more time reviewing the MSF.

IXP28X0 Media and Switch Fabric Interface

The Media and Switch Fabric (MSF) interface connects the IXP28X0 processor to a physical layer device (PHY), a switch fabric interface, or both. For more detail, see the *IXP2800 Hardware Reference Manual* (Intel January 2003). The MSF includes two interfaces, as follows:

- *Receive and transmit interfaces*. Each can be individually configured for either the System Packet Interface (SPI-4) Phase 2 to a PHY or the CSIX –L1 protocol to a switch fabric.

- *A flow-control interface*. A point-to-point connection passes CSIX-L1 flow control C-Frames either between two IXP2800 processors or between an IXP2800 processor and a CSIX-L1 switch fabric.

The MSF supports 16-bit low-voltage differential signaling (LVDS) for the SPI-4.2 data path channel. Both the fabric interface chip (FIC) and the network processor can be configured to support either low voltage TTL or LVDS signaling for the SPI-4 FIFO status channel. The MSF also supports 16-bit LVDS signaling for CSIX-L1 protocol and 4-bit LVDS signaling for the flow control interface. The fabric/processor can be clocked at speeds from 333 megahertz to 500 megahertz, providing up to 666 mega-transfers/second to 1000 mega-transfers/second. With a 16-bit wide bus, this capability equates to a full duplex bandwidth of 10.656 to 16 gigabits/second.

SPI-4.2 is an interface for packet and cell transfer between a PHY device (such as a SONET framer) and a link layer device, such as the IXP2800 network processor, for use in systems with aggregate bandwidths of OC-192 ATM and Packet-Over-SONET over SONET/SDH (POS) as well as 10 gigabits/second Ethernet applications. The SPI-4.2 protocol transfers data in variable length bursts, associating each burst with status information, such as a port number for a multi-port device, start-of-packet (SOP), or an end-of-packet (EOP). The MSF collects this information and passes it to the internal microengines.

The Common Switch Interface (CSIX_L1) defines an interface between a traffic manager (TM) and a switch fabric (SF) for ATM, IP, MPLS, Ethernet, and similar data communications applications. The Network Processor Forum (NPF) controls the CSIX_L1 specification. As defined by the NPF in this context, the traffic manager function actually is performed by internal actions of the IXP2800. The basic unit of information transferred between the IXP2800 processor and the switch fabric is called a CFrame. A number of CFrame types are defined, but all of them control the information about data, control, or lower layer flow control.

Associated with each CFrame is information such as length, type, and address. The MSF collects this information and passes it to microengines, as described in Chapter 4.

IXP2400 Media and Switch Fabric Interface

The IXP2400 MSF has the following major features:

■ Separate and independently configurable 32-bit receive and transmit buses.

■ A configurable bus interface. The bus may function as a single 32-bit bus, or it can be configured as independent channelized buses in one of these combinations: two 16-bit buses, four 8-bit buses, or one 16-bit bus and two 8-bit buses. Each channel can be configured to operate in either UTOPIA or POS-PHY (SPI-3) mode.

■ The Media bus operates from 25 to 133 Megahertz.

■ UTOPIA Level 1/2/3 and POS-PHY Level 2/3 single-PHY (SPHY) and multi-PHY (MPHY) operation. The IXP2400 MSF supports 8-, 16-, or 32-bit buses.

■ UTOPIA Level 3 multiple-physical layer (MPHY) master operation with a 32-bit wide bus. The IXP2400 MSF supports up to 32 slave ports in 32-bit mode and up to 31 slave ports in 16-bit mode.

■ POS-PHY Level 3 and SPI-3 MPHY master operation can be used when the bus is configured as either one 32-bit wide bus or two 16-bit wide buses. The master operation supports up to 32 slave ports in 32-bit mode and up to 31 slave ports in 16-bit mode.

■ Support for CSIX-L1 protocol with a 32-bit wide bus.

■ Support for an inter-processor CBus for communicating link level and fabric level flow control information between egress and ingress processors in CSIX mode.

■ Interface to internal buses, such as command, SRAM push/pull, and DRAM push/pull.

The MSF consists of separate receive and transmit interfaces. Each of the receive and transmit interfaces can be configured separately for either UTOPIA (Level 1, 2, and 3), POS-PHY (Level 2 and 3), or CSIX protocols.

The receive and transmit ports are unidirectional and completely independent of each other. Each port has 32 data signals, two clocks, a set of control signals, and a set of parity signals, all of which use 3.3V LVTTL signaling.

In UTOPIA and POS-PHY modes, each port can function as a single 32-bit interface, or any port can be subdivided into a combination of 16-bit or 8-bit channels. When running in channelized mode, each channel operates independently. Each channel is a point-to-point connection to a single PHY. This connection is also known as single-PHY (SPHY) mode.

In addition to SPHY mode, the IXP2400 processor also supports MPHY mode, in which the bus, whether configured in the 16-bit or 32-bit channel width, is shared by up to 32 ports with 32-bit wide channel or 31 ports in 16-bit wide channels. Following the UTOPIA Level 3 and POS-PHY Level 3 specifications, all ports must reside within one physical device. *Only master mode is supported in UTOPIA and POS-PHY modes; slave mode is not supported.*

In addition to the UTOPIA, POS-PHY, and CSIX interfaces, an interface called Cbus is used in CSIX mode to forward link level and fabric level flow control information from the egress processor that receives it to the ingress processor that transmits it.

For more detail, refer to the IXP2400 processor's hardware reference manual (Intel October 2002).

MSF CSIX Flow Control

The IXP2XXX processors have special hardware to send and receive flow-control messages from a switch fabric that adheres to the Network Processor Forum's CSIX framing specifications. These flow control messages are indicated in the cframe header as shown in Figure 3.13. Managing flow control elegantly with minimal latency requires a clean hardware interface and special software, which is a part of Intel IXA. CSIX flow control is communicated by Cframes that are specified as flow control frames.

CSIX supports two different types of flow control, as follows:

■ Link level flow control manages the lowest level link between the IXP2XXX processor and the actual fabric interface chip (FIC). In the CSIX Cframe header, Bits 14 and 15, called the ready bits, indicate this flow control message.

■ Virtual Output Queue (VOQ) flow control. VOQ flow control manages the scheduling of transmitted data to virtual output queues within an entire multi-blade system. A VOQ flow control message conforms to CSIX frame type 6.

Type	Frame Descripion	ExtHdr
0	Idle - Transmitted during inactivity	No
1	Unicast-Addressed to single destination TM	Yes
2	Multicast Mask - Transmit to masked address	Yes
3	Multicast ID - Transmit to group ID	Yes
4	Multicast Binary Copy - Transmit to 2 TMs	Yes
5	Broadcast - Transmit to all TMs	Yes
6	Flow Control - Controls flow between VOQs	Yes

Flow Control
CFrame Type
CSIXRsvd
Private

Base Header Format

Ready	Type	CR	P	Payload Length
15:14	13:10	9	8	7:0

Figure 3.13   CSIX Header

Figure 3.14 shows how the IXP2XXX processors receive these two different types of flow control.

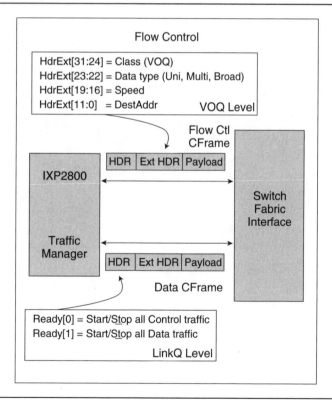

Figure 3.14   CSIX Flow-Control Messages

When the IXP2XXX processor receives CSIX frames, the MSF decodes the frames header to determine the type of frame and whether link level flow control is asserted. If the frame requires link level flow control, the ingress IXP2XXX processor prevents transmission of all data or control information to the FIC, which prevents overflowing the FIC's internal FIFO. When link level flow control is asserted, all data or control information ready to be transmitted from the network processor is stopped until flow control is released.

Whereas link level flow control manages the data flow from the network processor to the FIC chip only (chip-to-chip), VOQ flow control manages transmit scheduling to any output queue in the system no matter which blade in the system the queue resides in. Thus, VOQ flow control needs to support thousands of queues for robust systems. When VOQ flow control is asserted for a queue, the CSIX control mechanism prevents data transmission to only that queue.

Figure 3.15 illustrates a typical application example of the dual ingress/egress configuration. The egress process receives flow control messages from the fabric, but the ingress processor is the one that actually transmits the packets through the system. Thus, the egress processor receives flow control messages, then immediately sends it to the ingress processor to manage the flow of the packets transmitted through the fabric.

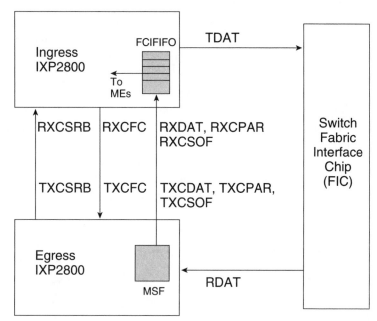

Flow-control is similar for the IXP2400 processor.

Figure 3.15   Flow-control Message Passing with the IXP2800

A special flow control interface is used to communicate flow control messages from the egress processor to the ingress processor. The TXCSRB/RXCSRB signal communicates link level ready messages. The egress processor decodes the CSIX header, and if link level flow control is true, this signal is asserted so the ingress processor can immediately stop transmission of all data or control information to the FIC.

VOQ flow control messages are communicated via the CBus. The egress processor's MSF unit decodes CSIX frames and sends flow control messages across the CBus to the ingress processor. The ingress processor receives these messages, placing them in a FIFO, and then signals the microengines that the FIFO has a message waiting. A transmit scheduling software algorithm uses this signal to read the message, decode it, then manage the flow for the particular VOQ contained in the message.

CBus is a 4-bit bus that is clocked at the same frequency as the primary MSF data path, for example 133 megahertz for the IXP2400 processor and 500 megahertz for the IXP2800 processor. Both the ingress and egress processors have an internal FIFO that buffers the messages prior to transmission and upon arrival. This 1-kilobyte FIFO is organized as 256 32-bit words. The CBus prevents FIFO overruns by using the TXCFC/RXCFC signal to control data flow into the ingress processor. The MSF transmission also contains a Start of Frame (SOF) delimiter as well as a parity signal.

Figure 3.15 shows only the fabric interface. A dual IXP2XXX-based system design also contains the network media interface. This interface also needs flow control, so these flow control signals are duplicated for that interface as well.

Note

You also can use the CBus for reasonably fast inter-processor communication. In normal operation, the CSIX flow control messages are put on the CBus directly by the MSF CSIX control circuitry. The IXP2XXX processors also allow microengines to put data directly into the transmit FIFO through CSR writes. The bandwidth for the IXP2400 processor is 532 megabits/second (133 Megahertz x 4 bits) while the IXP2800 processor supports 4 gigabits/second (1000 MT/s x 4 bits).

SPI-4.2 Flow Control

Flow control for the SPI-4.2 interface used on the IXP2800 processor deserves special attention due to the significant difference between it and SPI-3, POS-PHY, and UTOPIA flow control mechanisms that are used on the IXP2400 processor. These slower interfaces use simple on/off signaling. For transmit flow control, the PHY uses a signal (TxAvail) to tell the IXP2400 processor that its FIFO has ample room to receive data. For receive flow control, the IXP2400 processor uses a signal (RxEnable) to tell the PHY that its receive buffers have enough room to accept data from the PHY device.

Due to their higher OC-192 data rates, SPI-4.2 PHYs have more flexible capabilities than the slower interfaces. Due to their higher speed, multiple lower speed ports can be integrated into one physical device. In Figure 3.16, a single OC-192 framer device can have three OC-48 ports, three OC-12 ports and four OC-3 ports. Each port transfers data to and from the IXP2800 processor at its own average line rate. For example, the OC-48 port transfers four times the rate of data as the OC-12 port. Each port has its own FIFO, and the fullness of each FIFO varies according to traffic conditions. Designers implementing link layer flow control must take this flexibility into account. An implementation using the typical link layer flow control is inefficient in this case. For example, if two FIFOs for the OC-48 port are full, but the other ports can accept more data from the IXP28X0, a flow control mechanism that blocks data transfer to all of the ports is very inefficient. Thus, the SPI-4.2 flow control mechanism can assert flow control on a per port basis.

SPI-4.2 uses a more robust credit based flow control mechanism for a link layer device, like the IXP28X0, and a PHY, like a SONET framer, to communicate whether data can be sent over the interface and if so, how much data can be sent. A special serial FIFO status message allows the IXP28X0 processor and the PHY device to communicate their FIFO status. The IXP28X0 processor's MSF transmit logic can direct the flow on a per-port basis for the attached PHY. The MSF's receive logic can flow control on a per port basis or give a general state of overall RBUF buffer fullness to the PHY.

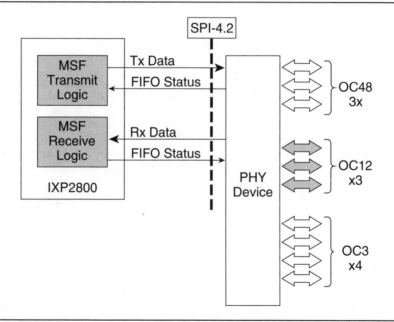

Figure 3.16   SPI-4.2 FIFO Status Interface

The SPI-4.2 interface uses a calendar-based scheduling mechanism. Each slot in the calendar indicates the port to which data is sent during a specific time period. Higher speed ports are represented more often in the calendar than lower speed ports. This calendar is loaded into the IXP2800 processor's MSF through a CSR, as shown in Figure 3.17.

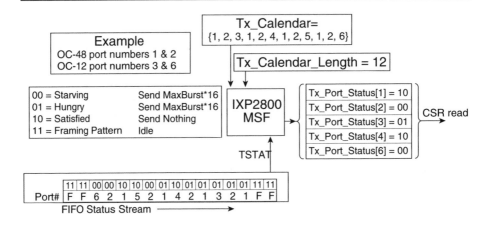

Figure 3.17   IXP2800 SPI-4.2 Transmit Flow-Control Messaging

In this transmit example, the SPI-4.2 device has two OC-48 ports (ports 1-2) and four OC-12 ports (ports 3-6). The calendar length of 12 indicates the OC-48 ports transmitting four times more data than the OC-12 ports. The particular sequence in the calendar ensures this transmission rate. The calendar tells the IXP28X0 MSF's transmit logic the order in which to transmit the packets to the PHY. This calendar in the PHY mirrors the calendar that is preloaded in the IXP28X0. The PHY indicates flow control by sending a continuous FIFO status serial stream to the IXP28X0 processor. The two framing bits define the start of packet and end of packet, delimiting the frame. Each pair of bits in this packet designates a particular port in the PHY. The coding of the bits indicates the FIFO's consumption status, as follows:

10 = full or a satisfied state

01 = needs a normal burst or hungry state

00 = needs an extra long burst or starving state

A satisfied state implies that the PHY's FIFO is full (satisfied) and doesn't require more data. A normal burst and extra long burst is user programmed in the IXP2800's MSF unit and matches what is stored in the corresponding PHY. The MSF transmit control logic decodes this continuous FIFO status stream and indicates the ports status via the Tx_Port_Status[n] registers. These registers are read by the Transmit Scheduler microengine, which determines which ports it can transmit to.

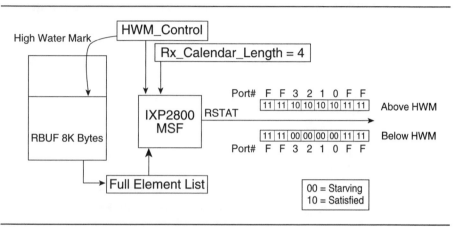

Figure 3.18   IXP2800 SPI-4.2 Receive Flow-control Messaging Using RBUF Status Mode

To manage receive-flow control, the IXP28X0 sends a FIFO status stream to the PHY that is very similar to the one that it receives from a PHY on the transmit bus. There are two modes for the receive calendar that is sent to the PHY. In the per port over-ride mode, it sends a status word to the PHY on a per port basis. Microengine software controls this value based the current RBUF buffer fullness available to receive additional packets from a specific PHY ports. The PHY then reads this calendar word to determine which of its ports it can send to the IXP28X0. Some applications may use this mode to flow control a specific PHY's port if there aren't enough processing resources available to process additional packets from the port. However, the software architecture should be designed so this isn't needed in the first place. Software should remove packets from the RBUF fast enough so RBUF overruns don't occur.

The second mode allows flow-control of a port to be based on the most conservative of three different values. In this mode, satisfied is defined to be more conservative than hungry, which is more conservative than starving.

■ *RBUF Status Mode.* The MSF maintains an average high water mark for the entire 8-kilobyte receive buffer (RBUF). This high water mark (HWM) is programmed via an IXP28X0 MSF CSR. When the total receive buffer is under the high water mark, the MSF sends the PHY a hungry or starving state message for all the ports. Then, the PHY can send data from any of its ports to the IXP28X0 processor. When the high water mark is reached, the MSF sets a satisfied status for all the ports and sends that calendar stream to the PHY. The PHY then stops sending data from *all* its ports as illustrated in Figure 3.18.

■ *Per Port Override.* Each port can be given a specific satisfied, hungry, or starving state as in the first method described previously.

■ *Global Override.* Software can globally set all the ports to a specific value of satisfied, hungry, or starving.

In this second mode, software can override a port's current flow control state with a more conservative value. For instance, suppose that the current buffer fullness is under the high water mark (HWM) and that the MSF is configured to send hungry status to the PHY for all ports while in this condition. If a microengine thread wants to flow control a particular port, it can override the current RBUF HWM status with a more conservative satisfied status message to flow control a particular port. This ability allows microengine software to have greater control over what ports it can service based on processor loading.

PCI Bus

The PCI bus provides the mechanism for IXP2XXX network processors to interface to control plane processors, Ethernet NICs during development, or other standard PCI devices. The PCI Controller provides a 64-bit, 66-Megahertz capable PCI Revision 2.2 interface. This controller is also compatible with 32-bit and/or 33-Megahertz PCI devices.

The PCI controller provides the following functions:

■ Target access giving the external bus master access to SRAM, DRAM, and CSRs

■ Master access for Intel XScale core or microengine access to PCI target devices

■ Three DMA channels

■ Mailbox and doorbell registers for communication from Intel XScale core to host

■ PCI arbiter

You can configure IXP2XXX network processors to act as a PCI central function. Alternatively, you can configure them to serve as an add-in device, such as an adapter board in a personal computer or an appliance-like motherboard.

IXP28x0 RDRAM

The IXP28x0 processor has controllers for three Rambus† DRAM (RDRAM) channels. Each controller independently accesses its own RDRAMs, and each can operate concurrently with the other controllers because they are not operating as a single, wider memory. DRAM provides high density, high bandwidth storage and is typically used for data buffers.

The IXP28x0 processor supports RDRAM sizes of 64, 128, 256, and 512 megabits; however, each of the channels must be populated by RDRAMs with the same number, size, and speed. Each channel can be populated with one to four RDRAMs per bank for a short channel and one RIMM for a long channel.

Up to 2 gigabytes of DRAM is supported. If less memory is available, the upper part of the address space is not used. To reduce system cost and promote area savings, a system design can have Channels 0 and 1 populated and leave Channel 2 empty, or have Channel 0 populated and leave Channels 1 and 2 empty.

Reads and writes to RDRAM are generated by microengines, Intel Xscale core, and PCI (external Bus Masters and DMA Channels). Controller cycles also refresh and calibrate the RDRAMs, transparently to software. RDRAM power-down and nap modes are not supported.

Hardware interleaving of addresses, also known as striping, provides balanced access to all populated channels. The interleave size is 128 bytes. Interleaving helps to maintain utilization of available bandwidth by spreading consecutive accesses to multiple channels. Hardware does the interleaving in such a way that the three channels appear to software as a single contiguous memory space.

IXP2400 DRAM

The IXP2400 processor also uses DRAM for packet buffering and for storing larger data structures, but the IXP2400 processor uses DDR SDRAM for these functions. The IXP2400 DRAM's features are:

- Supports one DDR SDRAM channel 64 bits wide without ECC or 72 bits with ECC.
- Supports DDR devices up to 300 mega-transfers/second.
- Supports 64-megabit, 128-megabit, 256-megabit, 512-megabit and 1-gigabit technologies for x8 and x16 devices, both DIMM and direct soldered.
- Hardware-controlled interleaving spreads contiguous addresses across multiple banks.
- All supported devices have four banks.
- Configurable optional error correction using ECC bits.
- Supports one single-sided DIMM or one double-sided DIMM.
- Supports up to 2 gigabytes of memory capacity using 1–gigabyte DRAM technology.

The memory controller is responsible for the off-chip DRAM and provides a mechanism for other functional units in the IXP2400 processor to access the DRAM. A 2-gigabyte address space is allocated to DRAM. From a software perspective, the memory space is guaranteed to be contiguous. If less memory is available, the upper part of the address space is aliased into the lower part of the address space, and the upper part should not be used by software.

Reads and writes to DRAM are generated by the microengines, by the Intel XScale core, and by PCI bus masters. These bus masters are connected to the controllers via the command bus and push and pull buses. The memory controller takes commands from these sources and enqueues them in command inlet FIFOs. The commands are dequeued and the accesses to the DRAM are performed. The controller also triggers refresh cycles to the DRAMs.

SRAM

The IXP2XXX network processors use SRAM for storing look-up tables, free buffer lists, buffer and queue descriptors, and other data structures that need access to fast, low latency memory. It also supports co-processors, such as TCAMs, and classification co-processors that adhere to Quad Data Rate (QDR) signaling. SRAM is used in conjunction with the DRAM to optimize memory utilization and lower costs. For example, when an IXP2XXX network processor performs a route look-up, it first searches through SRAM for an address match. The size of these tables is modest, around 4 megabytes for typical applications, but they must be accessed very quickly, with minimal latency, to optimize the software-based search algorithm. When found, the match contains a pointer to a flow or connection descriptor that is stored in DRAM. This descriptor can be several words long and consume considerable memory space for systems supporting 100Ks of flows.

The IXP2400 and IXP2800 processors have two and four independent SRAM controllers respectively, each supporting pipelined QDR synchronous SRAM and the option of adding or substituting a coprocessor that adheres to QDR signaling. Any or all controllers can be left unpopulated if the application does not need to use them. SRAM is accessible by the microengines, the Intel XScale core, and the PCI Unit. The SRAM unit has a programmable priority arbiter ranging from 1 to 32 levels to prevent the Intel XScale core from consuming an unfair amount of SRAM bandwidth.

The memory is logically four bytes (32 bits) wide; physically the data pins are two bytes wide and double clocked. Byte parity is supported. Each of the four bytes has a parity bit, which is written when the byte is written and checked when the data is read. Byte enables select the byte lanes to use for writes of less than 32 bits. Each SRAM channel is independent of the others so it can be clocked and configured differently from the others to suit the particular application.

Slow Port

The slow port is an external interface to IXP2XXX processors that is used for Flash ROM access and 8-, 16-, or 32-bit asynchronous device access. The slow port allows the Intel XScale core to do read/write data transfers to these slave devices. The address bus and data bus are multiplexed on a physical 8-bit bus to reduce the pin count. In addition, 24 bits of address space are shifted out on three clock cycles. Therefore, a program needs an external set of buffers to latch the address. Two chip selects are provided.

Serial Port

The IXP2XXX processors contain a standard RS-232 compatible Universal Asynchronous Receiver/Transmitter (UART), which can be used for communication with a debugger or maintenance console. Modem controls are not supported. If they are needed, GPIO pins can be used.

The UART performs serial-to-parallel conversion on data characters that are received from a peripheral device and parallel-to-serial conversion on data characters that are received from the processor. The processor can read the complete status of the UART at any time during operation. Available status information includes the type and condition of the transfer operations being performed by the UART and any error conditions including parity, overrun, framing, or break interrupt.

GPIO

The IXP2XXX processors contain eight General Purpose I/O (GPIO) pins. These pins can be programmed as either input or output, and they can be used for slow speed I/O, such as LEDs or input switches. They can also be used as interrupts to the Intel XScale core or to clock the programmable timers.

Chapter 4

Intel® IXA Microarchitecture

This chapter introduces the Intel IXA microarchitecture. It focuses on the critical functional units that are directly involved with touching packets in data plane processing, such as in the IPv6 packet flow described in Chapter 1. These units—the microengines, chassis, and MSF— are directly involved in the processing flow. While the Intel XScale core, PCI unit, SHaC, and DRAM unit are important functional units, their operation is either peripheral to the actual data plane processing or is already well understood and so is only briefly described here. The performance of the SRAM unit is very significant to maintaining high line rates and will be covered in more detail in Chapter 6. The goal of this chapter is not to explain all the details of the processor because you can find that information in the published documentation, such as the hardware reference manual for the respective processor (see "References"). The IXP2400 and IXP2800 processors are functionally the same, so they are explained separately only when they differ. For an excellent article describing more of the details of the Intel IXA microarchitecture, see "The Next Generation of Intel Network Processors" (Adiletta et al. 2002).

The eight main functional units of the IXP2XXX processors, with the IXP2850 processor's crypto core being the ninth, are:

■ Chassis—The chassis is the internal highway of the IXP2XXX network processors. It is the set of internal data and command buses that connect the functional units together.

■ Microengines—The microengines are software programmable processors that perform the bulk of network packet data processing.

■ Media and Switch Fabric—The Media and Switch Fabric Interface is where the IXP2XXX interfaces to MACs, framers, and fabric interface chips. It automates the reception of packets into the processor and offloads these tasks from the microengines.

■ Intel XScale core—The Intel XScale core is where the bulk of control plane processing and system initialization and control occur.

■ PCI Unit—The PCI unit is the interface between IXP2XXX network processors and control and management processors and PCI based I/O controllers.

■ SRAM Unit—The SRAM unit is used for high bandwidth and low latency data structure storage. It contains a sophisticated memory controller for automating linked list and ring buffer management.

■ DRAM Unit—The DRAM unit is used for packet storage and also for very large data structures.

■ SHaC—The SHaC contains the Scratch memory, Hash unit, and CSRs.

■ Crypto—The dual crypto unit in the IXP2850 performs DES, 3DES, AES, and SHA-1 algorithms.

Figure 4.1 shows the relationships between these units.

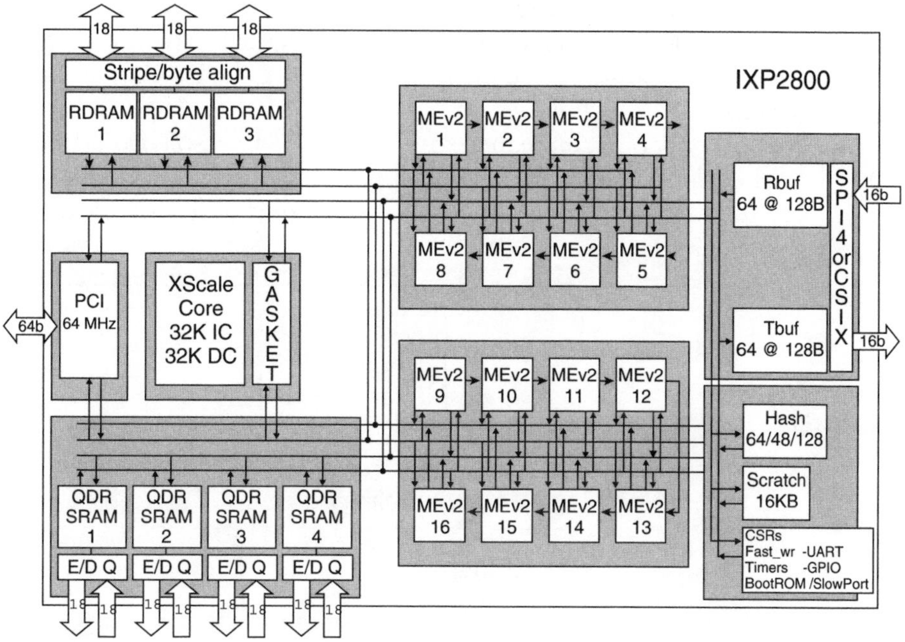

Figure 4.1   Internal Architecture for the IXP2800 Processor

Parallel Processing Paradigm

IXP2XXX network processors use multiple microengines (MEs) to solve complex packet-processing problems. The MEs process instructions internally, such as ALU operations. They make use of other functional units, called bus targets, in the network processor for transferring and processing data. Thus, multiple masters (the MEs, the PCI bus, and the Intel XScale core) must access multiple targets with high bandwidth and minimal latency. In a traditional single processor model, a typical pipeline might be: fetch, decode, execute, data write back. Should the particular instruction be a non-cached memory operation, like a read, the pipeline stalls until the data is read from memory. In a multiprocessor architecture, such as those based on IXP2XXX network processors, the various MEs continuously compete for memory and I/O resources, incurring latency when making multiple requests of a single resource.

If the MEs executed memory and I/O commands, using programmed I/O techniques, they would stall, perpetually waiting for theirs and previous memory operations to complete. For example, suppose 15 threads have issued memory commands to an SRAM channel, which can only execute these commands sequentially across the actual external pins. If programmed I/O techniques were used, all 15 threads would stall, waiting for the previous commands to complete. The result would be excessive latency and overall processing would slow. Therefore, special methods are needed to hide this memory latency and not slow down the processing.

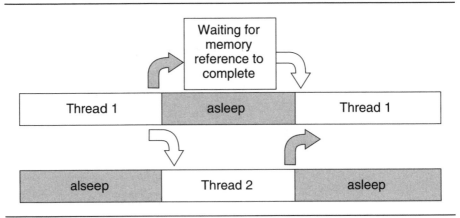

Figure 4.2 Multi-threading

The IXP2XXX network processors use special techniques to mitigate the problems of a multi-master and multi-slave system. To get around this latency problem, the MEs use multithreading and DMA type data transfers to decouple the execution of memory and I/O operations from microengine processing. The functional units (memory units, PCI, MSF, SHaC) execute the actual operation using DMA type techniques. By issuing the instruction to the memory and I/O units and having them execute the instruction, threads can continue processing or they can switch to another thread so more work can be done.

Having one process switch to another process to hide long latency operations is called multithreading. When a thread executes a long latency memory or I/O operation, it goes to sleep so that another process (or thread) can do some work while the original process waits for the memory operation to complete. The process of going to sleep is nonpreemptive because the thread has total control of its execution state.

It can continue executing instructions or it can go to sleep if it wants to. There is no RTOS or other mechanism that puts a thread to sleep. Multi-threading is described in more detail in Chapter 5 and illustrated in Figure 4.2.

The Chassis

The chassis forms the internal highway of IXP2XXX network processors. The chassis is designed to support the multithreading architecture of Intel IXA and allows memory latency reducing techniques to be implemented. It consists of the data paths, command paths and arbitration units that manage the flow of commands and data to and from the masters and targets on the bus. In the IXP2XXX network architecture, the supported masters are the microengines, Intel XScale, and PCI unit. The supported targets are the SRAM, DRAM, MSF, PCI, and SHaC. The sub-functions of the SHaC are also targets. Thus, there are 3 masters and 7 targets. This is illustrated in Figure 4.3.

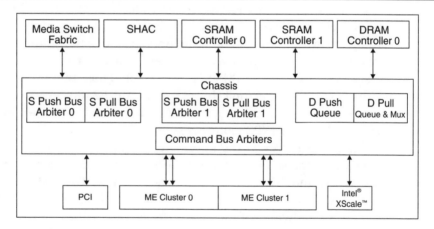

Figure 4.3   IXP2XXX Product Line Chassis

The architecture of the chassis assumes multithreading and multiprocessing. For example, when a microengine issues an SRAM memory-write command, the SRAM_write command is put out on a command bus and is directed to the targeted SRAM controller.

Note   The ME could decide to go to sleep to hide this memory operation and allow other threads to do some work.

The SRAM controller receives the command and buffers it into an internal command queue along with other SRAM_write commands that it has received from other masters on the chassis, such as other microengines, the Intel XScale core, or the PCI unit. The SRAM channel decodes the command, but first it must get the data that it is supposed to write to memory. As such, it pulls this data from the source microengine then writes it to memory.

If the original command was a DRAM memory Read command, for example, a similar process is used, but the data flows in the opposite direction. After receiving the command from the ME, the DRAM channel reads the data from memory, then it pushes that data to the source that is requesting the data. This pushing and pulling takes place on uni-directional buses to optimize performance and give full-duplex operation. Thus, the chassis uses a push bus for read data, a pull bus for write data, and a command bus for the commands.

The push and pull buses form the internal data paths, with a pair of S buses and a single D bus. The S bus serves as the internal data bus for SRAM, as well as PCI, MSF, and SHaC data transfers. All three of the supported masters—microengines, Intel Xscale core, and PCI—attach to this bus as well. The two S push/pull buses provide full-duplex operation. Each 32-bit wide push-and-pull bus operates at ½ the primary clock rate of the processor. The primary clock is 600 MHz for the IXP2400 processor and 1.4 GHz for the IXP2800 processor. Thus, the full duplex bandwidth of the S push/pull buses of the IXP2400 processor is 19.2 gigabits/second (2 x 32 bits x 300 MHz) and 44.8 gigabits/second (2 x 32 x 700 MHz) for the IXP2800 processor.

The D bus serves as the internal data bus for DRAM, as well as MSF and PCI data transfers. All three supported masters—microengines, Intel XScale core, and PCI—attach to this bus as well. The 64-bit D push/pull bus also operates at ½ the primary clock rate of the processor. Thus, the full duplex bandwidth of the D push/pull bus for the IXP2400 processor is 19.2 gigabits/second (64bits x 300 Mhz) and 44.8 gigabits/second (64 x 700 MHz) for the IXP2800 processor.

With commands and data being transferred between the masters and targets, the chassis has an arbitration mechanism to prioritize and grant access to the various buses. There are arbitration units for the D-Push and the D-Pull buses, for both pairs of S-Push and S-Pull buses, and for the command buses. All of these different buses interface to the bus targets using a common chassis interface.

These various buses have a common interface to the I/O functional units. The SHaC unit shown in Figure 4.4 is similar to the interface for the other units except that the SHaC unit uses the S_bus for data transfers. Commands from the bus masters fill a command inlet FIFO in the I/O or memory unit. This FIFO buffers commands from all the bus masters, allowing multiple masters to issue commands then do other work while the I/O or memory unit actually executes the command. This functionality is similar to traditional DMA operations.

If the command is a write operation, its data must come from the bus master before the functional unit can write it out. If the command requestor is a microengine, the SHaC unit must retrieve the data from the MEs S_Transfer Out (Xfer Out) registers. This data is pulled from these Xfer Out registers data across the S_Pull bus. Because other functional units might want to get pull data from other masters, the functional units need to request the data in the first place by generating a pull command and sending it across the chassis. This pull data is received and buffered in a pull data FIFO.

Note

> Each microengine has two sets of transfer registers, the S transfer registers and the D transfer registers. The S transfer registers directly attach to the internal S_bus and the D transfer registers directly attach to the D_bus. Because each of these buses provides a pull and a pull bus to support full-duplex operation, the MEs transfer registers are further divided into transfer In and transfer Out registers.
>
> ■ S_Xfer_out registers attach to S_pull bus
>
> ■ S_Xfer_in registers attach to S_push bus
>
> ■ D_Xfer_out registers attach to D_pull bus
>
> ■ D_Xfer_in registers attach to D_push bus
>
> Because some I/O functional units only attach to either the S bus or D bus—the SHaC only attaches to the S_bus, for example—software can communicate with these I/O units using transfer registers of the other bus. To do so, the transfer In buses have an input mux that allows either S or D transfer registers to be used for I/O transfers. For example, a SHaC Read command can transfer data on the S_push bus and deposit the results in either the S_Xfer_in or D_Xfer_in registers, based on the state of the input mux that is under software control. Thus, maximum transfer register flexibility is guaranteed.

If the command is a read operation, a process similar to the write command is used. After the memory or I/O unit executes the read command, the read data from those units, like scratch memory, is sent across the push bus and placed in an Xfer_In register of the microengine or in similar registers in the Intel XScale core or PCI unit. Of course, the push bus must be requested via a command sent to the push arbiter.

While the chassis provides a robust arbitration mechanism for multiple masters and multiple targets, it does consume cycles and impact overall latency. Depending on the command load from the various masters, the internal latency can consume 50 to 100 core cycles. This is why I/O latency to scratch memory ranges from 50 to 150 cycles while SRAM latency ranges from 70 to 160 cycles.

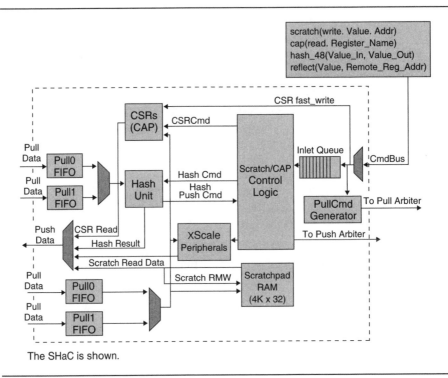

The SHaC is shown.

Figure 4.4 Typical Functional Unit of the IXP2XXX

The chassis contains two other buses. The ARM[†] Advanced Peripheral Bus (APB) supports standard APB devices, like GPIO, timers, UARTs, Global Chassis Registers, and the slow port controller. The full-duplex APB consists of 32-bit read and write buses combined with additional control signals. Also, a CAP CSR bus supports fast-write operations and standard read and write operations to the CSRs. The CSR bus is also full duplex and consists of 32-bit read and write buses with additional control signals.

Table 4.1 provides a summary of the buses.

Table 4.1   Bus Summary

Bus	Width	Arbitrating Masters	Attached Targets	Full-Duplex Bandwidth	
				IXP2400 600 Mhz	IXP2800 1.4 Ghz
D-Push/Pull	64	All	DRAM MSF, PCI	19.2 Gb/s	44.8 Gb/s
S0-Push/Pull	32	ME Cluster 1, PCI	SRAM MSF, PCI, SHaC	9.6 Gb/s	22.4 Gb/s
S1-Push/Pull	32	ME Cluster 2, Intel XScale core	SRAM MSF, PCI, SHaC	9.6 Gb/s	22.4 Gb/s
ARM Peripheral Bus (R/W)	32	Intel XScale core	UARTs, GPIO's, Timers, …	9.6 Gb/s	22.4 Gb/s
CAP CSR	32	Intel XScale core, MEs	Fast Writes and CSRs	9.6 Gb/s	22.4 Gb/s

More detailed views of the IXP2400 and IXP2800 chassis are shown in Figure 4.5 and Figure 4.6 respectively. The chassis frequency operates at ½ the microengine frequency.

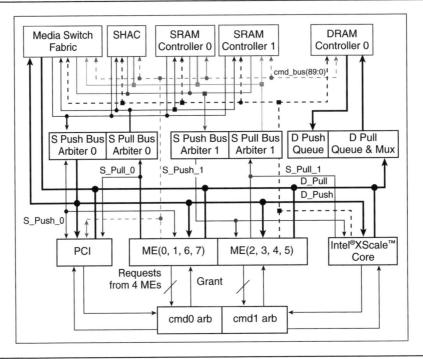

Figure 4.5   IXP2400 Internal Architecture

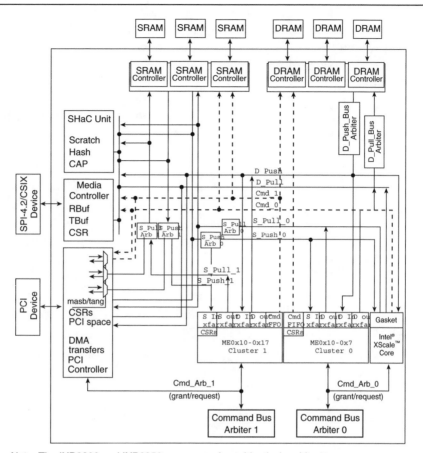

Note: The IXP2800 and IXP2850 processors have identical architectures, except for one thing: the IXP2850 processor has an internal crypto unit.

Figure 4.6 IXP2800 Internal Architecture

Microengines

The microengines do most of the programmable packet processing for an Intel IXA application. The IXP2400 processor has eight microengines and the IXP28X0 processor has sixteen of them. The microengines have access to all shared resources, including SRAM, DRAM, and MSF, as well as private connections between adjacent microengines, called "next neighbors," due to their proximate location.

The block diagram in Figure 4.7 is simplified for clarity. Some blocks and connectivity have been omitted to make the diagram more readable. Also, this block diagram does not show any pipeline stages; rather it shows the logical flow of information.

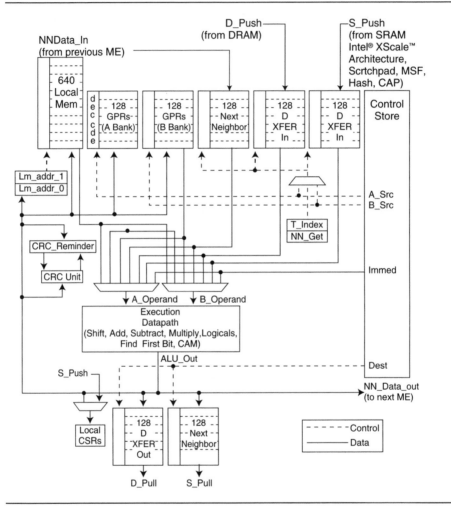

Figure 4.7   Microengine Detail

Control Store

The control store is an area of RAM that holds the application program that the microengine executes. Currently, the control store holds 4096 instructions, each of which is 40 bits wide. Subsequent variants of INTEL IXA network processors may have different size control stores. For example, the B revision of the IXP28X0 will have an 8-kilobyte control store for 8 of the 16 microengines. The Intel XScale core initializes this RAM. The control store is protected by parity against soft errors.

Contexts

Eight hardware contexts are available in the microengine. To allow for efficient context swapping, each context has its own register set, program counter and context-specific local register set. Having a copy for each context eliminates the need to move context-specific information between shared memory and the microengine registers for each context swap. Fast context swapping allows a context to do computation while other contexts wait to complete I/O, such as a delay for external memory accesses, or for a signal from another context or hardware unit.

Each of the eight contexts is in one of four states.

- Inactive—Some applications do not require all eight contexts. Therefore, a context can be disabled.

- Executing—A context is in an executing state when its context number is in the active state. The executing context's program is used to fetch instructions from the control store. A context stays in this state until it executes an instruction that causes it to go into sleep state. No hardware interrupt or preemption takes place; context swapping is completely under software control. At most, one context can be in the executing state at any time.

- Ready—In this state, a context is ready to execute, but it cannot because a different context is executing. When the executing context goes to sleep state, the microengine's context arbiter selects the next context to go to the executing state from among all the contexts in the ready state. The arbitration is round robin.

- Sleep—A context is waiting for one or more external events, as specified in a wakeup event CSR to occur. Typically, such events are related to an I/O access, but wakeup events are not limited to those.

The state diagram in Figure 4.8 illustrates the context state transitions. Each of the eight contexts is in one of these states. At most one context can be in executing state at a time; any number of contexts can be in any of the other states.

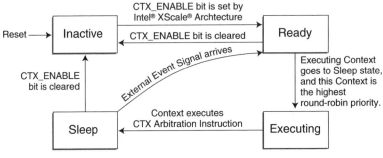

Note:
After reset, the Intel XScale processor must load the starting address of the CTX_PC, load the CTX_WAKEUP_EVENTS to 0x1 (voluntary), and then set the approriate CTX_ENABLE bits to begin executing Context(s).

Figure 4.8   Context States

Data Path Registers

As the block diagram in Figure 4.7 shows, each microengine contains four types of 32-bit data path registers:

- 256 general-purpose registers (GPRs)—GPRs are used for general programming purposes. They are read and written exclusively under program control. When used as a source in an instruction, GPRs supply operands to the execution's data path. When used as a destination in an instruction, they are written with the result of the execution's data path. The specific GPRs that are selected are encoded in the instruction.

- 512 transfer registers—Transfer registers, abbreviated as Xfer registers, are used for transferring data between the microengine and locations external to the microengine, such as DRAM, SRAM, etc.

- 128 next neighbor registers—The next neighbor registers allow one microengine to efficiently pass data from itself to its nearest neighbor. They can be written by the previous neighbor ME, or by itself. They can be configured as context relative registers or as a small ring buffer.

■ 640 32-bit words of local memory—Local memory is addressable storage located in the microengine. Local memory is read and written exclusively under program control. Local memory supplies operands to the execution data path as a source, and receives results as a destination. The specific memory location addressed is based on local memory address pointers, with two per context.

Execution Data Path

The execution data path can take one or two operands, perform an operation, and optionally write back a result. The sources and destinations can be GPRs, transfer registers, next neighbor registers, and local memory. The operations are shifts, add/subtract, logicals, multiply, byte align, and find first one bit.

Byte Align

The data path provides a mechanism to move data from source register(s) to any destination register(s) with byte aligning. Byte aligning takes four consecutive bytes from two concatenated values (8 bytes), starting at any of four byte boundaries (0, 1, 2, 3) and based on the endian type that is defined in the instruction opcode.

CAM

The block diagram in Figure 4.9 illustrates the CAM operation. Chapter 5 explains how the CAM is actually used in real applications to maintain locks across microengine threads. The CAM has 16 entries. Each entry stores a 32-bit value, which can be compared against a source operand by instruction:

```
CAM_Lookup[dest_reg, source_reg]
```

All entries are compared in parallel, and the result of the lookup is a 9-bit value that is written into the specified destination register.

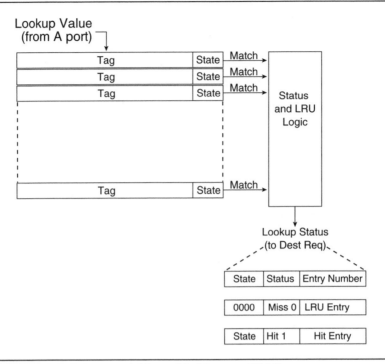

Figure 4.9   MEv2 Content Addressable Memory (CAM)

The 9-bit result consists of 4 state bits (`dest_reg[11:8]`), concatenated with a 1-bit hit-miss indication (`dest_reg[7]`), concatenated with 4-bit entry number (`dest_reg[6:3]`). All other bits of `dest_reg` are written with `0`. Possible results of the lookup are:

- Miss (0)—Lookup value is not in the CAM. The entry number is the least recently used entry, which can be used as a suggested entry to replace, and state bits are `0000`.

- Hit (1)—Lookup value is in CAM. The entry number is the entry that the value matches. State bits are the value from the entry that has matched.

- State Bits—The value is set by software at the time that the entry is loaded or that value is changed in an entry that is already loaded.

The Least Recently Used (LRU) logic maintains a time-ordered list of CAM entry usage. When an entry is loaded or finds a match on a lookup, that entry is marked as LRU.

CRC Unit

The CRC unit operates in parallel with the execution data path. It takes two operands, performs a cyclic redundancy check (CRC) operation, and writes back a result. CRC-16 and CRC-32 are supported.

Event Signals

Event signals are used to coordinate a program with the completion of external events. For example, when a microengine executes an instruction directing an external unit to read data that is written into a Transfer_In register, the program must ensure that the register does not try to use the data until the external unit has written it. This time is not deterministic due to queuing delays and other uncertainties in the external units, for example, DRAM refresh. No hardware mechanism raises a flag that a register write is pending, and then prevents the program from using the data. Instead, the coordination is under software control, with hardware support.

In the instructions that use external units (i.e., SRAM, DRAM, etc.) fields direct the external unit to supply an indication, called an event signal, that the command has been completed. An application can use 15 event signals per context and one local CSR per context tracks the pending event signals and the returned ones. The event signals can be used to move a context from sleep state to ready state. Alternatively, the program can test and branch on the status of event signals.

Event Signals can be set in nine different ways, as follows:

- When data is written into S_TRANSFER_IN registers
- When data is written into D_TRANSFER_IN registers
- When data is taken from S_TRANSFER_OUT registers
- When data is taken from D_TRANSFER_OUT registers
- By a write to INTERTHREAD_SIGNAL register
- By a write from previous neighbor microengine to NEXT_NEIGHBOR_SIGNAL
- By a write from Next Neighbor microengine to PREVIOUS_NEIGHBOR_SIGNAL
- By a write to SAME_ME_SIGNAL Local CSR
- By internal timer

Any or all event signals can be set by any of the above sources.

When a context executes a `ctx_arb` instruction or an instruction with `ctx_swap` token, it goes to sleep state. The context specifies one or more event signals that must be put in ready state. The `ctx_arb` instruction also specifies whether the operation needs the logical AND or logical OR of the event signal(s) to put the context into ready state.

Media and Switch Fabric Interface

In Chapter 3, you saw how the external interface of the IXP2XXX processor's Media and Switch Fabric (MSF) interfaces to MACs, framers, and switch fabrics using industry standard Utopia, SPI, or CSIX interfaces. This interface is the primary pathway on which network data flows through the chip. Unlike a network interface card (NIC) that has a direct data path from the media interface to memory, the IXP2XXX processor's MSF first buffers the packets as they are received. While a direct data path to memory, usually to DRAM, might seem like the simplest approach, buffering packets first has the advantage of giving the microengines direct access to the packets. If packets were directly buffered, microengines would consume additional bus bandwidth by reading the needed information from DRAM. Having direct access to the data prevents a round trip delay to/from DRAM, thereby increasing performance, especially at higher bit rates.

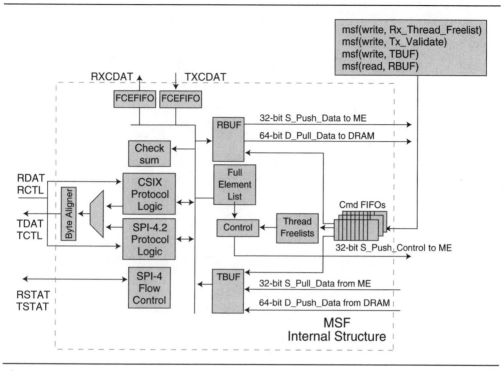

Figure 4.10   MSF Receive and Transmit Unit (IXP2800 Shown)

The MSF buffers packets into two structures: the transmit buffer (TBUF), which buffers data just prior to transmission, and receive buffer (RBUF), which buffers data just after receipt. The size of both the RBUF and TBUF is 8 kilobytes and both can be subdivided into elements that are either 64, 128, or 256 bytes wide. Thus, each buffer can contain 32 elements in a 256-byte buffer, 64 elements in a 128-byte buffer, and 128 elements in a 64-byte buffer. The elements' sizes are selected via CSRs in the MSF unit.

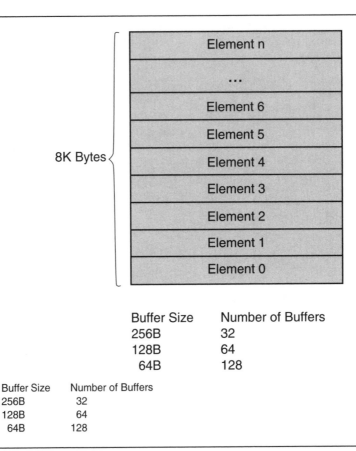

Buffer Size	Number of Buffers
256B	32
128B	64
64B	128

Buffer Size	Number of Buffers
256B	32
128B	64
64B	128

Figure 4.11   IXP2XXX Product Line RBUF/TBUF

The RBUF and TBUF can be partitioned so that different packet types can have their own buffer pool. The sizes of the partitions can differ, and each partition can have differently sized elements within it. A primary reason for buffer partitioning is to give priority to flow control messages from the CSIX fabric via dedicated buffers. Without a separate partition for flow control messages, the entire RBUF can become filled with data packets, and flow control messages wouldn't get through. The result is dropped packets at the congested line card that is receiving the packets. Partitioning also allows for optimizing the elements size according to the anticipated packet size, which may be different depending on the source. This partitioning is illustrated in Figure 4.12 for the IXP2800 processor and in Figures 4.13 and 4.14 for the IXP2400 processor.

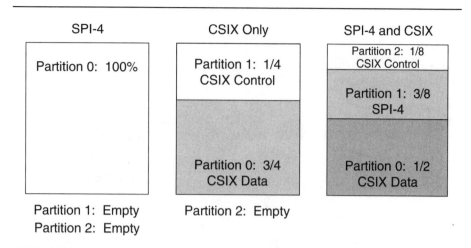

Figure 4.12   IXP2800 RBUF and TBUF Partitioning

In Figure 4.12, the first example dedicates 100 percent of the elements to SPI-4.2 data. The CSIX-only example has two partitions set up: partition 1 for CSIX flow control messages and partition 0 for CSIX data. In the third example, three partitions of differing sizes hold CSIX data, CSIX control flow messages, and SPI-4.2 data. A practical application for the partitioning shown in the first two examples is the dual processor ingress/egress configuration described in Chapter 3. In such configurations, the ingress for the IXP2800 processor receives data from MACs and framers via the SPI-4.2 interface—the RBUF would be 100 percent SPI-4.2—while the egress for the IXP2800 processor receives CSIX data streams and flow control messages. The partitioning shown in the third example would be used in single IXP2800 processor designs where a gasket chip interfaces to both SPI framers/MACs and CSIX fabrics.

The IXP2400 processor partitions the RBUF and TBUF a bit differently. The RBUF can be partitioned for both CSIX and Utopia/POSPHY/SPI, but not both together, as shown in Figure 4.13. Also, because the IXP2400 processor supports a channelized interface, the TBUF must be partitioned so that each channel can have its own buffering, as shown in Figure 4.14.

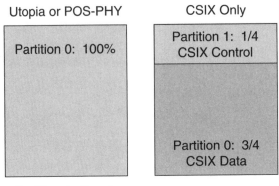

Utopia or POS-PHY

Partition 0: 100%

Partition 1: Empty

CSIX Only

Partition 1: 1/4
CSIX Control

Partition 0: 3/4
CSIX Data

Figure 4.13   IXP2400 RBUF Partitioning

The MSF hardware allocates packets to the different types of TBUF elements under software control. The MSF hardware loads the packets into the appropriate element based on its knowledge of where they should go. The MSF hardware allocates RBUF elements dynamically, based on the interface the MSF is configured for.

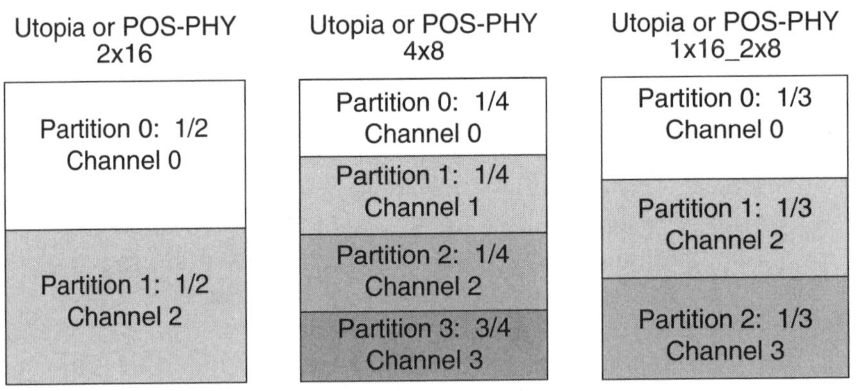

Utopia or POS-PHY
2x16

Partition 0: 1/2
Channel 0

Partition 1: 1/2
Channel 2

Utopia or POS-PHY
4x8

Partition 0: 1/4
Channel 0

Partition 1: 1/4
Channel 1

Partition 2: 1/4
Channel 2

Partition 3: 3/4
Channel 3

Utopia or POS-PHY
1x16_2x8

Partition 0: 1/3
Channel 0

Partition 1: 1/3
Channel 2

Partition 2: 1/3
Channel 3

Figure 4.14   IXP2400 TBUF Partitioning

MSF Receive Processing

After the MSF receives and buffers a packets one of several pre-specified microengine threads is notified. The thread reads the packet and processes it. After a thread finishes with the data stored in an element, software releases the element so the MSF can use it again for more packets. The MSF determines which thread to assign an element based on a thread free list, which is filled under software control. This list contains the thread IDs that are available to process packets. Each free list has a free list timeout that is programmed with the number of MSF bus cycles that must elapse in the absence of bus activity before the MSF auto-pushes a null packet status word to the next thread on the free list. This null packet indicator is needed because the threads that process packets might need to receive a steady stream of packets to function properly, especially if software-pipelining methods are used. The pipeline must be kept full of data for it to operate. Each partition has a separate thread free list with a maximum size, as shown in Figure 4.15.

IXP2400		IXP2800	
Freelist	Depth	Freelist	Depth
Rx_Thread_Freelist_0	64	Rx_Thread_Freelist_0	64
Rx_Thread_Freelist_1	16	Rx_Thread_Freelist_1	32
Rx_Thread_Freelist_2	32	Rx_Thread_Freelist_2	32
Rx_Thread_Freelist_3	16		

Figure 4.15   Thread Free List Maximum Size Per Partition

The format of a thread free list entry is shown below in Figure 4.16.

Rx_Thread_Freelist_#				
Reserved	Signal #	ME #	Thd ID	Xfer Register
31:18	14:13	11:7	6:4	3:0

Figure 4.16   Thread Free List Format

When a receive thread is finished processing a packet, the thread updates the RX_Thread_Freelist register with its thread ID number and other associated fields. The fields that define each entry help the MSF to assign an element to a thread correctly. These fields are defined in software by the originating thread that fills the free list. The microengine and thread ID indicates which thread of a particular microengine should process the packet. The Xfer register field indicates the Xfer register of a particular microengine in which the MSF should deposit a packet's receive status control word. The signal number field tells the MSF which Generalized Thread Signal (GTS) to use to signal the thread once the receive status word is pushed to the Xfer register.

The receive status word is formatted according to the specific interface on which the packet is received. From the status word, the thread receiving the status word determines what to do with the packet in an RBUF element. The status words vary from type to type, but in general, they have the following fields:

- Element number: indicates the element from which the software can get the packet

- Payload Length or Byte count: the number of bytes in the payload

- SOP: indicates whether this status word is a Start-of-Packet

- EOP: indicates whether this status word is an End-of-Packet

- Err: notification that the packet might have an error

- Channel: indicates the channel on which the packet or cell was received on (IXP2400 processor only)

- VCI/VPI: provides the VCI and VPI numbers of the received cell (Utopia mode of IXP2400 processor only)

- Parity: indicates whether the packet had a parity error

Figure 4.17 illustrates the process of receiving packets.

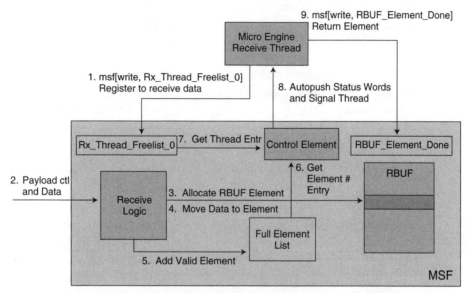

1. After a thread finishes processing a packet, the thread indicates to the MSF that it is available to process a packet by registering in the appropriate thread free list.

2. A packet arrives at the MSF where the receive logic starts taking control.

3. Based on the packet type—it can be the CSIX, SPI/Utopia, and so forth—the receive logic allocates an RBUF element in the appropriate partition.

4. The receive logic pulls the packet or cell from the framer, MAC, or FIC and deposits that packet or cell in the allocated element.

5. Once packet or cell buffering is complete, the full element list is updated with the newly full element number.

6. The control element is updated with the element number from Step 4.

7. The control element gets a thread ID from the thread free list.

8. The control element forms the receive status word and auto-pushes it into a Xfer register of the microengine thread that is indicated in the thread free list ID entry. The signal type, which is also indicated in the thread freelist ID entry, signals the thread. The thread then processes the packet.

9. After the thread finishes receiving the packet, it returns the element to the RBUF element done list. At this point, other packets that are coming from the network or fabric can use the element.

Figure 4.17　MSF Receive Processing

MSF Transmit Processing

When software transmits a packet, it fills a TBUF element number with the actual packet/cell data and also with pre-pend data. The pre-pend data is under software control and is often used for packet headers. Neither the pre-pend data nor the payload data need to be contiguous; they have their own offset and length into a TBUF element. The MSF transmits the first byte of the pre-pend data, and then concatenates the payload after the entire pre-pend data has been sent, as shown in Figure 4.18.

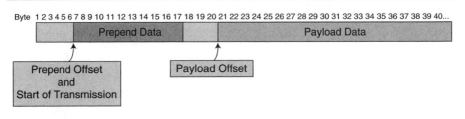

Figure 4.18   TBUF Element Format

Each TBUF element has a control word associated with it, similar to RBUF elements. While the MSF uses the receive control word to tell software what to do, software uses the transmit control word to tell the MSF how to transmit the packet. The transmit control word has many of the same fields as the receive control word, such as packet length, SOP, EOP, and channel ID (for IXP2400 processors). It also contains the TBUF offset for pre-pend and payload data, in addition to the pre-pend length.

Before the MSF actually transmits a TBUF element, that packet must be validated because certain conditions often have to be met before the packet is actually transmitted across the pins. A simple example is when a packet's payload is first written into a TBUF element, but its header is still being worked on. Once the header is updated, it is put into a TBUF element as pre-pend data. The TBUF element is now ready to be sent out by validating it. Validating occurs by writing the TBUF control word for the element (if enabled) or by setting a valid bit in the Tx_Validate CSR.

The process of transmitting packets ensures proper order and priority within each of the TBUF partitions. Figure 4.19 shows a TBUF with three partitions. The MSF transmits validated elements in round robin order within each partition and across partitions. Each partition has a running count of the number of packets sent. If an element is not validated and is next in the round robin sequence to be transmitted, the transmit sequence is blocked for that element and that partition. The transmit state machine cannot advance to the next element within that partition, but it does advance to the next partition and transmits the next element in the sequence, assuming it is validated. After transmitting an element from that partition, the transmit state machine advances to the next partition and transmits the next element in the sequence, assuming it is validated.

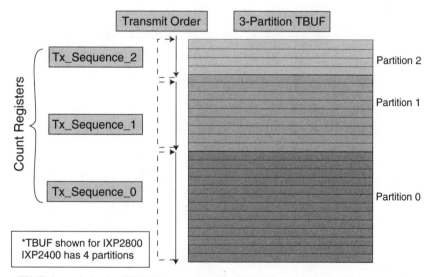

TBUF shown is for the IXP2800 processor. The IXP2400 processor has four partitions.

Figure 4.19   TBUF Transmitting Process

At a high level, the transmit hardware is under software control, as shown in Figure 4.20.

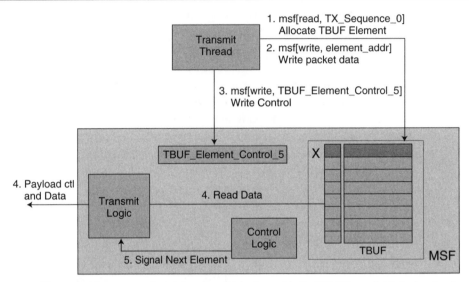

1. Transmit software must first determine which element in the TBUF is available by issuing the msf[read, tx_sequence_ID, …], then it allocates the element.

2. Software transmits the packet directly to the allocated element. The data can come from the microengine's transfer registers or via a direct path from DRAM.

3. The transmit control word is updated for that element. This action validates the element, if possible. If not, a separate CSR write sets a validate bit for the element.

4. The transmit state machine reads the data from the TBUF element and sends it across the pins to the MAC, Framer, or FIC.

5. The transmit state machine advances to the next element.

Figure 4.20   Transmit Flow

Intel® XScale™ Core

The Intel XScale core is an ARM V5TE compliant microprocessor of Intel IXA that provides for high performance and low power. To achieve the highest performance possible, the Intel XScale core incorporates architectural features that help mitigate the effects of memory latency, which is very similar to the goals of the microengines. These features include:

- The ability to continue instruction execution even while the data cache is retrieving data from external memory. This ability allows the processor to be kept as busy as possible by avoiding stalls during cache reads.

- The write buffer allows the processor to buffer data on chip so it can be kept busy without stalling. It coalesces several write operations together for the most efficient external bus operation.

- Write-back caching allows most efficient bus utilization by allowing the processor to write data back to external memory when its write buffer is sufficiently full.

- Various data cache allocation policies, which can be configured different for each application.

- Cache locking allows data and instructions to be locked in the cache for highest performance. This feature allows the data and instructions to stay in the cache when they normally would be evicted using the processors cache eviction policy.

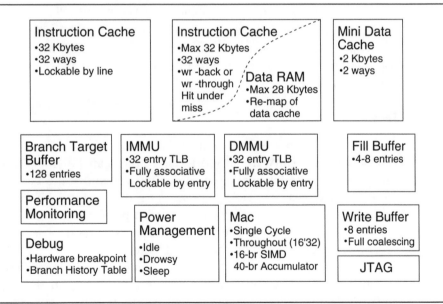

Figure 4.21   Intel® XScale™ Core Feature set

For a complete description of the Intel XScale core, refer to the *IXP2800 Hardware Reference Manual* (Intel January 2003).

Intel® XScale™ Core Peripherals

The Intel XScale core peripherals are the I/O units that are common to standard embedded microprocessors. These peripherals allow the Intel XScale core to interface to I/O units that are both internal and external to the IXP2XXX processors. Chapter 3 reviewed the GPIOs, timers, and slow port. The other core peripherals are the interrupt controller and timers.

Interrupt Controller

You can use the interrupt controller to enable or mask interrupts from a number of chip-wide sources, such as the following:

- Timers that normally are used by a real-time operating system.
- Interrupts generated by microengine software to request services from the Intel XScale core.
- External agents, such as PCI devices.
- Error conditions, such as DRAM ECC error or SPI-4.2 parity error.

Interrupt status is read as memory-mapped registers. The state of an interrupt signal can be read even when it is masked from actually interrupting. Enabling and masking of interrupts is done as writes to memory mapped registers.

Timers

The IXP2XXX processors contain four programmable 32-bit timers that can be used for software support. Each timer can be clocked by any of the following: the internal clock, a divided version of the clock, or a signal on an external General Purpose I/O (GPIO) pin. Each timer can be programmed to generate a periodic interrupt after a programmed number of clocks. The delay time can range from several nanoseconds to several minutes, depending on the clock frequency.

In addition, you can use the fourth timer as a watchdog timer. To do so, software must reload the timer value periodically. If the application software fails to do so and the timer counts to zero, it resets the chip. This event can be used to detect a condition that causes the software to hang or fail to reload the timer for some other reason.

PCI Controller

The PCI controller provides a 64-bit, 66-MHz interface that complies with *PCI Local Bus Specification Revision 2.2* (PCI SIG 1998). It is also compatible with 32-bit and/or 33-MHz PCI devices. The PCI controller provides the following functions:

- Target access—external bus master access to SRAM, DRAM, and CSRs

- Master access—the Intel XScale core access to PCI target devices

- Three DMA channels

- Mailbox and Doorbell registers for the Intel XScale core to Host communication

- PCI arbiter

SRAM Unit

The SRAM is probably one of the most, if not *the* most, sophisticated I/O unit in the IXP2XXX processors. SRAM is where the processor stores critical data structures such as route tables, free buffer pools, flow state tables, queue descriptors, and other important network information. To maintain high data rates, these data structures need to be accessed at the highest rates with the lowest latency. High bandwidth is achieved using the latest SRAM memory technologies, such as QDR and QDRII memory types. To minimize latency, one can optimize the way that the memory is used in the first place. The IXP network processor optimizes these functions according to the very specific ways that SRAM memory is used. The SRAM unit performs three classes of operations:

- Basic read/write commands

- Atomic operations

- Linked list and ring buffer management

Because these commands are so important to INTEL IXA applications, Chapter 6 provides a more thorough description.

Basic read and write commands are typical SRAM operations. The IXP2400 and IXP2800 processors transfer from 1 to 16 longwords to and from external memory. Data that is read from memory is placed on the push bus then transferred to the master that issued the command. The command master is signaled that the operation is complete after the last phase of the data transfer. For write operations, the SRAM unit pulls data from the command source, writes it to memory, and then signals the source that the operation is completed.

Atomic operations are very important for minimizing memory latency. These operations are often read-modify-write combinations that require exclusive access to memory so other processes don't access the data during the data update. The atomic operational nature of the SRAM controller ensures this exclusivity. The SRAM unit supports the following commands:

- Set bit
- Clear bit
- Increment
- Decrement
- Add
- Swap

The processor uses queues and linked lists frequently during the processing life of a packet, and using them with minimal latency is critical to maintaining the highest line rate. The SRAM unit has an integrated linked list and ring buffer controller that atomically enqueues and dequeues buffers to and from linked lists and ring buffers. These atomic commands also allow mutually exclusive processing without cumbersome locking mechanisms. The SRAM unit supports the following three linked list commands:

- Enqueue and dequeue
- Read queue descriptor
- Write queue descriptor

The ring buffer controller atomically puts data onto a ring buffer and gets data off a ring buffer. Normal ring buffers are supported, as well as journals, which are a variation of rings used for debugging purposes. The two ring buffer commands are:

- Put Data on ring
- Get Data from ring

DRAM Functional Unit

The primary job of IXP2XXX processors DRAM units is to serve as a memory controller for external DDR SDRAM on the IXP2400 processor and for RDRAM on the IXP28X0 processor. While these units are sophisticated, they don't require the robust command set that is available for the SRAM unit because DRAM is used primarily for packet storage and for storing large state tables. Both of these uses would require a significant amount of memory bandwidth, but they don't typically require the lowest latency data modification operations, such as happens in SRAM.

The SHaC

The SHaC unit is a multifunction block containing scratchpad memory and logic blocks that are used to perform hashing operations and to interface with Intel XScale core peripherals and chip CSRs through the APB and CSR buses, respectively. The SHaC also houses the global registers, as well as chip reset logic. The SHaC unit has the following features:

■ Communication to Intel XScale core peripherals, such as GPIOs and timers, through the APB bus

■ Creation of hash indices of 48-, 64-, or 128-bit widths

■ Communication ring used by microengines for inter-process communication

■ Scratch pad memory usable by Intel XScale core and microengines

■ CSR bus interface to permit fast writes to CSRs, as well as standard read and writes

■ Push/Pull Reflector to transfer data from the pull bus to the push bus for ME-to-ME communication.

Detailed information about CSRs is contained in the Intel IXA programmer's reference manual (Intel 2003).

Scratchpad Memory

The scratchpad memory is 16-kilobytes, organized as 4K 32-bit words, that is accessible by microengines and the Intel XScale core. The scratchpad memory provides the following operations:

- Normal reads and writes. From one to sixteen 32-bit words can be read or written with a single microengine instruction.

- Atomic read-modify-write operations, bit-set, bit-clear, increment, decrement, add, subtract, and swap. These operations can return the pre-modified data, at the application designer's option.

- Sixteen hardware-assisted rings for inter-process communication. Each ring is a FIFO that uses a head-and-tail pointer to store or read information in scratchpad memory.

Scratchpad memory is provided as a third memory resource, in addition to SRAM and DRAM, to be shared by the microengines and the Intel XScale core. The microengines and the Intel XScale core can distribute memory accesses between these three types of memory resources to provide a greater number of memory accesses occurring in parallel.

Hash Unit

The SHaC unit contains a hash unit that can take 48-bit, 64-bit, or 128-bit data and produce a 48-bit, a 64-bit, or a 128-bit hash index, respectively. Both the microengines and the Intel XScale core can access the hash unit, and this access is useful for table searches with large keys—L2 addresses, for example. Figure 4.12 is a block diagram of the hash unit.

Up to three hash indexes can be created using a single microengine instruction. These indexes help to minimize command overhead. The Intel XScale core can do only one hash at a time.

The hash unit uses a hard-wired polynomial algorithm and a programmable hash multiplier to create hash indexes. Three separate multipliers are supported: one for 48-bit hash operations, one for 64-bit hash operations, and one for 128-bit hash operations. The multiplier is programmed through control registers in the hash unit.

Control and Status Register Access Proxy

The Control and Status Register Access Proxy (CAP) contains a number of chip-wide control and status registers. Some provide miscellaneous control and status while others are used to communicate between microengines or between a microengine and the Intel XScale core. Rings in scratchpad memory and SRAM also can be used for inter-process communication, as follows:

■ Inter-thread signal—Each thread (or context) on a microengine can send a signal to any other thread by writing to the Inter-Thread_Signal register. This method allows a thread to sleep while awaiting completion of a task by a different thread.

■ Thread message—Each thread has a message register where it can post a software-specific message. Other microengine threads or the Intel XScale core can poll for availability of messages by reading the THREAD_MESSAGE_SUMMARY register. The processor clears both the THREAD_MESSAGE and the corresponding THREAD_MESSAGE_SUMMARY upon a read of the message.

■ Self-destruct—This register provides another type of communication. The microengine software can set individual bits in the SELF DESTRUCT registers atomically. These registers are cleared upon read. The meaning of each bit is software-specific. Clearing the register upon read eliminates a race condition when multiple readers exist.

■ Thread interrupt—Each thread can interrupt the Intel XScale core on two different interrupt 'pins' (these 'pins' are internal to the network processor). Usage is software-specific. Having two interrupts promotes flexibility. For example, one interrupt can be assigned to normal service requests and the other can be assigned to error conditions. To associate more information with the interrupt, you can use mailboxes, or you can use rings in SRAM or scratchpad memory.

■ Reflector—CAP provides a function, called reflector, where any microengine thread can move data between its registers and those of any other thread. In response to a single write or read instruction with the address in the specific reflector range, CAP gets data from the source microengine and puts it into the destination microengine. Optionally, both the sending and receiving threads can be signaled upon completion of the data movement.

IXP2850 Crypto Unit

Last, but not least, is the IXP2850 crypto core, which integrates two crypto units for performing bulk crypto operations. The IXP2850 has exactly the same architecture of the IXP2800 with the addition of the internal crypto functionality. Public key acceleration, for protocols such as IKE, can be done externally such as on the PCI bus. The IXP2850 crypto unit forms the basis of a whole new set of applications to be based on Intel IXA. The purpose of the IXP2850 is to do bulk encryption and decryption at 10 gigabits per second, providing supporting protocols for robust applications such as VPN/firewalls, SAN/NAS storage gateways, secure web servers, L5-L7 traffic management systems, and the like. Supporting software protocol blocks includes TCP/IP termination, IPSec, SSL, iSCSI, FCIP, and Layer 4+ load balancing. Adding crypto to the internal architecture has significant performance and cost benefits.

From a pure cost perspective, integrating the crypto unit saves the developer from having to use an external crypto device in the system. An internal crypto engine enables sharing multiple buses and memory subsystems. For example, IPSec state data can be stored in SRAM along with the free buffer lists, lookup tables, and Q descriptors for other applications. DRAM is also shared between the crypto and other functions for packet storage and security association (SA) data. Because of this integration, the added power consumption for crypto functionality is only 2 extra watts.

Integrating crypto inside the IXP2850 increases performance by minimizing memory bandwidth, often the most valuable chip resource. When a packet arrives in the network processor, the network processor first needs to do a first level classification to determine whether the packet is encrypted. If the network processor does not have integrated crypto, packets that need decryption must be sent across a bus (like PCI or QDR SRAM bus), decrypted, and then read back into the processor. The decrypted packet is processed, and written back to memory. In this basic flow, the packet makes two round trips through DRAM. This detour can drop performance in half if the DRAM bus is already close to its maximum capacity for normal, unencrypted traffic.

The IXP2850 has two crypto engines. Each engine supports the following in hardware, with MD5 and rc4 being supported in software on the microengines.

■ Two 3DES cores

■ One AES core, which supports a block size of 128 bits and key lengths of 128, 192, and 256 bits

■ Two SHA-1 cores

Each crypto unit supports a flow-through architecture. Each unit has multiple instantiations of the algorithms, so packets can be interleaved through the unit for highest performance. The core maintains state internally and a new state can be loaded as the cores are running. Anticipating the need for TCP termination in many applications, the unit can perform TCP checksum at the end of the processing flow. Figure 4.22 illustrates the internal blocks of the two crypto cores.

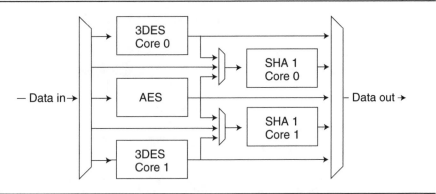

Figure 4.22   IXP2850 Crypto Core Blocks

Crypto Data Flow

Figure 4.23 shows the four basic data flow steps when processing encrypted or decrypted data.

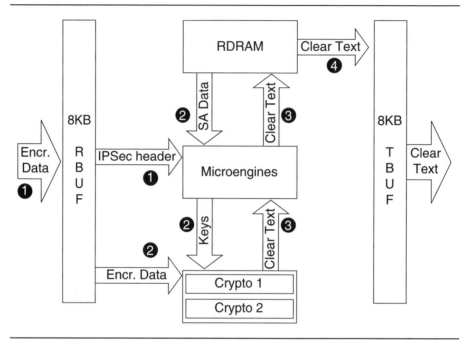

Figure 4.23   Crypto Data Flow

In this short example, you can see how an IPSEC packet flows through the IXP2850.

1.   Receive IPSec packet
   –   A thread receives the MSF status word about the new packet that was just stored in the RBUF unit. This status word is autopushed into an SRAM txfer register of the thread.
   –   Process RBUF status word.
   –   If this is SOP (RBUF has header)
      –   Read in packet header (including IPSec header)
      –   IPv4 verify
      –   Lookup the Security Parameter Index (SPI) field. This is used with the security association to authenticate the packet.

- – Allocate crypto unit
- – Allocate data buffer
- – Signal next thread in the pipeline.

2. Start Processing IPSec Packet

- – Start processing once signaled from stage 1
- – If SOP, then…
    - – Load SA from DRAM to microengine
    - – Move data from the RBUF to crypto RAM
    - – Check for SA parameters, algorithms, etc.
    - – Load cipher and HMAC keys into crypto unit
- – Signal next thread in the pipeline

3. IPSec Update

- – Start processing once signaled from stage 2
- – If SOP, then…
    - – Hash the SPI, sequence, and IV
    - – Hash and decrypt the payload data
    - – HMAC final processing
    - – Check authentication data
    - – IPv4 verify on internal header
    - – Move the data to decrypted data to memory
- – Signal next thread in the pipeline

4. Final IPSec processing for packet

- – Start processing once signaled from stage 3
- – Perform IPSec policy checks
    - – Anti-Replay
    - – Security policy database lookup
    - – Lifetime checks, time, and bytes
    - – Update counters
- – Signal next stage in the pipeline, usually a classifications stage on the internal header.
- – Once processing is finished, transmit out to MSF via a TBUF.

A great paper to read on the IXP2850 crypto core is "Security: Adding Protection to the Network via the Network Processor" (Feghali et al. 2002).

Summary

The IXP2XXX family of network processors is designed for flexible and fast data plane processing. The chassis, microengines, and MSF are directly in the data flow and provide the speed and functionality for the highest line rate possible. The microengines use multithreading techniques to hide the detrimental effects of memory latency so they can operate as efficiently as possible. The I/O units have the power to offload mundane tasks from the microengines, thus preserving valuable MIPS and avoiding long memory latencies. The whole architecture is based on a high performance chassis that provides multiple, full-duplex buses that provide the microengines, Intel XScale core and PCI unit with the highest bandwidth data paths to the I/O units.

Multithreading contributes to the throughput, but the introduction of parallel processing introduces several problems that must be addressed for the fastest packet processing. Chapter 5 provides an explanation of multithreading, the Serial Stream Processing problem, and special multithreading techniques that are used to squeeze the last ounce of performance from Intel IXA.

Chapter 5

Parallel Processing

Parallel processing and multithreading are how Intel IXA gets its high performance and form the foundational processing paradigm for the IXP2XXX network processors. The concepts aren't that difficult. As packets are received from the network, a microengine thread picks up a packet and processes it. Because the total time it takes for one thread to process one packet often exceeds the time that new packets arrive, additional threads pick up new packets as they are received. Because only one of the eight threads in a microengine can be executing at one time, the thread execution is time sliced with other threads, with one thread processing instructions while the other threads are idle, waiting for memory or I/O operations to complete. This multithreading technique is how the IXP2XXX network processors process packets at line rate. The system designer assigns the appropriate number of threads (and microengines) to handle the anticipated packet rate.

General-purpose processors were never designed for the unique demands of network traffic because they are not able to efficiently hide memory latencies found in networking applications. To provide the packet-processing capability needed for network traffic, the IXP2XXX network processors have special hardware to remove the damaging effects of memory latencies. However, not all memory latency problems have the same negative effect. Some memory latency problems require application specific mechanisms to solve them. Before you learn about the effects of memory latencies and how the IXP2XXX network processors solve them, a larger question needs to be answered in the next section.

Why Not Use a General Purpose Processor?

Network processors are primarily chosen for network applications over hardwired ASICs for their flexibility and time-to-market advantages. If this is so, why not use a general-purpose processor that seems to offer the same flexibility and time-to-market advantages? The reason is simple: general-purpose processors achieve their performance by using on-chip caches to hide memory latencies. But the unique characteristics of network traffic and related data minimize the benefits of this cache. These on-chip caches operate at the same speed as the core microprocessor itself, so data or instructions in the cache are accessed without the CPU stalling, which is waiting to access external memory. However, when this general-purpose processor needs to access external memory, it has to downshift to the speed of the external memory, which often is several times slower than the CPU itself. For example, if the CPU is operating at 2 gigahertz, but external memory is at 300 megahertz, the CPU actually slows to 300 megahertz when external data or instructions are accessed. Thus, for a general-purpose processor to run at the highest possible speed, data and instructions must be stored in its on-chip cache.

Because on-chip caches take up valuable silicon area and are thus expensive, their size is much smaller than external memory. For data to be cached in this limited memory space, the data must be grouped close together both in physical location and in time. Data without this characteristic is loaded in the cache the first time that the CPU accesses it, but eventually the data is evicted if it isn't used after a while. Typically, CPU cache eviction policies use Least Recently Used (LRU) algorithms to determine whether data stays in the cache or gets evicted. Data that was used least recently is evicted (or written back to memory) so newer needed data fit into the valuable and limited space of the cache. Thus, for data to stay in the cache, it must be grouped closely together, because the cache itself is relatively small, and it must be accessed often because of the cache LRU replacement policy. *Spatially associative data* is grouped close together physically whereas *temporally associative data* is close together in time.

General-purpose processors are not as fast as network processors at data plane network processing because network data is rarely spatially or temporally associative. For systems that process thousands of traffic flows, packets arriving from the network are statistically distributed with a wide variance. In other words, packets that are received one after another are rarely associated with each other. This dissociation is even truer at the higher data rates that support hundreds of thousands of flows or connections. If you have a faster packet rate and more supported flows, fewer of the packets are likely to be associated with each other. Thus, cached packets are soon evicted because a continual stream of unrelated packets forces the cache management unit of the CPU to evict infrequently accessed packets, even if more work can be done on them. Not only are the packets spatially and temporally dissociative, but network data structures also don't fit well in caches. For example, large routing tables to be processed using Longest Prefix Match (LPM) algorithms are extremely dissociative because the LPM algorithm has to hop throughout the table, use a value only once, then jump to another value that is likely very physically distant from the previous value. As a result, the CPU's cache is *thrashed*—data gets read once then is evicted a short time later. Because the CPU operates at its highest possible performance level when data that is in the cache is used more than once, this cache thrash forces the CPU to downshift to the speed of external memory. The result is that a 2-gigahertz general-purpose processor is now operating at the speed of the much slower memory, a significant performance degradation.

Because of this cache thrash problem and the need to optimize processing of network data streams, IXP2XXX network processors use multiprocessing, multithreading, and software pipelining techniques to achieve high performance by taking advantage of the uniqueness of the network data patterns. In later chapters, you will see that while these techniques do indeed give the network processor a critical performance enhancement over general-purpose processors, in some worst-case scenarios where received packets do have high associability, the very multiprocessing and multithreading techniques that are used to process dissociative packets can also cause performance degradation unless special techniques are used to solve these problems. The IXP2XXX family of network processors use special hardware and software techniques to process packets at line rate whether they are dissociative or not.

Multi-processing and Multithreading

The IXP2XXX network processors have multiple processing engines and multithreading to achieve high throughput for packet processing by taking advantage of the dissociative nature of the incoming data stream. Because the received packet stream isn't easily cached into a single CPU core, the technique of multi-processing is used with multiple CPU cores to process the independent packets coming from the network. Each microengine performs specific tasks on a packet. The concept of multithreading is to allow each ME to operate a process (or different processes) in multiple instances, time-slicing between processes to achieve the most efficient performance.

Multi-processing

The microengines process multiple independent streams of network packets. Each microengine's instructions are stored in a control store that gives the instructions single cycle access to the microengine's execution unit. These instructions are loaded once when the system powers up, and they do not follow a cached architecture to manage large programs. In the MEv2 architecture, the entire program fits into the control store. By storing all of the instructions locally, the microengines can operate at their full clock rate without waiting for slow instruction fetches from memory that occur in a cached system. Having multiple microengines allows application of significantly more MIPS-to-packet processing problems. For example, the IXP2800 has 16 microengines running at 1.4 gigahertz, or a total of 22,400 MIPS. The multi-processing characteristics of the architecture makes the IXP2XXX based system highly scalable because the internal chassis allows for groups of microengines to be added or removed for future IXP2XXX network processors, as described in Chapter 4.

Assigning packets and tasks to microengines depends primarily on the design of the application, but IXP2XXX network processors support two packet-processing paradigms, as follows.

- *Hyper Task Chaining* or software pipelining is optimized for homogeneous packet types where the packet processing is very similar for the vast majority of the packets. This paradigm leverages the advantages of pipelining and special hardware functions and is necessary for the highest line rates.

- *Pool of Threads* is optimized for flexibility where a more familiar run-to-completion programming paradigm is desired. This paradigm is best used with heterogeneous packet streams where the packet processing times vary widely from packet to packet.

Hyper Task Chaining utilizes several microengines to run different tasks, as illustrated below in Figure 5.1.

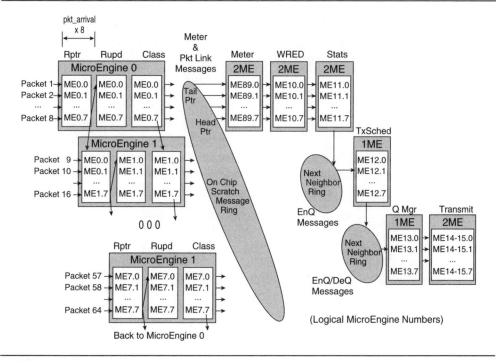

Figure 5.1   Hyper Task Chaining

In this software pipeline paradigm, a packet is processed by several tasks, with each task running on one or more microengines. The packet or the data that describes the packet—called context, state, or metadata—is passed from task to task until the packet is finally transmitted. To construct this software pipeline, each task or stage needs to be synchronized with the other tasks or stages. Each stage must be completed in a fixed time slot or else the packet is treated as an exception and sent to the core. This synchronization is not as hard as it sounds because it uses inter-thread signaling to transition from one stage (thread) to another. This software pipeline paradigm is called Hyper Task Chaining and is intended for the highest possible performance. The Pool of Threads (POTs) paradigm is optimized for flexible programming, where a more familiar run-to-completion programming method is used. The run-to-completion method allows all the tasks of packet processing to become a single program, as illustrated in Figure 5.2.

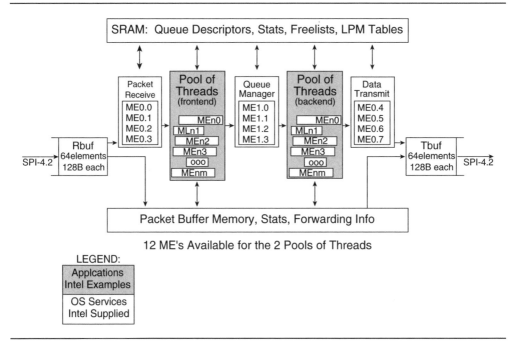

Figure 5.2   Pool of Threads

Each of these programs is independent of the other programs, with packet sequencing being managed after the threads complete their processing. This independence allows for much simpler programming than HTC because the programmer only needs to be concerned with one program and not with synchronizing each program with the other programs. While the POT method is simpler to implement for variable per packet processing time, it is not as fast as Hyper Task Chaining, which is optimized for speed for fixed processing times. Because IXP2XXX network processors are software programmable, either programming paradigm can be used. The uses of both HTC and POT paradigms are described in Chapter 7.

Multithreading

Multithreading allows multiple processes to run on a single processor, extracting the last bit of performance from that single processor. The Achilles heel for any processor is long latency memory, which can be 100 cycles for SRAM and 400 cycles for DRAM, respectively, and has to wait for that operation to complete before continuing, as illustrated in Figure 5.3 for a single processing thread.

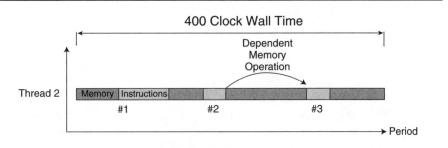

Figure 5.3   Single Processing Thread

In this example, a single thread executes internal ALU-type operations, which operate at one instruction per clock in typical RISC behavior. Then, the thread issues a dependent memory read operation to SRAM. Because this memory operation takes so long to complete, the instruction following the memory operation must wait. The microprocessor stalls, doing nothing, resulting in very inefficient performance.

Dependent Memory Operations

When a thread is waiting for a previous memory operation to complete before it can continue processing, that memory operation is called a dependent memory operation. Hiding these dependent memory operations is critical for the most efficient operation of the network processor. These operations impact performance in varying degrees, depending on the type of operation being performed. The least harmful operation is when a process launches a read or write and subsequent code needs to wait for the memory operation to complete. The next highest impact comes from read-modify-write critical sections. In these operations, an entire process prevents subsequent threads from operating until that initial process is completed. The worst-case dependent memory operations are where linked list or other data structure must be traversed or walked, which involved several dependent memory operations. Working around these operations is different for the various types of functions being performed.

Intel IXA is based on hiding these time-intensive operations. Multi-threading allows the memory latencies associated with one thread to be hidden behind the computations of other threads. The IXP2XXX network processors also have SRAM controllers that assist with automating complex operations. The SRAM unit automates ring buffer and linked list operations. Their atomic nature ensures mutually exclusive access and simplifies locking and unlocking operations. The SRAM unit also has several low-level atomic commands such as bit set, clear, increment, decrement, add, and swap. The scratch memory in the SHaC unit supports these commands in addition to ring buffer operations. Chapter 6 describes these special memory latency reducing commands in more detail.

The goal of multithreading is to remove memory latency inefficiency by having another process or thread operate while previously started threads are waiting for memory or other long latency operations to complete. The ideal case of multithreading is shown in Figure 5.4.

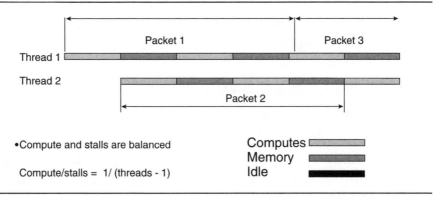

Figure 5.4   Ideal Threading

In this example, two threads are operating. Thread 1 operates a series of instructions then issues a memory operation. Then, thread 1 swaps out. *Swapping out* is when a microengine, under its own software control, goes from an executing state to a sleep state. The second thread is awakened (assuming it is in a ready state) and continues executing code while the first thread's memory operation is being processed. In perfectly balanced operation, the memory latency time of one thread equals the instruction execution time of the second thread, as shown in Figure 5.4. The equation that abstracts this operation for multiple threads is:

Compute/Stall = 1/(threads −1)

Thus, for 8 threads, the compute/stall ratio is 1/7 or 1 unit of execution time for every 7 units of stall time. This balanced situation isn't always the case. Most of the time, the memory latency time exceeds the instruction execution time, a situation called *latency bound*. Sometimes the instruction computation time exceeds the memory latency time, which is called *compute bound*. The latency bound situation is illustrated in Figure 5.5.

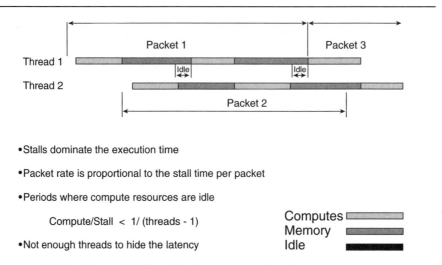

Figure 5.5 Latency Bound Threading

In the latency bound situation, the packet arrival rate is proportional to the memory latency time needed to process that packet for that micro-engine. Here's a helpful example to show you this situation. Thread 1 issues a memory operation (100 clocks in this example) then swaps out and goes to sleep. Thread 2 awakes and executes 70 instructions. After thread 2 finishes with its 70 instructions, it swaps out and goes to sleep. At this point, the microengine's arbiter checks to see whether the memory operation event for thread 1 is complete so it can wake up and continue execution. However, because the memory operation has not completed, thread 1 cannot be woken up. Because the memory operation in this example is 100 clocks and the compute time is 70 clocks, thread 1 will be idle for 30 clocks. Because the event needed to awaken thread 1 has not completed, the microengine's arbiter then checks for thread 2's event signal to complete. If it hasn't finished yet, the arbiter goes back to thread 1, checks for event completion, then goes to thread 2 and so on. The microengine's arbiter cycles through the event completion status for each of the threads and only awakens a thread when the appropriate event is complete. The imbalance in this latency bound scenario causes inefficiencies. A similar situation occurs in a compute bound situation, as illustrated in Figure 5.6.

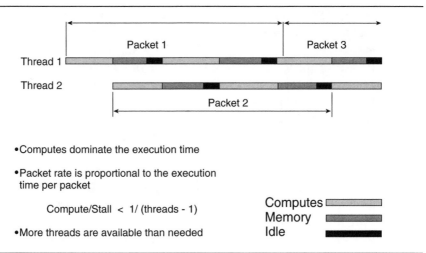

Figure 5.6   Compute Bound Threading

In the compute bound situation, the packet arrival rate is proportional to the instruction execution time needed to process that packet for that microengine. In this example, let's assume that both threads are executing a 120-clock task with 100 clocks of memory latency. Thread 1 runs for 120 clocks then swaps out after a memory reference is issued. Thread 2 awakes then and runs for 120 clocks before swapping out and going to sleep. During the 120-clock period that thread 2 was executing instructions, the 100-clock memory operation for thread 1 completed, so that thread was idle for 20 clocks.

Reducing the inefficiencies of both compute bound and latency bound situations is critical to maximize the utilization of the network processor. In the compute bound situation, fewer threads are required to balance system performance. To accomplish this balance, the MEv2 architecture supports a programmable number of threads per microengine. You can choose the number of threads per microengine, from 1, 2, 4, or 8, to give proper balance. For the compute bound scenario, having fewer operational threads is desirable. Because microengine resources are allocated on a per thread basis, more resources are available with fewer threads. Global and transfer registers are examples of these resources. Having fewer threads also allows for more efficient arbitration times for the microengines.

A more typical scenario, however, is the latency bound situation. Even with eight threads in MEv2, compute time might not be sufficient to hide the latency of all memory operations. With the higher clock rates of the IXP2XXX processors, the chance for memory latencies to exceed execution time is even greater. Execution time progressively gets shorter and shorter as semiconductor process improvements allow continual increases in processor clock rates. For this reason, the number of threads available in MEv2 architecture is 8, doubling the number in the MEv1 of the original IXP1200 network processor. In addition to increasing the number of threads in the microengine, other hardware mechanisms reduce the overall effects of memory latency, as explained later in this chapter.

This multi-processing and multithreading architecture solves the inherent problems with single-processor, cached CPUs. Parallel processing architectures achieve their highest performance when they operate on unrelated data—in our case packets. But, is this true for all network traffic? Are packets dependent and related to each other in some situations? Do the threads that process them need to be aware of any dependencies? The answer is a resounding YES!

The Serial Stream Processing Problem

Solving the serial stream process problem (SSPP) is critical for a network processor to experience high performance in the rich processing environments for which it is intended. This problem has two components, defined as follows:

■ *The Dependence Problem* occurs when interdependent, related streams of packets are associated with common data structures. This situation is typically known as a lock contention problem.

■ *The Independence Problem* occurs when independent and non-related packets are associated with common data structures.

As mentioned earlier, network processors use parallelism to achieve their high performance when packets are unrelated to each other. However, if multiple processes need access to common data structures, whether those structures are dependent or independent of each other, certain important and time-consuming operations can cause a parallel process to become serialized. Instead of being processed in parallel, several packets are processed one after another, serially. When the benefits of parallel processing are removed and the processing becomes serialized, overall performance can drop significantly and line rate performance can't be achieved. While the serial stream processing problem might seem obscure at first, it occurs commonly in networking applications. In several of these applications, significant per flow or connection state information is kept in memory. With tens or hundreds of thousands of flows to be managed, the problem is exacerbated.

■ *ATM and IP Flow Aggregation.* Often called the many-to-one or one-to-many problem, ATM and IP flow aggregation occurs when many thousand of independent ATM and IP flows are aggregated together, so they access a single common data structure. One such example is a transmit queue. Even though the packets and cells are processed independently, ultimately they might share common queues and data structures. When a single transmit queue is accessed by several threads concurrently, serialization results.

■ *Buffer Management.* Whether they are independent of or dependent on each other, when a stream of packets is received from the network, they must be buffered. To do this, the receive process requests a buffer from a common free buffer pool. This buffer pool is used for all packets arriving from the network.

■ *Classification, Metering, Policing, and Congestion Management.* When performing these tasks on an input stream, the algorithms employed can operate independently and in parallel if the packets themselves are unrelated. However, if these packets belong to the same interdependent flow, its data structure must be protected to prevent one process from accessing the data structure at the same time another is using it.

■ *Enqueueing and dequeueing* are two other situations where dependent packets need to be processed using special techniques. For example, when a packet is being enqueued to a transmit queue, that same queue must be protected if the transmit process attempts to dequeue from that same queue at the same time. In this case, the EnQ and DeQ process has to account for packet dependency.

■ *Traffic Scheduling and Shaping.* When shaping, scheduling, and transmitting traffic, the software or hardware functions that perform these tasks must be fully aware of, and allow for, packets that are dependent on each other. The scheduling and shaping algorithms must ensure that the packets don't access data structures belonging to the same flow at the same time.

At the core of the dependent and independent problems is a classical Read-Modify-Write (RMW) problem, in which one process needs to access a data structure from memory, modify it, then write it back to memory. Because another subsequent process can try to access and modify that same data structure, it needs to be locked down so mutual exclusivity can be given to the first process. This mechanism is triggered by a message that is associated with that data structure. Other processes can read that message to determine whether the data structure is being modified currently. This message is typically called a *mutex*, for *mut*ual *ex*clusion. This entire process of locking down a data structure and modifying it is called a *critical section*. When a process enters a critical section, the following six general steps are taken.

1. The mutex is first checked for locked status.
2. If locked, go to step 1; else set mutex to a locked status.
3. Read data.
4. Modify data.
5. Write back data.
6. Release the lock by setting mutex to unlocked status.

These six steps are followed in both the dependent and independent cases. Often times, the data to be modified is state information of the connection or flow, which can be accessed very quickly because the data is located within the processor. When thousands of flows or connections must be managed, the data structure is most likely to reside in external memory, which is much slower, requiring long latency reads. The worst-case situation, however, is when the data to be accessed and modified is stored in external memory in a linked list. Traversing this link list requires several dependent memory read and memory write operations to access the data. These dependent memory operations incur very long memory latencies because one memory access must finish before another one is started.

One common example is enqueueing a packet to a transmit queue, which takes three memory operations. In such operations, a queue descriptor is first read from memory so a tail pointer can be retrieved. With the tail pointer, the enqueue process writes a buffer link to the tail address memory location. The queue descriptor is then updated with the new tail address and is finally written back to memory. Thus, to enqueue a packet takes one memory read followed by two memory writes. Additionally, the second memory read is a dependent read operation, meaning the tail address cannot be read and modified until the first memory read operation is completed. The dequeueing operation is similar, requiring two reads followed by a write. Thus, to enqueue and dequeue a packet, a total of six memory accesses are required. This whole process is a critical section, meaning that the queue must be locked down, which adds additional time for memory access.

Application software must manage these critical sections properly, or significant performance degradation results. The RMW and locking process involves many accesses to or from memory, which is the source of high-speed packet processing problems. As packet rates continue to climb, the effects of memory latency become greater and greater. In fact, at the OC-192 line rate, memory latencies can exceed the packet arrival rate. This memory latency mismatch problem is the Achilles Heel of network processing architectures, whether they are hardwired ASICs, configurable hardware network processors, or fully programmable implementations. Table 5.1 shows the relation between packet arrival intervals vs. the access times of today's fastest currently available memory.

Table 5.1   Packet Arrival Interval vs. Memory Access Times

	OC-48	OC-192	OC-768
Cell Arrival Rate	~160 ns	~35 ns	~8 ns
DRAM Read Latency			~55-70 ns (DDR, RDR)
SRAM Read Latency			~10 ns (QDR)

At OC-48 data rates, memory access times are almost fast enough to keep up with packet interval period. However, as packet intervals decrease, memory access times struggle to keep up. The packet arrival interval of 8 nanoseconds for OC-768 is even smaller than 10 nanoseconds QDR SRAM memory technology.

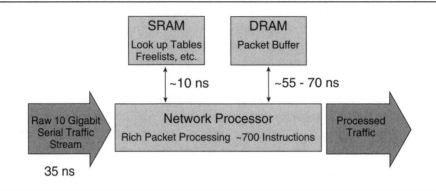

Figure 5.7   The Serial Stream Processing Problem

Overall, the serial stream-processing problem can affect pipelining architectures negatively when memory latencies are proportionately long relative to packet arrival rate. A pipelining architecture applies a series of tasks to an incoming packet stream and the pipeline is tuned so that each task completes in a fixed time period. Typically, this time period matches the arrival rate of the incoming packet. If the task-completion time exceeds the processing time, defined as instruction processing time plus memory latency time, the pipeline is broken and packets are dropped. As Table 5.1 shows, the OC-192 cell rate is 35 nanoseconds, implying the processing in one pipeline stage is only 35 nanoseconds, whereas DRAM access time is 55–70 nanoseconds and SRAM access time is 10 nanoseconds. From these figures, you can see that the pipeline period and memory accesses are almost the same speeds. If fact, processes operating on linked lists can break a pipeline due to their multiple, dependent memory operations.

Figure 5.8 shows the cumulative effect of memory latencies on an ATM cell stream without using special features of Intel IXA. In this example, the processing is broken down into three general stages:

■ Stage 1: When the first cell of VC1 is picked up by thread 1, its state information needs to be read. This state information also holds the mutex for VC1. Thread 1 checks this mutex and sets it to a locked state, assuming of course that it was previously unlocked. Just after VC1Cell 1 arrives, cell 2 arrives and is picked up by thread 2. However, the mutex for VC1 already has a locked status, so thread 2 needs to wait until thread 1 completes. This stage is the beginning of serialization.

- Stage 2: Thread 1 continues processing the cell and modifies it. This modification can include any number functions, such as ATM reassembly, policing, etc.

- Stage 3: This state information is then written back to memory where VC1's descriptor is located. The lock is then released so subsequent threads can use the same critical data.

In this example, threads 1, 2, and 3 experience lock contention because they are processing dependent and related cells. As such, these threads are serialized because the critical sections must be processed one at a time. Threads 4 through 8 do not experience lock contention because their cells are unrelated, so they can operate in parallel and can, in fact, process their five cells faster than threads 1 through 3, which are forced to operate in a serial fashion. Because memory latencies are difficult to hide in serial processing, processing time is extended and any thread that hasn't completed by the end of the pipe stage period is terminated and cells are dropped.

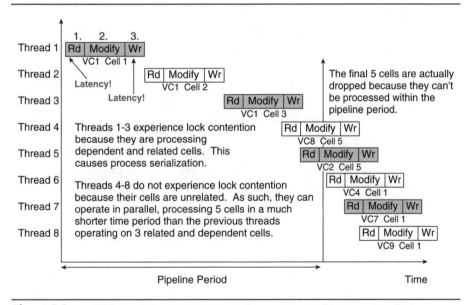

Figure 5.8   Effects of the Serial Stream Processing Problem on Pipelining

Distributed Cache

To solve the dependence or lock contention problem of packet processing within a single microengine, IXP2XXX network processors use a new approach, called a distributed cache, for checking for inter-thread dependency. Traditional methods employ a mutex in external memory, storing the state of a resource to determine whether that resource is locked or another resource can use and modify it. The resource itself is also stored in external memory. However, the time taken to lock, unlock, and check this mutex along with accessing the resource itself from external memory can become prohibitive due to the long memory latencies, so this method has a particularly negative impact for dependent packets at high line rate. The packets are serialized in time and can be dropped, as indicated in Figure 5.8. IXP2XXX network processors, on the other hand, bring the locking mechanism and the storage of the actual resource internal to the MEv2 microengine, forming the basis of the distributed cache. By localizing the dependency check in the microengine, the hardware can perform the check very quickly, in just a few cycles, which is significantly faster than the average 130 clocks of SRAM latency experienced by application software using a mutex in SRAM. The same is true of accessing data from local memory. By having the resource stored locally, the RMW can be done at the speed of the microengine itself. Thus, the distributed cache technique is completely scalable, extending the upper performance boundary as microengine frequencies increase with process technology improvements.

The distributed cache is analogous to a traditional microprocessor's cache tag RAM and cache data. Whereas a traditional cache tightly couples the cache tag with a line of cached information, Intel IXA decouples the tag from the actual data, allowing the tag to be used for various purposes and data types. In IXP2XXX processors, the equivalent of the cache tag is a 16-entry content addressable memory (CAM) that is maintained by software in the microengine. The cache data is the actual data resource to be modified. This resource storage can be in the 640 words of local memory in the microengine or in the SRAM or Scratch RAM Q_Array unit. Figure 5.9 illustrates how the CAM holds a flow identifier with the local memory storing the associated flows context or state information.

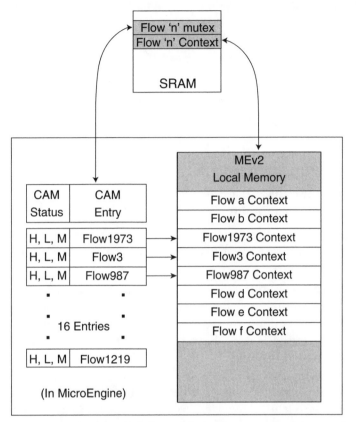

The CAM holds the critical data identifier and the local memory stores the associated state information. The CAM returns a status word on a CAM lookup. One bit of that status word indicates a hit (the data is stored locally) or a miss (the data is not stored locally). The status word also has 4 user-defined status bits that can be used for additional state information. In some applications, a locked status can be encoded in those user defined status bits. A locked status indicates that not only is the critical data already stored locally, but that another process is also working on that critical data. In other words, it is locked, meaning it is stored but can't be used.

Figure 5.9   MEv2 Distributed Cache

General Operation of the Distributed Cache

When a microengine enters a critical section of code, it stores an identifier for the critical data in the CAM then reads the packets actual critical data from SRAM to the MEv2 local memory. When a subsequent thread enters that same critical section, it performs a dependency check using the MEv2 CAM. The CAM returns to the thread one of two states of the critical data associated with the identifier:

■ *Miss*. When the result is a CAM miss, it can be assumed that the critical data is not saved locally and that the thread must read it from external memory. The miss status includes a least recently used (LRU) CAM entry number. The CAM miss helps a thread with a CAM replacement policy, which is described later.

■ *Hit*. If the result is a CAM hit, it can be assumed that the critical data resides in local memory and is currently locked by another thread.

By processing critical sections using the CAM, the modification of the critical data of interdependent packets goes very quickly. In fact, for a stream of dependent packets, only an initial memory read and a final memory write is done for all of the dependent packets. The packets are processed through at the internal clock rate of the microengine. What used to be a worst-case condition now becomes an optimal scenario. To achieve this highest level of performance for modification of critical data, a software technique called folding needs to be implemented.

Memory Bandwidth vs. Memory Latency

Reducing the effects of memory latency is central to Intel IXA. While the differences between memory latency and memory bandwidth is common knowledge, sometimes there is a misunderstanding of the intent of IXA's distributed cache. Memory bandwidth is simply the raw frequency of the memory or I/O units, whether measured in megahertz or gigabits per second. Memory bandwidth is measured at the pin interface between the network processor and the memory chip itself. Memory latency measures the total time it takes for a memory operation to complete. This total time includes:

- The source (microengine, Intel XScale core, PCI) issues a memory command to the memory unit.

- Memory unit decodes command.

- If write command, pull the data from the source, and write it to memory.

- If read command, execute command and push the data to the originating command source.

- When the operation is completed, signal the source.

This whole round trip delay defines the total latency of the memory.

Many Intel IXA features solve these memory latency problems. However, the distributed cache as it is described here solves only the memory latency problem, while not intending to minimize memory bandwidth. The distributed cache minimizes dependency checking and data modification, which can involve several dependent memory operations. When the CAM indicates that the critical data is stored locally, the long latency from these memory operations is significantly reduced. A side benefit is that external memory bandwidth is also minimized, but that is only a side effect. When Intel's highest speed OC-192 forwarding software applications are written, they assume that the CAM has 0 hits (no locally stored data) and 100 percent of the data accesses to external memory are made. Whereas traditional microprocessors use instructions and data caches to mitigate the problems of slow memory bandwidth, Intel IXA uses the distributed cache to mitigate the problems of memory latency time.

Folding

With the distributed cache architecture of the IXP2XXX network processors, a software technique called folding can increase performance significantly. To minimize the latency associated with modifying data in critical sections of dependent data streams, multiple read and writes can be folded into one memory read and write. The distributed cache architecture uses folding in all of Intel's data plane example software designs. Data plane functions, such as enqueueing and dequeueing, require this technique to maintain the highest possible performance. Folding is used to attack directly the memory latency problem associated with dependency checking in critical sections.

Figure 5.10 shows the effects of folding on a stream of eight dependent, related packets. Each of the eight threads of the microengine is assigned a packet as it is received from the previous microengine. Each thread is then responsible for processing the packet during this processing stage. For the sake of clarity, all eight packets are dependent, back-to-back packets that belong to the same connection, flow, queue, etc. In reality, this commonality is statistically improbable, especially for heavily loaded systems. Later, you will learn how the more common situation is handled, which is a mix of related and unrelated packets, where thousands of different flows or connections must be managed.

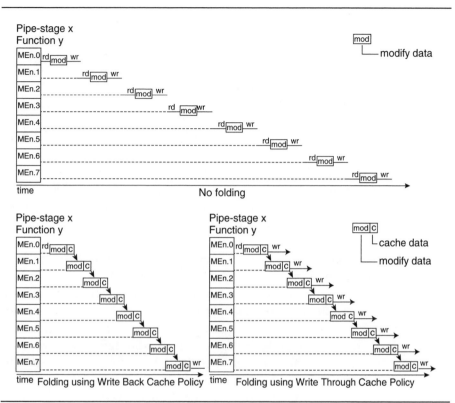

Figure 5.10 The Effects of Folding on Processing Dependent Critical Data

Without folding, each thread must read the critical data from memory, modify it, and then write it back along with the additional latency associated with checking a mutex, which also is in memory, to determine whether the data is locked in the first place. Thus, each thread has several dependent memory accesses, even if a thread uses the same modified data from the previous thread.

With folding, an initial read of the critical data by the first thread is stored in local memory. Then, the data is worked on, modified, and cached in local memory. The next thread checks the CAM to see if the critical data is cached and locked by a previous thread. If the critical data is cached and required by the current thread, this thread has immediate access to the data. The operation requires no read from external memory of this data, saving significant time. At some point, the cached data must be written back according to some cache replacement policy. For a write-back policy, the final thread writes the data back to external memory after all critical data for this dependent data has been modified. With a write-through policy, the data is written back to external memory by each thread after it has been locally cached. This write operation is hidden behind subsequent processing by other threads so its latency won't stretch out the overall processing time.

It should be noted that in Figure 5.10 all of the threads are working on packets of the same flow. A more realistic scenario is when the threads are working on different flows or connections. This situation is described in the next section. Figure 5.10 shows the worst-case situation if the mutex is in external memory while operating on packets of the same flow. By using folding, the mutex is stored and performed locally in the microengine, at a significantly faster rate then if performed in external memory.

The cache eviction policy is required to write stale data from local memory back to external memory. Because of the relatively small size of local memory, the processor evicts data that hasn't been recently used. Determining which data is stale occurs when the CAM returns a miss state after a lookup operation. Along with this miss state, the CAM returns a pointer into one of the CAM's 16 locations. This pointer is the least recently used entry of the CAM, which is also used to point to the stale critical data in local memory. The thread that issued the CAM lookup in the first place can then write back the locally stored critical data associated with the identifier back to external memory or wait until all the threads have completed, as described earlier.

Two mechanisms implement the folding technique. Figure 5.11 illustrates the two-stage process.

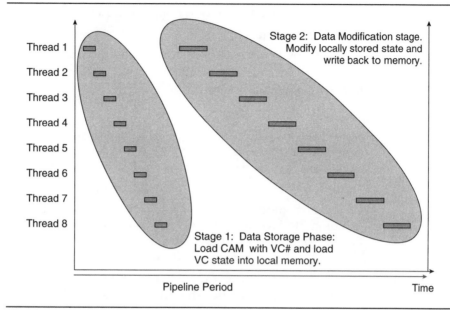

Figure 5.11   Dual Stage Folding Example

Each of the eight threads is assigned a packet as the microengine receives them from the previous microengine or directly from the MSF. Folding has two phases: the data storage phase and the data modification stage. The data storage phase is responsible for loading critical data into local memory and managing the CAM. The data modification stage is responsible for modifying the locally stored critical data and for evicting the data back to memory when processing is complete.

Data Storage Phase

The sequence is:

1. Thread begins when it receives a signal from previous microengine.

2. CAM is checked to see if critical data is currently loaded in local memory.

3. If critical data is loaded—that is, CAM responds with a hit for that critical data—this phase is complete for this thread. Jump to step 7.

4. If the critical data is not loaded in the CAM—CAM returns a Miss—the thread reads the critical data from SRAM and stores it in local memory. Stale data can be written back at this time according to the cache eviction policy, as described later.

5. Signal next thread.

6. Repeat steps 1 to 5 until all 8 threads have completed this stage.

Data Modification Stage

The sequence is:

1. Thread begins after it gets signaled from thread 8 of the previous data storage phase. Data is now stored in local memory of microengine and can be worked on.

2. Perform modification of data in local memory.

3. Data is now modified, processing is complete, and the data must be committed to memory, which can be done after all threads are finished or as part of an LRU process (described earlier).

At this point, you may be saying, "What is this all about? Why go through this complicated process just to read data, modify it, and write it back to memory." Just remember the original reason, which is to reduce the effect of memory latencies. As described earlier in this chapter, IXP2XXX network processors reduce memory latencies using multithreading techniques where one thread's memory references can be hidden behind another thread's computations. In the case of processing dependent packets in critical sections, however, the next thread can't proceed until the previous thread is completed, causing serialization. In this case, the memory reference is totally exposed and the RMW process takes excessively long.

Reducing serialization requires very fast dependency checking so one thread can see if any other threads are working on the same critical data. The role of the CAM allows a thread to determine very quickly whether data is being worked on or not while local memory allows very fast access to the critical data itself.

Managing thousands of connections, flows, queues...

The folding technique achieves its high performance by having the critical data stored in local memory and its identifier cached locally in the microengine CAM. However, the CAM is only 16 entries deep. So it may appear as if only applications having16 associations or less can be used. You might say, "This is fine for these smaller applications, but most applications manage thousands of connections, flows, queues, etc. So this whole folding business is only applicable in the statistically small chance that the processor receives a short burst of back-to-back interrelated packets. This won't work for most applications!" On closer examination, however, the Intel IXA distributed cache can manage thousands of flows, connections, queues, etc. using the MEv2 CAM and local memory.

Remember, the primary issue is reducing memory latencies. For situations where the critical data is stored in local memory and associated with the 16 entries in the CAM, very fast processing is achieved because the MEs have near instant access to the locally stored data. While processing is serialized (threads operate one after another), the processing occurs very quickly because no external memory accesses are required because the data is locally cached. However, for the statistically more common situation where thousands of independent flows are being processed, the threads need to access their critical data and mutex from external memory. However, because the flows are independent, the threads can operate in parallel and achieve the benefits of parallel processing. In summary, if the packets are dependent, the distributed cache is utilized and processing is serialized; if the packets are independent, packets are processed in parallel.

Interleaved Threading

As described in the previous section, threading is the mechanism used to hide the memory references of one thread behind the compute cycles of other threads. In the ideal case, the total time of the computes covers the memory references. However, memory references often exceed the total computes so they can't be hidden—especially when a thread issues several dependent memory references and the total compute time of the other threads is less than the total completion time of the memory reference. As the clock rate of Intel network processors increases and the total computation time relative to external memory latencies decreases, this problem needs continued attention.

For example, in Figure 5.12, each thread executes a short program of 10 instructions with a memory operation taking 100 clocks. We'll assume one instruction equivalent to one clock, the ideal RISC behavior. The last instruction of Thread 1 issues a dependent memory read, which is followed by an instruction that operates on the returned data. The thread goes to sleep on the memory read and is put into the ready state when the reference is completed. The other seven threads execute their instructions, covering 70 total clock cycles. Because the memory reference is 100 clocks and only 70 clocks have elapsed, Thread 1 won't wake up because the memory reference that it is waiting for hasn't completed yet. If the other seven threads are performing the same instructions as Thread 1, they will be in the same situation. They too wait for a memory reference to complete before execution can resume. In this example, 30 idle cycles occur before the execution on any of the threads can resume. For time-sensitive applications such as context pipelines, which are described in Chapter 7, the total pipeline can be exceeded.

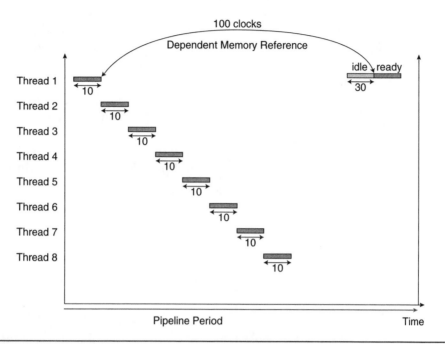

Figure 5.12 Problems with Latency Bound Threading

The fundamental problem results from too few computes to hide the dependent memory operation. The solution is to add more computes, but how? While the application may be hundreds of lines of code, there are not enough instructions between the dependent memory reference and the next instruction in the program. The same thread cannot perform additional processing on that same packet because it has to wait for the dependent memory reference to complete. The solution is to use *interleaved threading*, which assigns two or more processes, called phases, to each thread so the thread can operate on multiple packets. The idea is that each thread processes more than a single packet so that the total instruction cycle time allows the memory reference to be hidden behind the computes of the other threads, which also are processing multiple packets. This solution is called interleaved threading because the processing of two or more packets is interleaved on a single thread.

The concept of interleaved threading is illustrated in Figure 5.13. This diagram shows each thread operating on two packets, with thread 1 operating on packet n and $n+8$. With interleaved threading, each thread processes two or more packets. In phase 1, thread 1 begins to work on packet n, and then it issues a dependent memory reference when processing that packet. Thread 1 then starts processing packet $n+8$, but only goes to sleep after the completion of this first phase. Threads 2–8 follow in the same manner. After thread 8 completes, phase 1 is complete and phase 2 begins execution with thread 1. Because more computes have been added to each thread, the dependent memory reference from processing packet n has been completed prior to thread 1 entering phase 2. As such, this thread can begin immediately executing without having to wait.

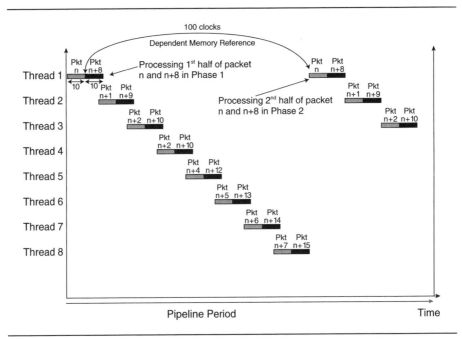

Figure 5.13   Interleaved Threading with Two Phases

Interleaved threading allows for the highest performance when even the smallest memory references need to be hidden for most efficient use of the microengine's compute resources. Interleaved threading, however, has some shortcomings that need to be considered. For example, the total execution time must be less than the packet arrival rate. Also, each phase adds its own complexity with more local states that must be stored in registers, local memory, etc. The programming model is more complex because actual instructions need to be counted relative to anticipated memory latencies. Also, this technique increases the amount of latency in the microengine and the number of packets in flight. However, these complexities do not outweigh the performance gains that are achieved.

Summary

The purpose of this chapter was to help you understand the basics of parallel processing and why Intel IXA works better than a general-purpose microprocessor for processing network data. Intel IXA's parallel processing uses multithreading and multiple microengines to process several packets simultaneously. These techniques are used when packets are independent and unrelated. When packets are dependent and related to each other, parallel processing can become serialized, which is a traditional problem with parallel processing techniques. The IXP2XXX network processors use a distributed cache to solve these serialization problems. Distributed cache uses folding and interleaved threading techniques to hide the memory latencies that occur during critical sections. The distributed cache uses a CAM in the microengine to check for inter-thread dependencies and local memory to hold the data that is to be operated on. This local memory is either stored locally in the microengine, or in the SRAM Q_Array. The features of the SRAM Q_Array are some of the most powerful of the chip, and they are described in greater detail in the next chapter.

Chapter 6

Managing Data Structures

ntel IXA is fully software programmable and uses memory for storing data structures and buffering packet data. Specifically, IXP2XXX network processors use ring buffers and linked lists to pass messages and data between microengines and buffer packets in DRAM. This technique is illustrated in the packet flow example in Chapter 1. Quickly accessing data structures with minimal latency in SRAM (and internal scratch memory) is very critical. When a software application is right in the middle of a complex processing algorithm and needs to access a data structure before processing can continue, memory access needs to be very quick or else processing stalls and packets may get dropped. In Intel IXA, linked lists and ring buffers are used extensively throughout the packet processing cycle. These linked lists and ring buffers are very complex memory operations that involve several read and write operations to manage the data structure. Because they are right in the middle of the processing flow, they need to be turned around very quickly. As such, these operations are fully automated in IXP2XXX network processors to reduce programming burden and minimize memory latency so high line rates can be achieved. The goal of this chapter is to give you a fundamental understanding how IXP2XXX processors manage linked lists and ring buffers.

Using Memory

Figure 6.1 illustrates the basic processing flow of packets as they are received, processed, and transmitted in the various types of data structures in a packet processing application.

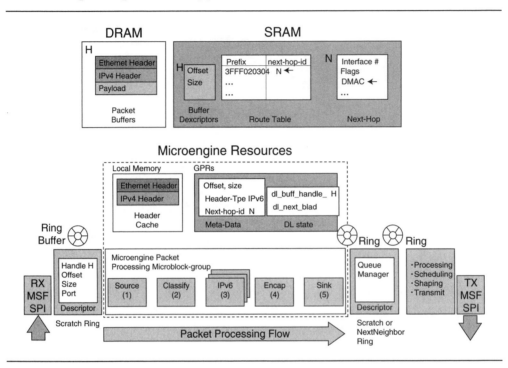

Figure 6.1   Memory Resource Utilization in Processing a Packet

Packets are first received by the MSF, reassembled by the RX microengine, and stored in DRAM. When they are first received, the processor must allocate a buffer from a free buffer pool. This free buffer pool is a linked-list structure consisting of hundreds or thousands of buffers that are pulled off for packet storage. Once buffered, the RX microengine passes a buffer descriptor to the packet processing microengines via a ring structure. This ring buffer is located in either external SRAM or internal scratch memory. The microengines in turn read the ring to get the buffer descriptor so they can then bring in the packet's header, and payload, if necessary, for processing. During the packet processing stages, microengines sometimes pass data from themselves to another microengine with minimal latency using next neighbor registers. To en-

microengine with minimal latency using next neighbor registers. To ensure that the next microengine knows that data has been given to it, generalized thread signals are used to signal between one microengine or thread to another. Once all receive processing is complete, the packet must be placed on a transmit queue. The receive process hands off a packet descriptor to an enqueue (EnQ)/dequeue (DeQ) microengine via another ring. The EnQ/DeQ microengine reads the packet descriptor, then adds the packet to the transmit queue which is a linked list structure. The EnQ/DeQ stage then takes a buffer off the linked list and communicates to the TX microengine via another ring where it takes a packet descriptor and finally transmits the packet.

To summarize, during this whole chain of packet processing steps, a number of mechanisms are used to step the processing through in an orderly fashion and also to buffer the actual packets, descriptors, and state information. Ring buffers were used to communicate from one microengine to another. GTS was used to signal one microengine to another. Linked lists were used to store the data packet buffers for hundreds or thousands of queues. Finally, next neighbor registers were used to provide a low latency microengine to microengine data path for pipelining tasks. To maintain high line rate, all of these mechanisms, especially linked lists and ring buffers need to be very fast and easy to use by the programmer, as you'll see in the next sections.

Linked List Management Structures

Buffering data using linked lists is a critical part of processing packets and this buffering is especially difficult to do when high line rates must be achieved. In fact, this difficulty contributes to the serial stream processing problem, defined in Chapter 5 for independent packets. As an example, this independence problem occurs when several flows must be aggregated into one common transmit queue. Depending on the application, this aggregation might require adding several packets to the end of a linked list. The software application must access this linked list very quickly with minimal latency. Enqueueing and dequeueing packets that are moving to and from a linked list are difficult because each packet involves dependent memory references with critical data to be protected. These operations are, in fact, some of the most difficult problems for a network processor to solve if they are handled with traditional software methods.

IXP2XXX network processors automate linked list management using a *Q_Array* controller in each of the SRAM channels. The Q_Array controller performs an entire enqueue or dequeue operation on a linked list with one command, such as:

```
SRAM [enqueue, --, src_op1, src_op2], opt_tok
```

The Q_Array also caches frequently used descriptors for very fast, low latency access. Because the Q_Array controller automates a function that is typically implemented in software, it must assume a certain structure for the queue descriptor. Table 6.1 shows the five fields that are of primary interest here, with Figure 6.2 illustrating the actual linked list.

Table 6.1   SRAM Q_Array Controller Descriptor Field Definition

Field	Description
Head Pointer	Points to the head of a linked list. Packets are dequeued from the head.
Tail Pointer	Points to the tail of a linked list. Packets are enqueued to the tail.
Q Count	Number of total packets on the linked list
Cell Count	Number of cells in a multi-cell packet. The cell count field is only relevant to the packet that is presently pointed to by the head pointer.
EOP	The EOP field indicates that the packet presently addressed by the Head pointer is the last cell in a multi-cell packet.

To understand how the SRAM Q_Array controller automates these operations, you first must understand how a single cell packet is buffered, then how buffering a multi-cell packet differs, and finally how both single cell and multi-cell packets are dequeued. In the following examples, the specifics of caching aren't described to simplify the explanation. Instead, all examples assume that the packet descriptors all reside in external memory.

For more detail about linked lists, refer to the *IXP2800 Hardware Reference Manual* (Intel Corporation 2002).

Enqueueing a Packet

In this first example, the Q_Array controller enqueues a single-cell packet. As defined here, frames are composed of either one or multiple cells. Cells are also called segments and are not implied to refer to ATM cells. Figure 6.2 illustrates the enqueueing of packet buffer Z to a queue structured as a linked list. A real-life application can require many thousands of queues. A linked list is composed of a descriptor followed by buffer pointers. Each buffer pointer provides an address of the data buffer's location in memory. The queue descriptor has several fields that define the list. The head pointer indicates the first buffer in the list. In Figure 6.2, the head pointer is address A. The data contained in memory location A is itself an address (B) that points to the next buffer in the list, which is buffer C. At this point, you might be thinking that this sequence is just a list of pointers from one value to the next, and you might ask, "Where is the actual data buffer? For example, where is buffer B?" Buffer B is actually found in DRAM and its location is determined by a base address (address B) and a predetermined offset. Software simply computes an offset to the base address to point to the actual buffer location in DRAM.

The tail pointer provides the address for the last buffer in the list. The Q_Array controller also contains a count that indicates how many packet buffers are on the list and a cell count that indicates how many cells are in a packet pointed to by the head pointer. The last buffer on the list indicated by the tail is not really a buffer but a no-link value. The data that is contained in the no-link memory location is typically all zeroes, serving as an additional signal of end-of-packet status. The no-link serves as a place holder for the next packet to be buffered.

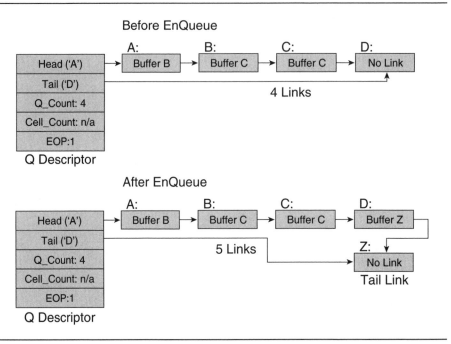

Figure 6.2 Enqueueing a Packet to a Linked List

In a completely software-based enqueue/dequeue process, as used in an ASIC or fully programmable gate array (FPGA), when a buffer is added to a queue, the queue descriptor first must be locked down because it is a shared resource to which multiple processes can require access, as you have with the lock contention between a receive process enqueueing to the list and a transmit process dequeueing from the list. As such, the EnQ and DeQ process is a critical section. However, because the SRAM Q_Array controller, as used in IXP2XXX network processors, implements these enqueue/dequeue instructions as atomic operations, the hardware can guarantee mutual exclusivity. No cumbersome software locking mechanisms need to be implemented.

Because the descriptor does not need to be locked down, the first operation that occurs is reading the queue descriptor to retrieve the tail pointer and count fields. Reading the head pointer is not needed for an enqueue operation, which is important because valuable memory cycles aren't wasted reading information that isn't needed. The buffer to be added, BufferZ, is placed at the tail address that was previously occupied by the no-link placeholder, which is shown in Figure 6.2 at address D. The BufferZ pointer points to a new no-link placeholder, and the tail is updated to point to the new no-link address, which is now address Z. The count is incremented to indicate the additional buffer on the list. In this example and the immediate ones that follow, the cell count field for the packet descriptor is not applicable; it only becomes a concern during a multi-cell dequeue operation.

In general, the following steps are taken to enqueue a packet:

1. Read queue descriptor to obtain the tail pointer and packet count. Remember: the head pointer is not needed to enqueue a packet.

2. Write the new buffer address at the memory location indicated by the tail pointer.

3. Modify the queue descriptor with a new tail address and incremented packet count.

4. Write back the modified queue descriptor to memory.

This example showed you how a packet is enqueued to a linked list. The packet was contained in a single cell buffer. Many times, however, a packet is segmented so that a single packet consists of several smaller cells, with one buffer being allocated to one cell, as shown in Figure 6.3.

MultiCell Packet

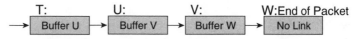

A multi-cell packet. 4 cells make up this packet.

A multi-cell packet made up of four cells.

Figure 6.3 Multi-Cell Packet

When the SRAM unit enqueues this multi-cell packet, it defines all the cells as one packet, so it only increments the queue count by 1. However, the cell count for this packet is 3. The two steps for the SRAM unit to enqueue a multi-cell packet are:

■ First, the SRAM unit must replace the previous no-link address with a pointer to the start of the new packet, using the SRAM command `Enq_Tail_and_Link`. This command updates address D to point to the new packet, the address T, and it increments the packet count by 1.

■ Second, the SRAM unit must update the tail address with the `Enq_Tail` command. This command does not increase the packet count because that value has already been incremented. This command only updates the tail with the new address.

These two steps are shown in Figure 6.4.

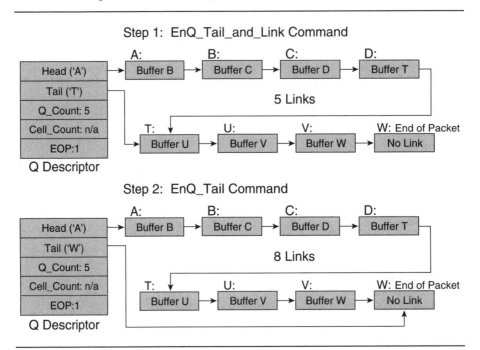

Figure 6.4   Enqueueing a Multi-Cell Packet B

Enqueueing a multi-cell packet takes two SRAM instructions. The format for these instructions is:

```
SRAM [cmd, --, src_opt1, src_opt2], opt_tok
```

The parameters for this command are shown in Table 6.2.

Table 6.2   SRAM Enqueue Command Parameters

Parameter	Command	Description
Cmd	Enqueue	This command is used to add a single buffer to the queue or to add the start-of-packet buffer of a multi-buffer frame to the queue. It adds a buffer to the queue contained in the Q-array entry and sets the tail to point to the buffer. If necessary, a link is established from the old tail buffer to the new buffer.
	Enqueue_Tail	This command updates the tail pointer only. This command must be preceded by an enqueue command to the same entry. This adds the end-of-packet buffer of a multi-buffer frame to the queue. No intervening commands should occur in a queue array entry between an enqueue and enqueue_tail command.
--	All Commands	Must be '—'
Src_op1, Src_op2	All Commands	Restricted operands that are added (src_op1 + src_op2) to define the following: [31:30] SRAM channel [29:24] Queue array entry number [23:0] Q_link pointer The Q_link pointer must be a 4-byte word address.
Opt_tok	All Commands	For indirect_ref, see the programmer's reference manual.

Note: For further information, see the programmer's reference manual.

Dequeueing a Packet

Dequeueing a packet is the opposite of enqueueing a packet. Typically, a transmit process dequeues a packet from a list prior to actually transmitting it. Whereas a packet is added to the end or the tail of a list for enqueueing, a packet is removed from the beginning or the head of the list when dequeueing. Dequeueing a packet requires a single instruction; just like enqueueing a packet requires only the enqueue command.

The following steps are taken to dequeue a packet, as shown in Figure 6.5:

1. Read queue descriptor to obtain the head pointer and cell count and EOP status. Remember: the tail pointer is not needed to dequeue a packet.

2. Read memory location pointed to by head pointer to obtain the address of the packet buffer to be dequeued.

3. Modify the queue descriptor with a new head pointer and with the packet count decremented by 1.

4. Write back the modified queue descriptor to memory.

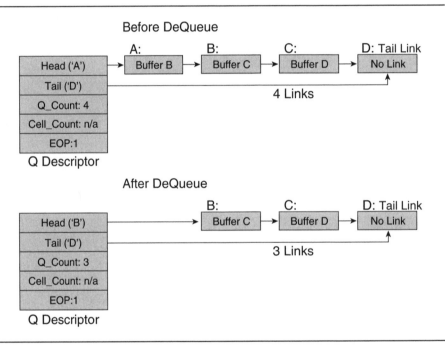

Figure 6.5   Dequeueing a Buffer from a Linked List

The next example shows you how a multi-cell packet dequeue operates. The queue in Figure 6.6 has five packets, with the packet pointed to by the head (A) consisting of four cells. The head points to address A and the tail points to address W. This list has a total of eight links.

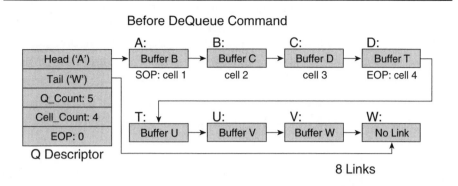

Figure 6.6   Link List Prior to Dequeueing a Multi-Cell Packet

When the Q_Array controller dequeues a packet, it first reads the head address, EOP, and cell count fields of the descriptor. The head address points to the packet to be dequeued while the EOP field indicates whether this buffer is the last one of a multi-cell packet. If reset to a value of zero, the count field indicates how many cells are in the packet. In this example, the cell count is 4 so the hardware has to dequeue one buffer at a time. To remove this entire packet requires 4 dequeue operations. In this example, one cell of the packet is dequeued at a time (although the Q_Array controller supports dequeueing an entire multi-cell packet at time). Figure 6.7 illustrates the state of the descriptor after the first buffer is dequeued.

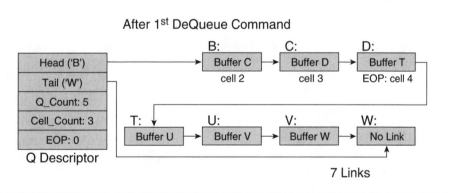

Figure 6.7   Linked List After the First Dequeue Operation

After this first dequeue on the packet, the head pointer is incremented to point to the next buffer. The Q_Array controller then checks the EOP status, which is still in a reset state (value of 0) because the entire packet hasn't been dequeued yet. Therefore, the Cell_Count is decremented by 1 while the Q_Count remains at 5. The Q_Count is only decremented after the entire packet is dequeued, and it remains the same as long as cells remain on the queue for that packet. This process continues until the last cell for this packet is reached.

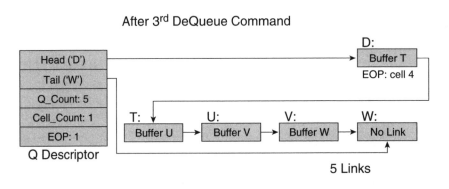

Figure 6.8   EOP is Reached for Multi-Cell Packet

After the third dequeue operation, the last buffer in the packet is reached, as indicated by EOP being set to 1. The Cell_Count is now 1 while the Q_Count remains at 5 because the last cell hasn't been removed yet. The EOP status bit tells the Q_Array controller that it can decrement the Q_Count on the next dequeue operation, as shown in Figure 6.9.

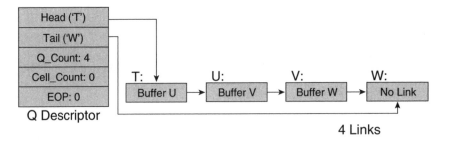

Figure 6.9   Next Packet is Ready to be Dequeued

After the last cell of the packet is dequeued, the Q_Count is decremented to show that four packets are now on the list. Also, the head pointer is updated to point to the next packet. For this example, assume that packet U is a single cell packet, so it has a Cell_Count of 0 with an EOP of 1 because it is the end of a 1 cell packet.

The format for the SRAM dequeue instruction is:

```
SRAM [dequeue, xfer, src_op1, src_op2], opt_tok
```

Table 6.3   SRAM Dequeue Command Parameters

Parameter	Command	Description	
Cmd	Dequeue	This command is used to remove a q_link from the queue. If the q_count is zero (nothing on the queue), the value of zero is returned. If the q_count is NOT zero (something on the queue), and the seg_cnt is 0 in the head q_link (buffer only has one segment), the q_link is removed from the linked list and it is returned. If the q_count is NOT zero (something on the queue), and the seg_cnt is NOT 0 in the head q_link (buffer holds multiple segments), the seg_cnt is decremented and the q_link NOT is removed from the linked list. If the q_count is not 0, the entire q_link is returned.	
xfer	All Commands	S or D transfer register where the q_link is returned.	
Src_op1, Src_op2	dequeue	Restricted operands that are added (src_op1 + src_op2) to define the following: [31:30] SRAM channel [29:24] Queue array entry number [23:0] Ignored	
Opt_tok	dequeue	Indirect_ref	Defer[sig_na me]
		ctx_swap [sig_name]	Sig_done [sig_name]

Note: For more details, see the programmer's reference manual.

SRAM Q_Array Controller

In the previous examples, the packet descriptor was assumed to be in external memory, and it had to be read and written for each enqueue or dequeue operation. For low speed applications, this may be acceptable, but to ensure line rate performance at the highest speeds, to continuously read and write descriptors to and from slow, external memory would be problematic, especially if many flows are mapped to a single transmit queue. Oftentimes called the "Many-to-One" problem, having to store single or few queue descriptors in external memory is very wasteful.

To solve these problems, the SRAM Q_Array controller caches frequently-used descriptors in the on-chip Q_Array structure, which resides in the IXP2XXX network processor's SRAM channel. The SRAM Q_Array is a hardware structure that automates enqueueing and dequeueing packets onto linked lists as well as controlling ring buffers and journals. The SRAM Q_Array can have any combination of *resident queue descriptors*, *cached queue descriptors*, and *ring/journal buffers*, up to a maximum of 64 total entries. Each SRAM channel has a separate Q_Array controller. Thus, the IXP2800 processor, with its four SRAM channels, can cache up to 256 queue descriptors, with the IXP2400 able to cache 128 descriptors in its two SRAM channels. The Q_Array controller is shown in Figure 6.10.

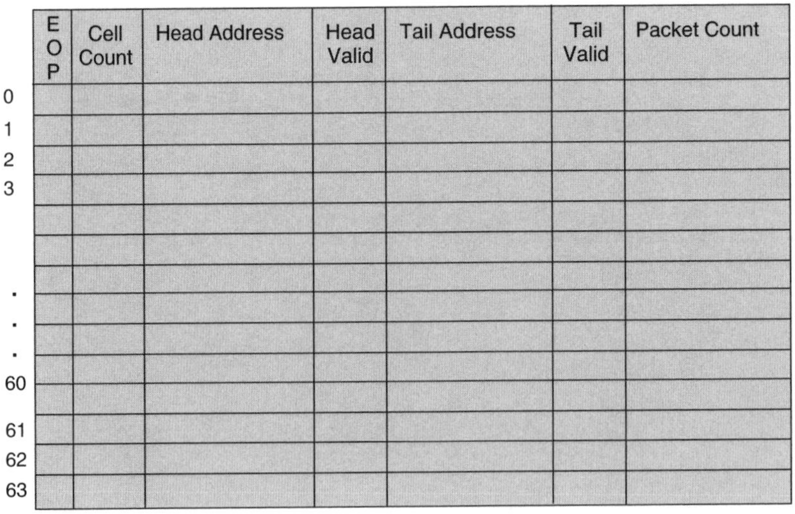

	EOP	Cell Count	Head Address	Head Valid	Tail Address	Tail Valid	Packet Count
0							
1							
2							
3							
·							
·							
·							
60							
61							
62							
63							

Figure 6.10   SRAM Q_Array Controller

The Q_Array utilizes the following format for the queue descriptor, as shown in Table 6.3.

Table 6.3 SRAM Q_Array Controller Descriptor Definitions

Field	Longword	Bit	Description
EOP	0	31	The EOP field indicates whether the packet currently addressed by the Head pointer is the last cell in a multi-cell packet. If this cell is the last in a multi-cell packet, the Q_Count is decremented on the next dequeue operation.
Cell count	0	30:24	Number of cells in a multi-cell packet. The cell count field is only relevant to the packet that is presently pointed to by the head pointer. This 8-bit value supports up to 256 cell packets.
Head	0	23:0	Head Pointer: 24-bit value that points to the head of a queue.
Tail	1	23:0	Tail Pointer: 24-bit value that points to the tail of a queue.
Q_Count	2	23:0	The number of packets on the queue.
SW_Private	2	31:24	9 bits that microcode software can use for storing list parameters, state, etc.
Head valid	N/A		Cached head pointer valid-maintained by hardware.
Tail valid	N/A		Cached tail pointer valid-maintained by hardware.

Three basic ways of using the SRAM Q_Array are:

■ *Resident queue descriptors* always stay in the Q_Array and are never flushed or evicted. They are loaded at boot time. An example of the resident queue descriptor linked list is a free buffer list that is established at the very beginning and is constantly used by all programs.

■ *Cached queue descriptors*. In many applications, hundreds or thousands of linked lists can be stored in SRAM, so the Q_Array only caches up to 64 of these locally. Cached queue descriptors only hold the most recently used descriptor. Therefore, software uses the microengine's CAM to discover whether a needed queue descriptor is stored locally in the Q_Array. The queue numbers of 16 queue descriptors that are locally stored in the Q_Array are loaded into the 16 entries of the CAM. Software then checks the

CAM to determine whether the needed queue is stored locally or in external memory. Cached queue descriptors are another implementation of the Intel IXA distributed cache.

■ *Resident Ring Buffers.* The Q_Array can also store the head and tail pointers for managing up to 64 ring buffers as well as journals.

The examples shown in the previous sections assumed a descriptor structure, but the caching mechanism wasn't described. The descriptor was always assumed to be in SRAM memory. With the Q_Array caching mechanism, the most recently used descriptors are locally cached. Because of this caching, the descriptors have to be loaded into the Q_Array, either at power-up for resident descriptors or during an eviction and replacement sequence for cached descriptors. The Q_Array has a special command to load and evict a Q_Array entry to and from its back-end SRAM store.

Three commands load a descriptor:

■ Read queue descriptor head

```
SRAM [rd_qdesc_head, …], opt_tok
```

This command partially loads a full descriptor in Q_Array entry. Only the head pointer, Q_Count, cell count, and EOP bit are loaded. Typically, this command is executed just prior to a dequeue operation on a non-cached descriptor. The tail pointer is not loaded to save memory bandwidth because the tail pointer is not needed for a dequeue operation. The Q_Array hardware sets the Head Valid (HV) bit to true, while the Tail Valid (TV) bit is set false because only the head value has been loaded.

■ Read queue descriptor tail

```
SRAM [rd_qdesc_tail, …],opt_tok
```

This command partially loads a full descriptor in the Q_Array entry. Only the tail pointer and Q_Count are loaded. Typically, this command is executed just prior to an enqueue operation on a non-cached descriptor. Because the head pointer is not needed for an enqueue operation, the head pointer is not loaded to save memory bandwidth. The Tail Valid (TV) bit is set true, while the Head Valid (HV) is set false.

- Read queue descriptor other

```
SRAM [rd_qdesc_other, …],opt_tok
```

This command is used to finish loading a descriptor so that its entire contents are valid. It is only used if either the head or tail is valid. For example, if the head is valid, this command loads the tail pointer to its assigned location in the array. If the tail is valid, this command loads the head pointer, Cell_Count, and EOP bit into their specified locations.

Two commands are used to evict a Q_Array entry back to memory. Both are used as part of a cache replacement policy where the least recently-used queue descriptor must be evicted to make room in the Q_Array for new entries.

- Write queue descriptor

```
SRAM [wr_qdesc, …], opt_tok
```

This command is used to evict an entry from the Q_Array. Only valid fields are evicted to save SRAM memory bandwidth. If the head is valid, only the head pointer, cell count, EOP bit, and Q_Count are returned to SRAM. If the tail is valid, only the tail and Q_Count are returned to SRAM. If both the head and tail are valid, all four fields are returned. If neither the head nor tail is valid, nothing is returned to SRAM.

- Write queue descriptor count

```
SRAM [wr_qdesc_count, …],opt_tok
```

This command is used to evict the Q_Count entry in the Q_Array and return its contents to SRAM memory.

To illustrate how the Q_Array works in general and how the cached mechanism works in particular, here are four examples of their use.

Example 1:   Enqueueing to a Cached Descriptor

The following examples can have hundreds or thousands of linked lists in SRAM. However, in this first example, the hardware enqueues a packet buffer when the queue descriptor is already cached in the SRAM Q_Array. The CAM is already loaded by the EnQ/DeQ applications software with the 16 most recently used queue descriptor identifiers, which is simply the queue number. Each identifier is uniquely associated with a queue number, or Qnum. In this example, the Q1 identifier is in CAM entry 0, the Q3 identifier is in CAM entry 1, and so on with the Q26 identifier stored in the last CAM entry (15).

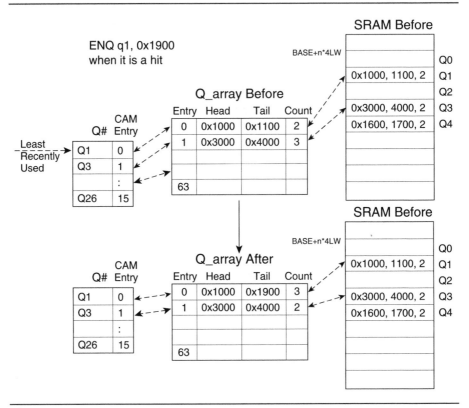

Figure 6.11   Enqueueing to a Cached Queue Descriptor

The first example is enqueueing from a cached queue descriptor, as shown in Figure 6.11. To begin the enqueue process, the EnQ/DeQ software, instantiated in a single microengine, receives a command to enqueue a packet that is buffered at location 0x1900 to Qnum 1. The EnQ/DeQ software first checks whether the Q_Array descriptor for Q1 is cached locally in the Q_Array. It does so by issuing a CAM lookup using the Qnum 1 identifier. In this situation, the Qnum 1 queue descriptor is already cached locally so the CAM lookup instruction returns a hit status. The Q_Array hardware performs the enqueue operation described earlier. The tail address now contains address 0x1900 and the packet count is incremented by 1. The queue descriptor for Qnum 1 is modified in the

Q_Array, but not in external memory. The Q_Array and external memory can be incoherent so long as software knows where the latest valid queue descriptor is located. The queue descriptor should be kept valid only in the Q_Array to minimize unnecessary memory accesses.

Example 2: Enqueueing to a Non- Cached Descriptor

This second example follows the model shown in Figure 6.12. The EnQ/DeQ software receives a command to enqueue to a queue that isn't resident in the Q_Array. In this case, the command enqueues a packet buffer at location 0x2000 to Qnum 4.

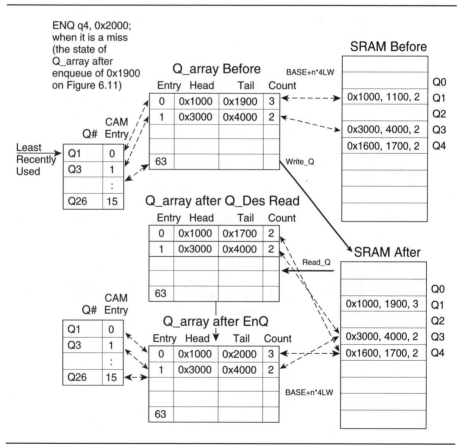

Figure 6.12   Enqueue to a Non-cached Descriptor

The following steps are taken:

1. EnQ/DeQ software receives a command to enqueue the packet buffer at location 0x2000 to Qnum 4.

    Software needs to determine if the queue descriptor for Qnum 4 is cached in Q_Array. It issues a CAM lookup command with Qnum 4 identifier.

2. The CAM lookup command returns a miss status. A CAM miss return state always returns a pointer to the least recently-used of the 16 CAM entries. In this case, it is CAM location 0, which holds Qnum 1.

3. Before the Q_Array hardware can perform the EnQ to Qnum 4, it needs to evict Qnum 1 descriptor to SRAM. This eviction is performed with a queue descriptor write command.

4. Once this Q_Array entry and CAM location are freed up, they must be filled with the data associated with Qnum 4. Software loads CAM entry 0 with the Qnum 4 identifier. Software issues a queue descriptor read command to load the Q_Array entry with the tail and count for Qnum 4.

Note | Only the tail and count, and not the head, are read because the head isn't needed for an enqueue command. As such, the hardware marks the tail valid and the head invalid for this Q_Array entry.

5. Once the queue descriptor for Qnum 4 is loaded into the array, the actual enqueue can take place. Software issues an EnQ command to the SRAM unit, shown below. The tail is updated with the new packet buffer pointer (0x2000) and the packet count is incremented by 1. As described earlier, only the queue descriptor in the Q_Array is modified; the descriptor in SRAM is left unmodified after the enqueue.

Example 3: Dequeueing from a cached descriptor

Figure 6.13 is a diagram of the actions taken to dequeue a buffer from a descriptor that is already cached in the Q_Array.

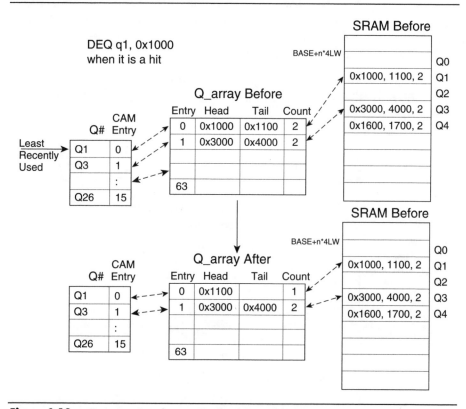

Figure 6.13   Dequeueing from a Cached Descriptor

This sequence of events is very similar to those in Example 1. In this situation, the command is to dequeue a packet buffer at location 0x1000 from Qnum 1. Here are the specific steps:

1. EnQ/DeQ software receives a dequeue command for packet buffer at location 0x1000 from Qnum 1.

    EnQ/DeQ software must determine whether Qnum 1 descriptor is cached locally in Q_Array. It issues a CAM lookup using Qnum 1 identifier.

2. The microengine CAM returns a HIT state indicating that the Qnum 1 descriptor is currently cached in the Q_Array.

3. EnQ/DeQ software issues a DeQ command.

4. Q_Array hardware modifies the head pointer to point to the next buffer pointer in the list (0x1100) and decrements the count. In this example, the count is one, so the tail pointer isn't valid because the head and tail point to the same location. The Q_Array now has the latest descriptor value for Qnum 1.

Example 4: Dequeueing from a non-cached descriptor

Figure 6.14 shows the sequence of steps taken when the EnQ/DeQ software receives a command to dequeue from a queue that isn't resident in the Q_Array.

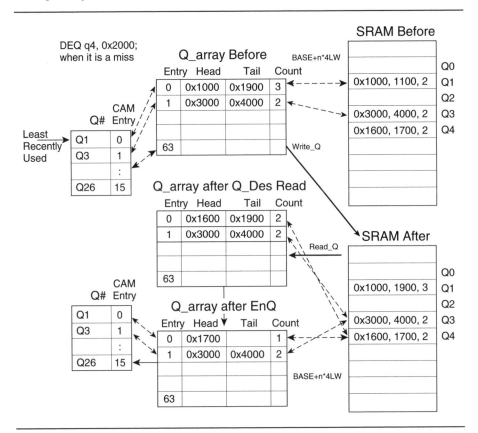

Figure 6.14 Dequeueing from a Non-cached Descriptor

In this case, the command is issued to dequeue a packet buffer at location 0x1600 from Qnum 4. The following steps are taken:

1. EnQ/DeQ software receives a command to dequeue packet buffer at location 0x1600 from Qnum 4.

    Software must determine whether the queue descriptor for Qnum 4 is cached in Q_Array. It issues a CAM lookup command with Qnum 4 identifier.

2. The CAM lookup command returns a miss status. A CAM miss return state always returns a pointer to the least recently-used of the 16 CAM entries. In this case, it is CAM location 0, which holds Qnum 1.

3. Before the Q_Array hardware can perform the EnQ to Qnum 4, it evicts Qnum 1 descriptor to SRAM. This eviction is performed with a queue descriptor write command.

4. Once this Q_Array entry and CAM location are freed up, they must be filled with the data associated with Qnum 4. Software loads CAM entry 0 with Qnum 4 identifier. Software issues a queue descriptor read command to load the Q_Array entry with the head and tail count for Qnum 4.

Note

> Only the head and cell count, and not the tail, are read because the tail isn't needed for a dequeue command. As such, the hardware marks the head valid and the tail invalid for this Q_Array entry.

5. Once the queue descriptor for Qnum 4 is loaded into the array, the actual dequeue can take place. Software issues a DeQ command to the SRAM unit, as shown below. The head is updated with the next packet buffer pointer (0x1700) in the list and the packet count is decremented by 1. Because only 1 packet is left in the queue, the packet count is 1, and only the head pointer is meaningful because the head and tail are the same value. As described earlier, only the queue descriptor in the Q_Array is modified; the descriptor in SRAM is left unmodified after the enqueue.

Ring Buffers

Ring buffers are the primary mechanism by which a microengine communicates messages and packet descriptors to other microengines. Rings allow a program running on one microengine to be decoupled from other microengines or the Intel XScale core. This provides a very modular programming model to an engineering team. One engineer can write software for one microengine while another engineer can write software for another ME with both of them using a ring structure to provide isolation and elasticity. Ring buffers follow a producer/consumer model with one microengine producing data to the ring while another microengine consuming the data. Rings allow a producer microengine to temporarily burst data to the ring faster than the consumer can pull it off. This elasticity means that the two programs don't have to be tightly synchronized.

Decoupling the software tasks running on the MEs makes life much easier for software programmers so they don't have to maintain tight synchronization between their programs. The ring buffers provide the isolation and elasticity needed so the software that was developed by different engineers has a common mechanism to communicate with each other.

The SRAM Q_Array controller has very efficient hardware support for implementing ring buffers. These hardware-based mechanisms allow single instruction access to the rings, which makes life much easier for the programmer. Also, because they are atomic, single instructions, lock contention isn't an issue and removes the need for cumbersome locking software. Minimizing the overhead of critical section management is vitally important to maintain high line rates. Now that you understand why rings are so important, you'll need to know what they actually are and how they work.

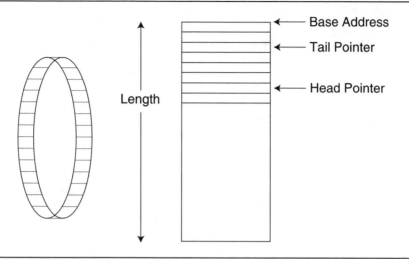

Figure 6.15   Ring Buffer Organization

Each SRAM channel's Q_Array can hold any combination of 64 ring buffer descriptors, cached linked list descriptors, or journals. Unlike linked lists where thousands of lists are stored externally and only the 64 most recently-used are cached in the Q_Array, each SRAM channel supports a maximum of 64 ring descriptors internally. A ring buffer descriptor consists of a tail pointer, a head pointer, and a length (a base address is initially loaded in a CSR). Producers "put" 1 to 16 longwords at the head of the ring while consumers "get" 1-16 longwords from the tail of the ring. The tail essentially follows the head as data is inserted at the head and removed from the tail. If the software doesn't remove data from the tail fast enough, it is possible for the head to wrap around the entire ring to the tail. To prevent an overflow condition when a put command is issued to the SRAM unit, it returns a 4-byte status word that indicates how many longwords are currently on the ring and if the put command was successful in the first place. The 4-byte status word is placed into a transfer register contained in the SRAM put instruction. Putting and getting data is an atomic operation so mutual exclusive access is guaranteed. The SRAM unit supports 8 different ring lengths, from 512 longwords to 64K longwords in power of 2 increments.

The format of the SRAM put and get instructions is:

```
SRAM [cmd, xfer, src_op1, src_op2, ref_cnt], opt_tok
```

Table 6.4   SRAM Ring commands

Parameter	Command	Description
cmd	Get	Get the data from the ring specified in the address and return it to the specified transfer registers.
	Put	Put the data into the ring specified in the address from the specified SRAM transfer registers.
xfer	Get	S or D transfer register
	Put	S-transfer register. The write transfer registers holds the data that is put onto the ring. The read transfer register holds the full status word which has the format: [31] Success = 1, Fail = 0 [30:16] Always 0 [15:0] Number of 4-byte words on the ring before the put operation.
Src_opt1, Src_opt2	All commands	Restricted operands that are added (src_op1 + src_op2) to define the following: [31:30] SRAM channel [29:8] Ignored [7:2] Ring number [1:0] Ignored
Ref_cnt	All commands	Reference count. Specifies the number of transfers (1 to 8) in increments of 4 byte words. If the indirect_ref token is specified, ref_cnt can be a keyword max_nn (where nn = 1-16).
Opt_tok	All commands	Defer[sig_name] Indirect_ref
	Put	Sig_done[sig_name2]
	Get	Sig_done[sig_name] Ctx_swap Ignore_data_error

Note: For further information, see the programmer's reference manual.

The internal scratch memory in the SHaC unit also supports ring buffers. A similar format of head, tail, and length are used. Up to 16 scratch rings are supported. Each scratch ring length can be 0, 128, 256, 512, or 1024 longwords. Each put or get command can burst from 1 to 16 longwords. Because the scratch memory size is 4K words, configurations that would exceed the total memory size aren't allowed. For example, having 8 rings that are 1024 longwords in length exceeds the total memory size. Before putting anything on to the ring, software should test if the ring is full or not. The first 12 rings support a full input state that can be tested with software (via the `br_inp_state` or `br_!inp_state`). The other 4 rings do not support a hardware mechanism to indicate full state so other methods, such as a credit counter scheme, need to be used.

The format of the scratch put and get operation is:

```
Scratch [cmd, xfer, src_op1, src_op2, ref_cnt], opt_tok
```

Table 6.5   Scratch Ring Commands

Parameter	Command	Description
cmd	Get	Get the data from the ring specified in the address and return it to the specified transfer registers.
	Put	Put the data into the ring specified in the address from the specified SRAM transfer registers.
xfer	Get	S or D transfer register
	Put	S-transfer read register
Src_opt1, Src_opt2	All commands	Restricted operands that are added (src_op1 + src_op2) to define the scratch ring address (0-15). Bits[1:0] are ignored.
Ref_cnt	All commands	Reference count. Specifies the number of transfers (1 to 8) in increments of 4 byte words. Valid values are 1-8.
Opt_tok	All commands	Ctx_swap[sig_name] — sig_done [sig_name]
		Indirect_ref — Defer[n] (n= 1 to 2)
	Get	Ignore_data_error

For further information, see the programmer's reference manual.

The seven basic steps to putting data on a ring are:

1. Initialize SRAM ring.

2. Signal consumer that SRAM ring is initialized.

3. Check to see if the ring is full.

4. If not full, put the data onto the ring.

5. Check to see whether the Put was successful.

6. If not, keep trying.

7. Go back to producing (Step 3).

The five basic steps to getting data from a ring are:

1. Wait for signal that the producer has completed ring initialization.

2. Get item from the ring.

3. Check if ring was empty.

4. If not, use the data.

5. Repeat from step 2.

The "Many-to-One" Problem

A common problem with data plane processing is called the "Many-to-One" problem. This problem occurs when flows or connections are aggregated together, causing serialization during the transmit process. To understand this problem, the much simpler "Many-to-Many" situation is illustrated below in Figure 6.16.

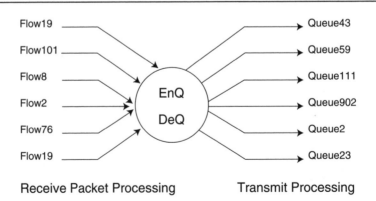

Figure 6.16   Mapping flows to transmit Queues: "Many-to-Many"

Figure 6.16 show multiple flows being enqueued to multiple transmit queues. The receive packet processing is implemented with the multi-processing and multithreading techniques inherent in Intel IXA. Packets associated with the various flows are processed independently. As you learned in Chapter 5, the serial stream processing problem occurs when different threads need to operate on related data, causing serialization. In Figure 6.16, let's assume that two threads are both processing packets associated with flow19. The distributed cache in the IXP2XXX processors manages lock contention in this situation to avoid the significant performance degradation associated with serialization. The serial stream processing problem also manifests itself during the enqueueing and dequeueing of packets to and from transmit queues. This is shown below in Figure 6.17, which illustrates the many-to-one problem.

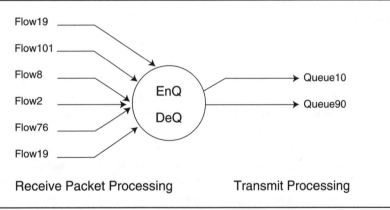

Figure 6.17   Mapping flows to transmit queues: "Many-to-One"

In the many to one problem, several flows are aggregated to one transmit queue. Aggregating to a common queue forces serialization by nature, as only one packet can be enqueued at a time and packet order must be preserved. Most systems have more than one transmit queue, so a generalized software architecture needs to be implemented that manages aggregation to either a single or multiple queues. To manage this situation, the SRAM Q_Array caches the most used queue descriptor so the hardware can immediately perform an enqueue or dequeue without immediately reading the descriptor. In this example, the descriptors for queue90 and queue10 are cached in the local Q_Array. While enqueues to the same queue are serialized, the hardware performs the hardest work of adding a packet to the tail of a linked list, as described earlier.

Because the enqueue operation is atomic, the actual queue descriptor data does not need to be locked down. Also, the enqueue/dequeue functions are performed sequentially as the hardware forces packet order. By caching the queue descriptors and performing the enqueue and dequeue in hardware, the only real limitation is the pin-side memory bandwidth. With today's memory technology, the IXP2800 processor can perform 60 million enqueue/dequeue operations per second with the IXP2400 processor performing 15 million enqueue/dequeue operations per second.

Because Intel IXA is based on parallelism, it needs to directly attack packet-processing problems that would force any kind of serialization. The architecture does this in a unique way by assuming there will be serialization and then building the necessary hardware to solve the problem in the first place.

Summary

Efficiently buffering data is critical to maintaining high line rates that are expected of IXP2XXX network processors. Because IXP2XXX network processors utilize a store and forward architecture, they have a heavy dependence on memory for buffering packets and critical per packet state information and general data structures. The threads that access these data structures often need exclusive access to them to prevent simultaneous access by other threads, which can cause data corruption. The SRAM Q_Array controller of IXP2XXX network processors automate many of these complex buffering tasks, such as enqueueing or dequeueing to/from a linked list or adding or taking data from a ring buffer. These operations can be quite complex when performed solely in software, such as that done by general-purpose processors. Not only is the process of managing them complex, but they also need to be protected as critical sections. Because the Q_Array controller automates these tasks and performs them atomically, the software burden on the programmer is significantly reduced.

Chapter 7

Mapping Tasks to Microengines

In Chapter 5, you learned the basics of multithreading and how a single microengine can perform multiple tasks to increase performance. However, one of the biggest questions software engineers have is how to map several tasks across several microengines. This task might seem challenging, given the eight and sixteen microengines of the IXP2400 or IXP28X0 processors, respectively. With process technology enabling even more transistors on a chip, more microengines could become available in the future. Therefore, it is critical to have a programming model that can be readily programmed and is optimized for the end application.

Because IXP2XXX network processors are fully software-based, the programming model can be chosen to suit the application at hand. In one approach, called *Pool of Threads*, the network processor is programmed much like a standard microprocessor in what is commonly called "run-to-completion mode." Another approach is a pipelining architecture called *Hyper Task Chaining*. Regardless of the approach taken, two programming challenges inherent in parallel packet processing must be addressed: maintaining packet order and ensuring exclusive thread access to critical sections.

After reading this chapter, you may have questions about implementing your application using one of these programming models. For that information, refer to *IXP2400/2800 Programming* (Johnson 2003).

Mutual Exclusion and Ordering

No matter what approach you take, your program must preserve mutual exclusion of critical data and maintain the ordering of packets. As you learned in Chapter 5, maintaining critical data sections ensures mutual exclusive access to them. As one thread is updating data in memory, software must prevent another thread from trying to modify that data at the same time. In Chapter 5, mutual exclusion was discussed in the context of a single microengine. In many applications, where several microengines are used in parallel, software mechanisms need to preserve mutual exclusivity across all the microengines performing similar tasks.

Maintaining packet order is another challenge that the software model needs to manage. The network processor receive packets from the network in a certain order, and they need to exit the processor in the same order. One example is ATM AAL5 reassembly. When an IXP2XXX network processor receives individual ATM AAL5 cells, software reassembles them into one larger frame. The process must ensure that each cell is reassembled in the frame in the order that it was received. Another example is IP header compression where a packet's header is compressed to minimize packet length, especially where the header is long and the payload is relatively small, like in VoIP. In this example, to uncompress a header, software uses the header of the previous packet to determine the current packet's header. Not all packet-processing applications need to maintain packet order, however, so it is up to the programmer to determine how best to optimize the system.

HTC uses folding and inter-thread signaling to insure critical data coherency and proper packet ordering. Folding was discussed in detail in Chapter 5 so these concepts will not be duplicated here. Because POTs uses software mechanisms (vs. hardware MEv2 CAM and signaling) to address data coherency and packet ordering, these concepts will be described in detail later in this chapter. As such, this chapter goes into greater detail with POTs than with HTC.

Hyper Task Chaining

Hyper Task Chaining (HTC) is a pipelining approach to packet processing. HTC is given deterministic performance because each stage in the pipeline has predetermined time duration. HTC is best applied when the processing time is roughly the same for the majority of the packets, which makes for a simplified pipeline. HTC is also best used when you find a certain likelihood that the incoming packets belong to the same flow or connection. In these situations, you have a higher probability of multiple threads requesting simultaneous access to critical data, which requires a fast and efficient mechanism for locking down critical sections. Let's first look at the basics of HTC, before the benefits and limitations will become clear.

With Hyper Task Chaining, an overall networking application is broken down into a series of tasks, as follows:

Network Function = Task1 + Task2 + Task3 + ...+ Taskn

Based on the characteristics of the function being applied to the packet, the packets can be chained in two different ways:

■ *Function Chaining.* A function chain typically performs the heavy packet processing on a packet or cell. A function chain is a series of tasks that are applied to a packet that run on several microengines. Function chaining is used when many different operations need to be done that will modify the packet.

■ *Context Chaining.* With context chaining, one task runs on one microengine. Typically, the software task operates on the state or descriptor of a packet, not the packet itself. However, for simpler packet processing tasks, a context pipe stage can do a minimal amount of packet modification.

Function Chaining

Typically, function chaining occurs just after a packet is received and before it is enqueued for transmission. Function chaining does the heavy lifting on the packet, and because several tasks are performed on it, function chaining is more complex and slower than context chaining. As a result, several microengines are used in parallel to increase performance. As described in Chapter 5, when a thread's processing time exceeds the packet arrival time, multiple threads and microengines are used in parallel to maintain line rate.

With functional pipelining, the actual packet header, and oftentimes the payload, gets worked on and modified. Therefore, one thread processes all of the tasks for the entire packet in the functional stage. It can be said that "One Thread, One Program" processes the entire packet in a functional pipeline, as illustrated in Figure 7.1. Packet state is kept in context-relative local registers, so when the packet passes from task n to task $n+1$, the relevant state data is readily accessible.

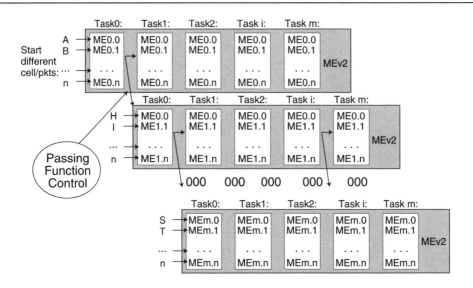

Figure 7.1   HTC Function Chaining

With function chaining, each thread of a microengine processes a series of m tasks on the packet. Each task time is structured to complete in one packet arrival time. The program that each thread executes is identical. This one program processes each of the tasks, 0 through m. With functional chaining, the software maintains inter-thread critical sections by using the MEv2's local memory and CAM using the folding techniques described in Chapter 5. Folding is the fastest way to lock critical sections and perform Read-Modify-Write operations.

The application maintains mutually exclusive access to critical sections across microengines through inter-thread signaling. While using the microengine's local CAM and local memory is much faster than using external memory, the state of the microengine CAM and the local memory isn't visible to other microengines. Critical data and its lock state must be visible to all processes in all microengines that happen to be working on that critical data at any particular point in time. To get around this condition, microengines are staggered in time by one pipe-stage time, or *task time*, to ensure that only one microengine is operating on any one particular task at any one time. For example, when the second microengine is working on critical data associated with the first task, the other microengines are processing other tasks. This ensures that only one microengine has exclusive access to that critical data.

Packet ordering using function chaining is obtained by strict ordering of threads to incoming packets. Thread 1 works on the first packet; thread 2 works on the second packet, and so on. Because of the strict ordering of packets to threads, the threads will complete processing in order and will then fill the MSF's thread free list with their thread ID. This mechanism allows the threads to be assigned to newly received packets in proper, sequential order. As packets are received by the MSF, the next thread that is signaled to pick up the next packet in the proper thread to maintain ordered sequence. With HTC, if one thread completes processing before the preceding thread completes, it needs to wait until the earlier thread completes. This delay is one of the disadvantages of the pipelining approach.

In a functional pipeline, the total number of tasks must equal the total number of microengines. You might ask why this restriction exists. If the number of tasks is greater than microengines, there won't be enough threads to pick up packets as they arrive, and packets will be dropped. For example, let's say the application has four tasks and two microengines. The first 16 packets are picked up by the 16 threads of these microengines. However, when the 17th packet arrives, the first microengine starts working on packets 1–8 on the third task, while the second microengine is working on packets 9–15 for the second task. When the 17th packet arrives, it will be dropped because no thread is available to pick it up.

Not only can the tasks not exceed the microengines, the number of microengines cannot exceed the number of tasks. With more microengines than tasks, two microengines can be processing the same task at the same time and accessing the same critical data for a flow or connection. Because critical data and state are kept local in the microengine's CAM and local memory, one microengine cannot know if another has taken out a lock on the same critical data, so it could inadvertently modify and update the same data and potentially cause data corruption errors.

So, how long can each task be? In a pipelining architecture, each pipeline stage, or *pipe stage*, needs to have the same time duration (or less), which is the packet arrival rate. Because of the strict ordering of packets to threads and the requirement that the number of microengines equals the number of tasks, the software developer needs to guarantee that a task time fits into a relatively fixed period of time. Because each microengine processes eight packets and each packet has eight threads, each task must finish within eight packet arrival times.

To help explain this, let's assume we are processing OC-192 POS traffic with an IXP2800 processor running at 1.4-gigahertz. This data stream has an approximate packet arrival rate of 35 nanoseconds or about 50 clocks. The actual value is 41 ns, or 57 equivalent clocks. The 50 clock value is an approximation and helps simplify the analysis. The formula for calculating the equivalent number of ME clocks is: $50 = 35 \text{ ns} * 1.4 \text{ GHz}$. In other words, for every OC-192 POS packet that arrives in 35 ns, 50 IXP2800 clocks elapse. As such, each task must compete within 400 total clocks: (8 threads x 50) clocks. After the eighth packet is processed by microengine 1, that microengine signals microengine 2, the next in the chain, to pick up the ninth packet.

This 400 clock period is called the *wall time* and is defined as the total elapsed time period for a thread to process a packet. Wall time is a combination of instruction processing time and memory latency time. Assuming a perfect balance of instruction processing to memory latency, as described in Chapter 5, each thread is allocated 50 instruction cycle times and 350 equivalent memory latency cycle times. Further, assume one instruction per clock, and each task is allocated 50 instructions.

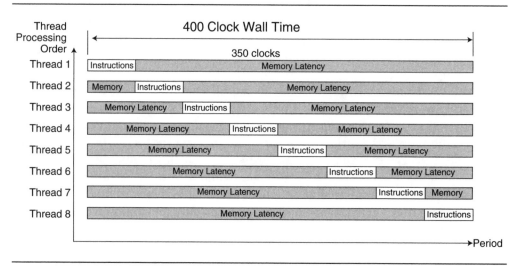

Figure 7.2   Single Task IXP2800 Wall Time for OC192 POS

Figure 7.2 illustrates the wall time for a single task. This task must finish in eight packet arrival times because each of the eight threads processes a packet as fast as they are received from the network. Each thread is allocated 50 clocks for instructions and 350 clocks for memory accesses. When a thread issues long latency memory instructions, it swaps out to allow other threads to have processing time. In reality, this long period of memory latency almost never follows one large block of instructions. Typically, the pattern is a few instructions, followed by a dependent memory operation, followed by more instructions waiting for the memory operation to complete. This pattern is illustrated in Figure 7.3.

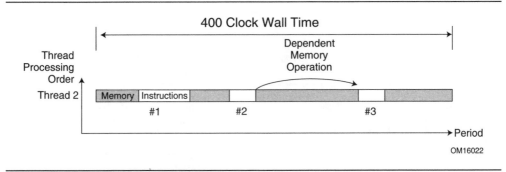

Figure 7.3 Single Thread Task Wall Time

In this illustration, thread 2's budget of 50 instructions is spread in three blocks. Block 1 typically finishes by initiating a memory reference and swapping out. After the other threads in the microengine do some work, thread 2 is awakened in the executing state and does more work in block 2. In this example, block 2 initiates a dependent memory operation, then goes to sleep. This memory operation must complete before it is awakened. Even though this dependent memory operation consumes only a small percentage of total memory bandwidth, the overall latency is many times the actual time it takes the data to transfer across the pins. With instructions in block 3 waiting for the previous memory reference to complete, the total wait time could be very long. Because average SRAM memory latency is often about 130 clocks, each pipe stage has a budget of three dependent SRAM memory operations, and a total of 390 clocks, calculated as: 3 pipe stages x 130 clocks = 390 clocks for the thread/block. 390 clocks is very close to our 400 clock pipestage budget. Table 7.1 shows the specific task times for the OC192 POS example design for the IXP2800 processor. This software design utilizes eight microengines to perform eight tasks in a functional pipeline.

Table 7.1   Instruction Cycle and Dependent Memory Operations Budgeting for IXP2800 OC192 POS Example Design

Function	Pipe Stages Allocated	Function Execution Time (in nanoseconds)[1]	Function MEv2 Execution cycles[2]	Dependent SRAM read operations per thread[3]
RPTR-Reassembly pointer search[4]	1	291.2	400	3
RUPD-Re-assembly information update[4]	1	291.2	400	3
PKT_PROC-packet processing[4]	6	1747.2	2400	24

Notes

1. Processing is based on 40-byte IP packet for POS arrival rate of 36.4 ns for OC192 bit rate. Function Execution Time is 36.4 ns x ME threads (8) x number of pipe stage periods.
2. Based on a 1.4-GHz ME clock rate and 50 cycles per 40-byte packet arrival time.
3. Based on a 130 cycle average SRAM latency.
4. These processing stages are the names given to the IXP2800 processor's OC-192 POS example design and are documented in that reference design's CD, listed in "References."

Note

> This example is based on OC192 POS with a 40-byte packet. For 10-gigabit/second Ethernet, with its minimum sized 64-byte packet, 12-byte inter-packet gap, and 8 byte preamble, the packet arrival rate is 67 nanoseconds, or 94 equivalent clock cycles for a 1.4-gigahertz IXP2800 processor. Thus, Ethernet allows for about a 50-percent increase in headroom due to the lower packet arrival rate.
>
> This analysis also applies to the IXP2400 processor. Only the packet arrival time changes. The packet arrival rate is 97 clocks (163 nanoseconds per OC48 40-byte IP packet carried in a PPP frame) and the IXP clock rate is 600 megahertz.

When a functional pipe-stage task completes, it must write packet state or metadata back to memory. This write-back is important so other threads on other microengines can access the state. If the pipe stage is implemented using the folding techniques described in Chapter 5, the packet state can be written back to memory at the end of the pipe-stage time (the write-back technique) or written to memory by each thread as soon as a thread completes its processing task (the write-through method). Using these methods ensures access to state information for subsequent threads if they are processing related packets belonging to the same flow or connection.

Pipe-stage Transitioning Using GTS

In a hardware-based pipeline, such as used in an ASIC or microprocessor, the pipeline stages transition on hard boundaries, typically driven by a master clock. Each task is implemented in hardwired gates, so the design can guarantee that one task pipe stage finishes before the next stage begins. The HTC functional pipeline does not have these fixed constraints, primarily because the functional pipeline stages do not have hard, predetermined wall times because memory latencies can never be predicted with 100-percent accuracy. While the average SRAM latency is 130 cycles, sometimes it can be 100 cycles, and other times it can be 150 cycles. As such, the pipe-stage processing time fluctuates about an average centered on the packet arrival rate the pipeline was designed for.

Because of this fluctuation, the functional pipeline uses generalized thread signaling (GTS) under program control to transition from one stage to the next. After a pipestage completes, the application signals the next microengine performing the task in the pipeline using GTS so the signaled thread knows that it can start processing. GTS greatly simplifies pipeline design because it enables the HTC functional pipeline to be implemented without hard time boundaries. In fact, because of the flexible nature of GTS, one pipestage (N) can borrow cycles from the next stage ($N+1$). If the N+1 stage requires only a few instruction cycles, the previous stage can use them.

Context Pipelining

Context pipelining is much simpler than functional pipelining because a single microengine is operating on a single task. Therefore, no mutual exclusion issues occur across multiple microengines. A microengine running one task need not worry about another microengine performing the same task, with the potential for updating the same critical data and corrupting it. A context pipeline is illustrated in Figure 7.4.

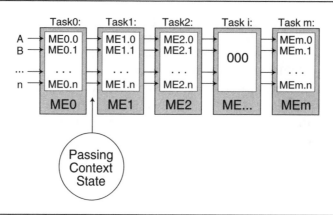

Figure 7.4   Context Pipeline

While a functional pipeline modifies the actual packet data and moves the packet from task to task, a context pipeline usually operates on state or descriptor data that describes the packet. A context pipeline can also modify a packet. Because one context stage is assigned to one microengine, the processing budget for that task is limited to just one packet arrival interval, so only the fastest packet processing tasks can fit in a context pipe stage. An example of a context pipeline is an enqueue-dequeue task where a packet is added to a queue and removed from the queue by a queue manager. The actual packet isn't modified, but its state is. For example, the packet is added to a queue then removed with its packet descriptor (which is a linked list queue descriptor), and then given to a transmit scheduler for eventual transmission. Because a single microengine executes each task, the microengine's CAM can maintain lock state for the entire task. This capability significantly minimizes the negative effects of using external memory for holding MUTEXs.

Context pipelines utilize the SRAM and scratch ring buffers, as well as next neighbor registers, to pass packet state data from one task to the next. These mechanisms are elegant and simple to use for context pipelines, because packet state information is typically smaller than the actual packets. This practice makes for relatively efficient communication between stages in a context pipeline.

Hyper Task Chaining Diff Serv Example

In a real application, both functional pipelines and context pipelines are used to process a packet from the moment it is received to the time it leaves the processor during transmission. Figure 7.5 shows a diff serv software example that can be used in a line card application.

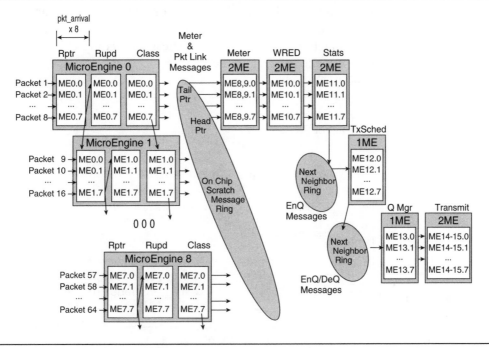

Figure 7.5   HTC Diff Serv Example

In this diff serv example, eight packet-processing tasks or stages are required in a functional pipeline. Because eight pipe stages are required, eight microengines are also needed to implement this pipeline. These stages include two packet-receiving stages, Rptr and Rupd for POS reassembly, and six generic stages for classification, or packet processing. The front-end functional pipeline interfaces with the context pipelines running on the other microengines using the on-chip scratch memory ring buffers. After the heavy lifting of the packet reception stage, the packet's state is sent to two metering microengines, one for performing congestion management, such as WRED, and another for statistics. After this metering is completed, the statistics task sends an enqueue message via a next neighbor ring to the transmit scheduler. Once scheduled, the transmit scheduler notifies the queue manager, which takes the packet and signals the transmit microengine for eventual transmission to the network.

Pool of Threads

The Pool of Threads (POTs) model is a more intuitive programming model that programmers of traditional processors may find more familiar. It implements what is commonly termed the run-to-completion model. Figure 7.6 illustrates the general concept.

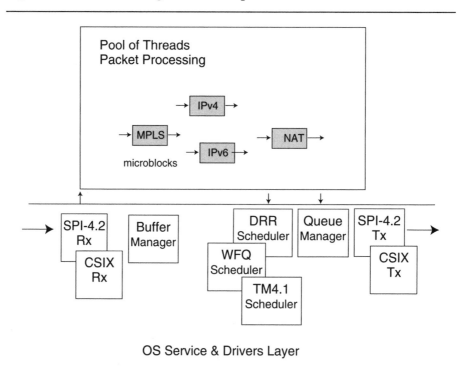

Figure 7.6   High Level View of the Pool of Threads Model

With POTs, one program does most of the packet processing, from the time the packet is received to the time it is enqueued. After a packet is received, the packet finds an available thread from a free thread pool and assigns the packet to that thread. That thread can perform any number of software tasks on/for the packet, such as MPLS label insertion, IPv4/IPv6 forwarding, and NATing. This program relies on lower level blocks for packet reception, buffer management, queue management, and packet transmit, among other things. While shown as merely a driver in this diagram, the traffic scheduling tasks are usually very sophisticated algorithms. Designers usually implement their own for their unique applications. These lower layer blocks are analogous to OS services and drivers in more traditional systems.

POTs is implemented as shown in Figure 7.7. In this diagram, memory is used in the typical fashion, with DRAM storing the packet buffers, statistics database, forwarding info, and the like. SRAM is used to store queue descriptors, state metadata, freelists, Longest Prefix Match (LPM) tables, and similar information. When a packet is first received, it is buffered in one of the Rbuf elements of the MSF. Then, MSF signals the packet receive block so it can pull the packet out of the Rbuf, and the packet dispatcher reassembles it.

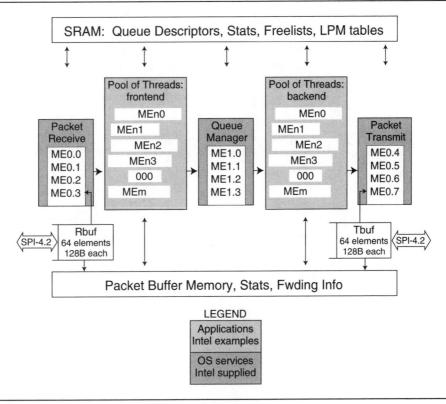

Figure 7.7   POTs Mapping to Hardware Resources

The packet receiver stage runs on one microengine and has three primary jobs.

■ If packets are arriving from the SPI interface, the first task of the packet receiver is to reassemble the mPKTs from the MSF interface into a complete frame.

■ The second function of the packet receiver is assigning a sequence number to the incoming packet. As described earlier, it is required for many applications to maintain packet order through the network processor. By assigning a packet sequence number, later processing stages can order the packets correctly. Packet ordering is done in the middle (defined as partial packet ordering) and at the end of the POTs processing stage, so when the processing moves to the next step—for example, the queue manager or data transmit stage—the packets are already in order.

■ Thirdly, the packet receiver assigns the packet to a thread from a pool of free threads. It can do packet assignment in a couple different ways. One way is for the packet receiver to maintain a list of free threads. When a packet arrives, it assigns it to one of the free threads on the list. A second method of packet assignment is to put the packet (actually, the packet descriptor) on a circular queue. As threads are freed, they pick up a new packet from this circular queue to work on them.

Functional Thread Assignment

Packets can be assigned to the pool of threads in a couple of ways. In one mechanism, each thread processes a certain type of packet, such as MPLS, NAT, IPv4, as shown in Figure 7.8.

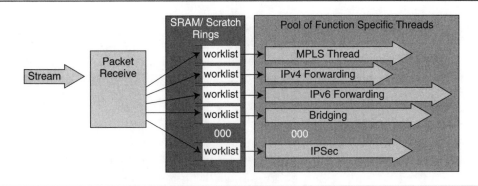

Figure 7.8   POTs Functional Thread Assignment

In the function specific assignment, threads are grouped according to a certain function they perform. The packet receiver must do a first-level classification on the packets as they arrive. The packets are put on a work list, which is just an SRAM or Scratch ring buffer. Each functional group of threads has its own work list. This method minimizes instruction code space requirements and processing time because the MEs in one functional group only have to process a subset of the total number of anticipated tasks.

General Thread Assignment

The second method of assigning packets to threads is to enable any of the threads to process any packet that arrives from the network, as shown in Figure 7.9.

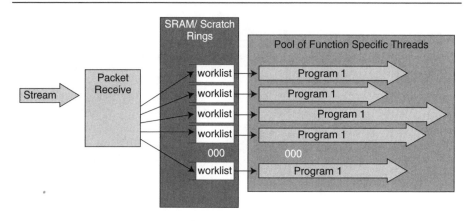

Figure 7.9 POTs General Thread Assignment

A benefit of the general thread assignment is that the packet receive block doesn't need to pre-classify the packet to assign it to the appropriate threads. Using general thread assignment, the packet receiver simply assigns a packet, no matter what type it is, to any free thread in the pool. A disadvantage of this approach is that the code storage can be large and the processing time a bit longer because the threads now need to handle any protocol or task that is thrown at them.

Packet Ordering with Pool of Threads

Two kinds of packet ordering scenarios must be considered when writing packet-processing software. One scenario, called *partial packet order*, deals with packet order during the middle of a processing flow. Maintaining packet order at the end of packet processing is called *end-to-end packet ordering*. End-to-end packet ordering ensures that packets leave the system in the same order that they entered it, which is illustrated in the flow graph in Figure 7.10. This IPv4-to-IPv6 example illustrates the different processing stages through which a packet travels. The blocks that are marked with bold lines are the ones that require packets to be processed in the order that they arrived. These bold-marked blocks are the ones where partial packet order needs to be maintained. The enqueue stage at the end does require the packets to leave the application in the same order that they entered it. What this example shows is that in many paths packet order does not matter and order is required in only a few. Regardless, you need a method of maintaining partial packet order, even if a small percentage of packets require it.

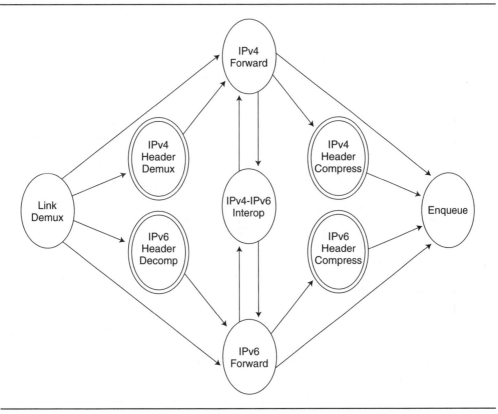

Figure 7.10   Processing Flow Graph Showing Packet Ordering

End-to-End Packet Ordering with Pool of Threads

Maintaining end-to-end packet ordering is managed by a software mechanism and data structure known as *Asynchronous Insert, Synchronous Remove* (AISR). With the POTs programming model, packets can be processed out of order by the various threads in the pool. The processing of one packet may end before a packet that was received earlier has finished. With HTC, packet ordering is guaranteed because of the strict assignment of threads to incoming packets. This ability is a significant benefit of HTC. With POTs, this strict packet assignment is removed, which means that you must use other mechanisms. This mechanism is AISR, as shown in Figure 7.11.

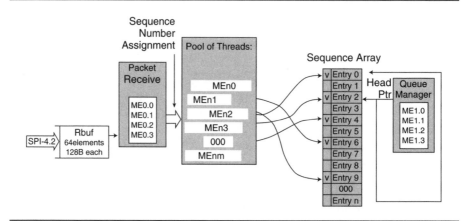

Figure 7.11   Maintaining End-to-End Packet Ordering with AISR

AISR uses a *packet receive* block to assign a sequence number to the packet when it is received. Along with other packet descriptor data, such as buffer location or reassembly state, the sequence number is carried by the thread for the duration of the processing. When processing is complete, the packet is inserted into the appropriate location into the AISR sequence array. The AISR array is implemented as a circular array in SRAM. If a packet is assigned sequence 89, location 89 in the AISR array is filled with the packet's buffer handler and the location is validated after it has been processed. As other packets are received and processed, they are inserted into the AISR array according to their sequence number entry and their associated valid bit is set. When a producer thread has inserted all packets into the array, the thread places itself via a thread ID number into a free thread pool, or it grabs another packet from the work list.

It is important to realize that threads do not fill the AISR array sequentially in the order that the packets arrive. Because packet processing varies from packet to packet, this strict sequencing can't be ensured, and, in fact, AISR is designed to handle exactly this problem. The producer inserts packets into the array asynchronously. The consumer of the AISR array is responsible for maintaining synchronous removal from the array. In Figure 7.11, the queue manager polls the AISR array in a round robin manner and removes the packets in order, according to their sequence number and whether the entry is validated. This consumer maintains a head pointer to the current expected entry. When the expected entry is valid, the consumer removes the packet and the pointer advances to the next entry. If this next entry is not valid, the consumer waits for it to be validated. This condition causes a head of line blocking problem, described later in this chapter. Once validated, the consumer removes the packet and goes to the next entry. By removing only validated packets from the AISR array, the consumer forces packet ordering.

Managing Large Programs

With POTs, packet processing is done by a single program that is processed with one thread. Because the available threads in the pool must be able to accept any packet that comes along, the program must have the functionality to handle any type of packet. So, a problem can occur if the program should outgrow the 4-kilobyte words of available program space of the MEv2 control store. For example, the IXP28X0-B rev could have an 8-kilobyte control store in eight of the sixteen microengines. One way to solve this problem is to have two pools of threads. This solution doubles the functional processing capabilities, but halves the number of threads in the pool. Because fewer threads are in the pool, each thread needs to complete in half the time. Thus, the average packet rate drops in half compared to the single pool implementation that is twice the size. This relationship is illustrated in Figure 7.12.

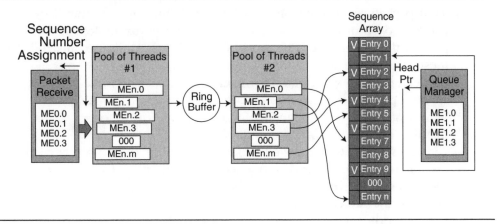

Figure 7.12   Two-stage POTs Design

In a two-stage POTs design, the AISR array ensures the proper packet sequence across both pools. The first group of threads perform the first half of the overall functions while the second pool completes the processing. Packets are passed from one pool to the next via a ring buffer in SRAM.

Head of Line Blocking

Head-of-line blocking occurs when the AISR consumer, usually the queue manager, is forced to wait for packets to be validated in the AISR array to ensure proper ordering. Head-of-line blocking causes packets to back up in the AISR array, and overall performance can suffer if those packets aren't removed fast enough and the lost time isn't somehow regained. In most situations, the pool of threads produces entries into the AISR array while the queue manager continuously consumes them. If head-of-line blocking occurs due to a producer thread processing an especially complex packet, the AISR consumer has idle times and isn't kept fully utilized. While the packet processing threads are fully utilized, the head-of-line blocking condition won't enable the consumer to be fully utilized. Packets clump up in the AISR array. Once the block condition is removed, a consumer like the queue manager needs to catch up. However, at the highest line rates the queue manager needs to be fully utilized to prevent the AISR array from overflowing. In a sense, the problem is just being pushed from one end to the other, similar to squeezing a balloon at one end only to see a bulge on the other.

The way to minimize this blocking situation is to have two or more classes of sequence arrays. With just one AISR array, completely unrelated packets are likely to be blocked while waiting for other unrelated packets to be ordered. To consider one unusual example, suppose the pool of threads is processing both ATM and IPv6 traffic streams and that these streams are completely unrelated. With just one AISR array, a situation can develop where an ATM packet was blocked while it waited for an IPv6 packet to arrive in order. Because of the single AISR array, and hence, only one set of sequence numbers, ordering is forced on packets that don't need to be ordered in the first place.

The solution to this false blocking situation is to group related packets together with separate sequence numbers and separate AISR arrays for each group. Every packet that belongs to a related group of packets is assigned the same *aggregate_ID* number. As packets are received from the network, they are given an aggregate_ID and a sequence number within the aggregate_ID. The aggregate_ID would specify which sequence group and AISR array a set of packets should be associated. Even though multiple related flows might result in multiple AISRs, the application still has a single pool of threads to process the packets. Each thread in the pool produces entries into the appropriate AISR, based on the packets aggregate_ID number. Also, there is only one ordering block, the queue manager in this case. This block maintains two pointers in the array, as illustrated in Figure 7.13.

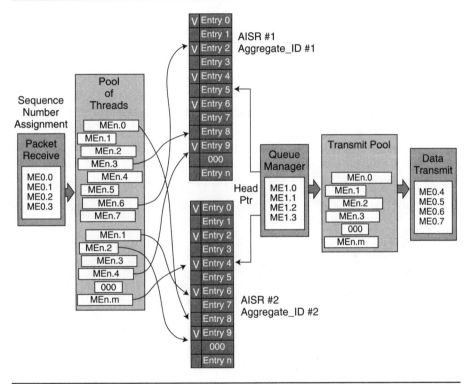

Figure 7.13   Dual AISR Arrays to Minimize False Blocking

Determining the Size of an AISR

Determining the size of the AISR array can give you a lot of insight into packet flow of the pool of threads programming model. While some implementations might assume 1- or 2-kilobyte entries, the size is very much dependent on the application. POTs assumes diverse packet-processing times, as not all threads are completed in the same amount of time. In fact, the possibility exists that the duration of a single thread could be many times longer than the average packet-processing period, as illustrated in Figure 7.14.

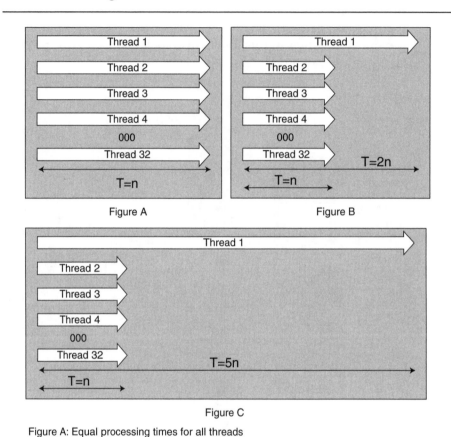

Figure A

Figure B

Figure C

Figure A: Equal processing times for all threads

Figure B: Thread 1 processing time is 2x others threads

Figure C: Thread 1 processing time is 5x other threads

Figure 7.14 POTs Processing Times

The size of the AISR array must accommodate the total number of outstanding packets that are waiting to be consumed by the queue manager. If the array is too small, the AISR array could wrap around and overwrite earlier entries. This overwriting of earlier entries is taken care of in the POTs implementation, but there is a performance penalty. If the AISR array is too large, it consumes valuable memory space. For example, Figure 7.14 shows a total of 32 threads in the pool. In Figure 7.14a, the threads are processing packets that require equal processing time. In this situation, the threads are completed in the same amount of time so the ASIR array could be minimally set at 32. However, in Figure 7.14b, Thread 1 takes twice as long as the other threads. Thread 1 would cause a blocking situation, holding up the queue manger from processing both this thread and the other threads following it. As thread 1 continues to process its packet, the other threads have already finished theirs, have entered and validated them into the array, and have already picked up a second packet. However, the queue manager is blocked, waiting for thread 1 to complete and validate its entry in the AISR array. In this situation, the AISR array has to be 64 entries deep to prevent wrapping around.

Figure 7.14c shows another example of this length, with the first thread taking five times the minimum processing time. An AISR array would need to be 5x31 threads or 155 entries deep. Thirty-one threads, not 32, are used in this calculation because one thread is already processing the complex packet. So the calculation is (N-1) threads x M, where M = maximum expected processing time. If the pool of threads has 64 threads, all these numbers are doubled. For instance, the AISR array in Figure 7.14c has to be 315 (63 x 5) entries deep. You can have a situation where the ratio between the maximum processing time and the minimum processing time is 10x when implementing 64 threads on the IXP2800 processor. This ratio would require a 630-entry deep AISR, and, to be on the safe side, the array might require 1,000 entries.

AISR Data Structure

The data structure of the AISR array allows both AISR producers and consumers to pass the needed information from one to the other. Because the consumer process, which could be the queue manager, pulls packets directly from the AISR array, this data structure needs to have all the information that the consumer needs to enqueue the packet. The consumer must know where the packet is, what queue to put it on, and whether the entry is valid or not. This AISR array structure is defined by software. As such, many variations depend on the unique objectives of the application. Figure 7.15 provides an example of an AISR array data structure.

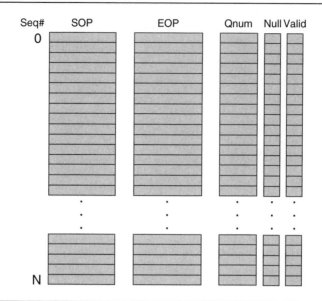

Figure 7.15   AISR Data Structure

The SOP and EOP are 32-bit pointers that indicate the start-of-packet and end-of-packet, respectively, for multi-packet frames. The Qnum identifies the transmit queue on which the packet should be placed when processing is complete. The Null field indicates to the consumer that the packet, which was assigned that particular sequence number, is not valid. If the null field is set, the consumer bypasses this particular entry. An entry may be null for a number of reasons. A process that flags a packet as containing an error and subsequently drops it sets the null field. A process that sends a packet to the Intel XScale core as an exception also enters null for the entry for that particular sequence number.

Another example is managing a multi-packet frame. Remember that each packet gets a sequence number from the packet receive block. However, some applications might assemble multiple packets into a larger frame. Only the assembled frame is entered into the AISR array. The sequence numbers that are associated with all but the first packet are set to null because they are already associated with the frame of the first entry. The SOP field points to the first packet of the frame while the EOP field points to the last packet of the frame.

Implementing AISR

Accessing and managing the AISR array quickly with minimal latency is very important because it lies right between the producers and consumers, which access it often. A typical AISR array can be 1,000 entries long, with each entry being 8–10 bytes. As such, the entire AISR array does not fit into the local memory of the microengine and must be stored in SRAM. However, with a typical latency of 130 clocks, SRAM can be a bottleneck. The solution for this problem is caching the most needed AISR entries in the local memory of the packet ordering microengine—the queue manager, for example—and have SRAM be the backup store for the entire array. Because the microengine's local memory is much faster than external SRAM, the packet reordering function can be much more efficient.

Caching the AISR entries into a packet-ordering microengine's local memory implies that only a subset of the entire array is stored locally. Because the microengine's local memory is limited in size, it can hold up to 211 AISR entries, assuming a 12-byte AISR entry size for the 640 32-bit words of local memory, with the current implementation caching 32 entries. Caching 64 and 128 entries are also possible choices. This AISR array is implemented in a circular queue both in local memory and in SRAM. Figure 7.16 illustrates this cached mechanism.

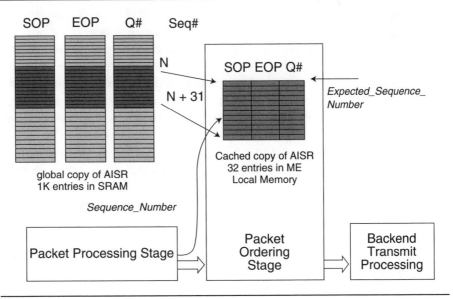

Figure 7.16   Caching AISR in Local Memory

The 32 AISR entries are stored sequentially, starting with the current head pointer N, which points to the current entry in the array. The packet ordering microengine has AISR entries N to $N+31$ stored locally. The packet-processing stage produces entries and sends them in possibly arbitrary order to the packet ordering stage ME, which examines the packet's Sequence_Number. The packet ordering stage compares the sequence number of the incoming packet to a counter called the Expected_Sequence_Number, also called the head pointer or N. If these numbers match, the incoming packet is arriving in order and can be enqueued (assuming that the packet-ordering stage is the queue manager) and the Expected_Sequence_Number N is incremented. Because the head pointer is new, the head pointer in the locally cached AISR array now points to entry 0, which is the $N+32$ entry. So, a new AISR entry must be read from SRAM and stored locally at the $N+31$ location.

If the sequence number of the incoming packet does not match the Expected_Sequence_Number, the packet is arriving out of order and the entry must be entered into the AISR array. If the packet's sequence number is within the range of N to $N+31$, the packet can be cached in the AISR array in the microengine's local memory. If it is out of the range of local memory, the entry is stored in SRAM.

Maintaining Partial Packet Order with Pool of Threads

Maintaining partial packet order is required only if certain processing stages in the middle of a program require ordering. This requirement is the main difference between partial packet ordering and end-to-end packet ordering, where all packets need to leave the system in the same order as they entered it. With partial packet ordering, some packets have to be ordered while others do not. Determining which packets are to be ordered or not is one of the main challenges. To help you understand the steps, Figure 7.17 represents them in a simple flow graph of four processing stages. Nodes 1, 3, and 4 do not require packets to be processed in order, whereas node 2 does require ordering. If a packet steps from node 1 to 3 to 4, ordering need not be maintained. However, all packets that enter node 2 do need to be processed in order. Node 2 is thus called an *Ordered Processing (OP) node*.

The big question in this processing flow is: How does node 2 know when to wait for an out-of-order packet to arrive and when does it skip an out-of-order packet because that packet isn't needed at that node? For example, suppose packet 15 is the last packet that node 2 has processed. Then node 2 receives packet 21. In this instance, five outstanding packets (16, 17, 18, 19, and 20) must be accounted for. Are these five packets still being processed earlier in the flow graph and they just haven't reached node 2 yet? Or have they bypassed node 2 completely, taking the node 1-3-4 path? If the packet has taken this later path, then node 2 doesn't need to wait for the packets and can skip over them. However, if it can't know the packet's path, node 2 has to wait until it does know.

Pool of threads uses a simple method to keep track of those packets needing to be processed in order and those that can be skipped. It uses a data structure with an integer value called *last_seq_num* and a bit vector called a *skip-vector*. The last_seq_num integer represents the last packet sequence number that an OP node has processed. The bit vector represents packet sequence numbers that the OP node might need to process and those that should be skipped.

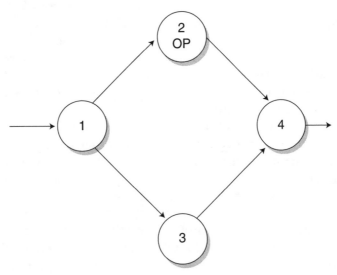

Node 2 requires packets to be processed in order.
Nodes 1, 3, and 4 do not require ordering.

Figure 7.17   Simple Flow Graph Showing last_seq_num

This data structure is illustrated in Figure 7.18. Each OP node maintains its own skip vector and last_seq_num. In a system with n OPs, there are n skip vectors and n last_seq_nums. Each entry of the skip vector corresponds to a packet sequence number, which is the same one that was given to the packet upon entering the pool of threads and is the same one that the AISR array references. As such, it can be viewed as another data structure alongside the AISR array. The semantics of the skip vector are:

1:      This packet may visit this OP module.
        The skip vector is initialized to all 1s.

0:      This packet will not be visiting this OP module.

When a new packet visits the OP node and it is the next one following the last_seq_num, the packet is in order, processed, and the last_seq_num is incremented. When a thread travels through the flow graph and it knows that it will not visit the OP node (such as when it visits node 3 in Figure 7.17), the thread sets its sequence entry in the skip vector to a 0 for that OP node. By setting the skip vector to a 0, the thread tells the OP node that this packet can be skipped and subsequent threads that visit the OP do not have to wait for its packet to arrive for processing to continue.

If the new packet that arrives at the OP node is not in sequential order, the thread processing that out of order packet checks the skip vectors to see whether any 1s lie between it and the last_seq_num. If a 1 is set for any of the sequence numbers, the thread that processes this packet is blocked as it waits until those outstanding packets arrive or it is later found that those outstanding packets can actually be skipped because they took a path around the OP node. Once all the earlier out-of-order packets arrive to the OP node or it is determined that the earlier out-of-order packets can be skipped, the current packet can be processed. Once the current packet is processed, the last_seq_num is set to this last processed packet sequence number. The method described here keeps track of out-of-order packets so threads that enter the OP nodes know when to wait for correct packet ordering and when they can proceed.

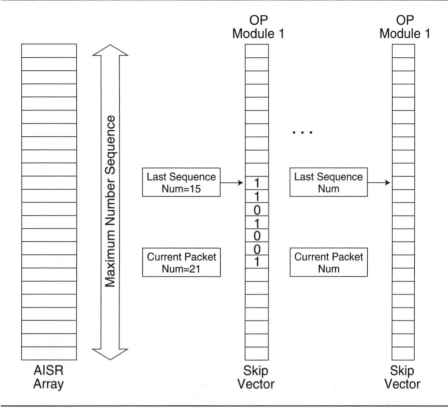

Figure 7.18 OP Module Processing

To show how OP module processing works, let's follow some packets using the flow graph in Figure 7.18. In this example, the last_seq_num is 15 and the current packet number entering the OP is 21. The threads processing packets 16 through 21 take the following steps through the flow graph:

1. The thread-processing packet 21 checks the skip vectors between it and last_seq_num (sequence 15). It detects at least one out-of-order packet outstanding. So, it has to wait and is blocked.

2. As packets 16–20 flow through the flow graph, the last_seq_num and skip vector are set appropriately. For example, suppose that packet 16 enters the OP node. Because it is in sequence, packet 16 (actually, the thread processing the packet 16) increments the last_seq_num to 16.

3. Next, packet 17 enters the flow. However, it does not enter the OP node, taking the path through unordered node 3, instead. Because it enters this node, packet 17 won't enter OP node 2. Then, it sets the skip bit for its sequence number to 0.

4. Next, packet 20 arrives at the OP module. Because packet 20 is an out of order packet, the thread blocks and waits. However, the thread finds out that packet 17 is a skip and therefore, updates the last_seq_num to 17.

5. Packet 18 enters the flow, but takes the unordered path through node 3. It then sets its skip bit to 0.

6. Packet 21 is still blocked because there is still a *1* value set (for sequence 19) in the skip vector between it and the last_seq_num (17).

7. Packet 19 arrives in the OP 2 node. Because the last_seq_num is 17, and the skip bit is set for 18, packet 19 can be processed. The last_seq_num is then set to 19.

8. Packet 20 can now be processed because it is now in order relative to the previous sequence numbers (the last_seq_num = 19). The last sequence number is set to 20.

9. The thread processing packet 21 then does another check to see if it can continue processing. Because the last_seq_num is now 20, it determines that packet 21 can be processed because it is now in order. The last_seq_num is now increased to 21.

10. Packet 22 now enters the flow and takes the unordered path through node 3. It then tells node 2 to skip this packet by updating its skip vector to a 0.

11. Packet 23 enters the flow through OP node 2. It checks the last_seq_num and the skip vector. Because only one skip vector entry, which is 0 for sequence 22, lies between this packet 23 and the last_seq_num 21, the thread processing packet 23 determines that its packet can be processed. Packet 23's thread updates the last_seq_num to 23 and processes the packet.

12. This process continues as packets flow through the system.

13. As packets exit the overall pool of threads, they ensure that their skip bits are set to the default state of 1 for all the OP nodes.

Non-Blocking Packet Ordering

In the previous example, if a thread arrives at the OP module and needs to wait for previous packets to arrive or for packets to be skipped, that thread is blocked. It can't do any work while it waits for these ordering conditions to be met. To maintain the highest possible performance, threads have to be constantly working on a packet. To keep blocked threads constantly busy, the POTs architecture has a non-blocking version of the partial packet-ordering algorithm. Developers don't need to implement this version of the algorithm it is purely optional. The non-blocking version improves thread efficiency while introducing a bit more complexity. It also solves a problem of deadlock that can arise in the blocking version when packets arrive out of order in the packet processing pipeline. The blocking version can deadlock with all threads blocking, and no progress made. The non-blocking version has no such deadlock problem.

The main objective of the non-blocking implementation is to free a blocked thread so it can do other work. This occurs with the thread placing the packet in a queue and then the newly freed thread goes off to do more work. The enqueued packet is worked on later when the blocking condition has been removed. The actual queue is a list of packet handles. The handle describes everything about the packet so when it is ready to be processed the thread has all the needed information to continue processing the packet. This list of packet handles is called the *packet data array* and is indexed by the packet sequence number. Remember that the packet sequence number was assigned by the packet dispatcher just prior to being picked up by the thread. In most implementations, the packet data array is most likely the AISR array itself because it is already a common data structure among all of the threads in the aggregate_ID. Another data structure is called the *status vector*. The status vector is associated with each OP module and indicates that the packet was delivered to the OP module by the previously blocked thread and it is now waiting to be processed. The packet is also indexed by the sequence number. The semantics of the status vector are:

0:    The packet has not arrived yet at this OP module.

1:    This packet has arrived and is waiting to be processed.

Thus, each OP module has a status vector, a packet data array (AISR), a skip vector, and a last sequence number, as illustrated in Figure 7.19.

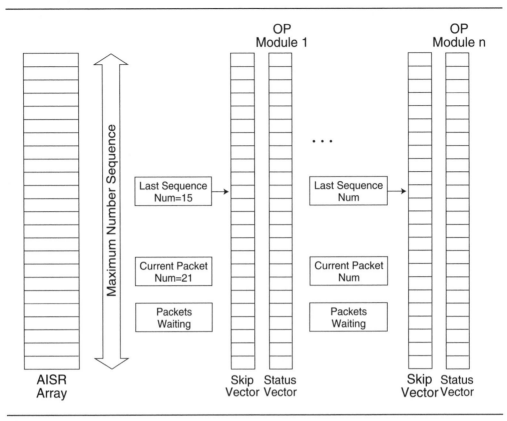

Figure 7.19 Non-Blocking Packet Ordering

Once a blocked thread has left its packet in the packet data array (AISR) and has indicated that it has done so by setting the corresponding bit in the status vector, the thread is now free to do more work. The thread needs to find work to do, but where? Should it pick up a completely new packet that just arrived from the network? Or should the free thread search through every OP module queue to find a packet that is ready to be processed. Having the thread poll every OP module packet data queue can be very time-consuming because it would have to access the queues (AISR) in external SRAM and the resulting latency would significantly slow down the thread. Implementing a centralized scheduler that would do the polling for the threads could be a solution, but it would consume a whole microengine and add complexity. The fastest and most efficient method is for each microengine to have a packet data queue state stored locally.

The algorithm that allows free threads quickly to determine where to find packets to work on depends on another data structure in each microengine. This data structure allows a thread to ascertain quickly which OP modules have packets that are ready to be processed or packets that are just waiting to be processed. Packets that are waiting to be processed, but are not yet ready, still have the blocking condition present. The data structure also indicates whether any one OP module has a large number of packets that are waiting to be processed so it can give that OP module a higher priority. The specifics of the data structure are three bit vectors. Each vector consists of one bit per OP module. The semantics of the OP module are:

■ *Waiting Vector.* A set bit indicates that packets might be waiting to be processed by the corresponding OP module. A waiting state suggests that the blocking condition still exists for some packets in the queue.

■ *Ready Vector.* A set bit indicates that packets might be waiting which are ready to be processed by the OP module. A ready state indicates that the blocking condition has been removed for some packets in the queue.

■ *Threshold Vector.* A set bit indicates that a large number of packets might be waiting to be processed by the corresponding aggregate ID block. The "large" designation is defined by a pre-set threshold value.

Be aware that these vectors only provide hints about the state of the queues. The conditions causing a packet to be blocked are very dynamic. For example, a delay occurs when a thread sets the skip bit and when that resulting state is reflected in the ready, waiting, and threshold bit vectors in the microengine. Also, these vectors are only updated by a thread for its own microengine. The bit vectors in other microengines do not represent exactly the state of all the OP_modules packet array queues. However, they are better than nothing, having a thread poll all the OP_modules' packet data queues or the AISR array. Thus, these vectors provide simple hints that help a newly freed thread quickly find more work to do.

Software algorithms can use these three bit vectors in the microengine several ways. Here is an example of one method. After a thread enqueues a packet, to find more work to do it:

1. Takes the bitwise AND of the ready and threshold vectors. If any bits are set, go to the indicated queues to process a packet. If no bits are set, proceed to step 2.

2. Looks at the ready vector. If any bits are set, go to the indicated queue. If no bits are set, proceed to step 3.

3. Looks at the *threshold* vector. If there are any bits set, go to the indicated queue. If there are no set bits, proceed to step 4.

4. Looks at the *waiting* vector. If any bits are set, go to the indicated queue. If no bits are set, proceed to step 5.

5. Grabs a new packet from the packet receiver.

The reason for a thread to look for a waiting packet in an OP module, as indicated in step 4, is the chance that the blocking condition for the waiting packet has been removed and the resulting state hasn't yet been reflected in the microengine.

Once a thread goes to an OP module to find a packet to process, it has to grab the right packet whose blocking condition has cleared and is ready to be processed. The three steps that the free thread goes through are:

1. Read the latest sequence number processed and the status and skip vectors.

2. Determine the smallest sequence number above the latest sequence processed that does not have its bit set in the skip vector. If the corresponding bit in the status vector is set, that packet is ready to be processed. The thread should use the atomic SRAM instruction test-and-clear to check the bit in the status vector. This check ensures that if multiple threads are looking at this queue at the same time, only one processes the packet.

3. If the conditions in steps 1 and 2 are not met, the thread should update the latest sequence number processed, setting it to a value immediately prior to the next sequence number that has not been skipped. With that update, the thread does not have to repeat the same work and it is once again a free thread.

Updating the bit vectors in the microengines is a core function of the non-blocking algorithm. These bit vectors are updated at two times: when a thread enqueues a packet for later processing at an OP module, and when a thread finishes processing a packet at an OP module. To facilitate updating these bit vectors, another data structure is added.

This field is an integer value and indicates how many packets are waiting to be processed for each OP_module. Hereafter called the *packets waiting integer*, this integer is incremented every time a thread queues a packet for later processing and is decremented every time a previously queued packet has been processed.

When a thread queues a packet for later processing, it sets the waiting vector bit for that OP module in its own ME. When a thread finishes processing a packet that was previously waiting and finds that no more packets are waiting, as indicated by that OP_modules packets waiting integer,) it resets the waiting vector for that OP_module in its microengine.

When a thread has finished processing a packet through an OP_module, it checks the status vector of the next packet in the sequence to determine whether that packet is ready to be processed. If it is ready to be processed, the thread sets that OP_module in its microengine. If the packet isn't ready to be processed, the thread resets that OP_module's ready vector.

When a thread increments the packets waiting integer and finds that it exceeds some predetermined threshold, the thread sets that OP_module's threshold vector bit. If a thread decrements the number of packets waiting and finds that it is below that threshold, it resets the threshold bit within its microengine.

Here's an important point regarding the coherency of these bit vectors and how they relate to the state of each OP_module. Because the bit vectors are updated for just one microengine, the one that just enqueued a blocked packet, the rest of the microengines do not share the latest state of the OP_modules. After the thread reads the bit vectors and visits the appropriate OP_module, the state of the OP module possibly won't correlate to the bit vectors of that microengine. This mismatch results in the thread searching for a packet in an OP_module with out-of-date state information. When it visits the OP_module, the thread needs to find out exactly whether a packet is ready to be processed or not. The role of the bit vectors is to provide best effort hints at the state of packets that are ready and waiting to be processed at each OP_module. While these bit vectors are not exactly 100-percent accurate, they do enable newly freed threads to determine more quickly which of the OP_modules have packets ready to be processed.

Critical Sections

Protecting critical sections using POTs is just as important as in HTC, but the developer needs to handle it in a much different manner. With HTC, the pipeline is sequenced in a way that only needs to maintain locking across a single microengine. With POTs, there is no strict ordering of packets, so the CAM's use is limited because the critical section identifiers are not globally visible. To address this problem, the mutex must be globally visible to all the threads that are processing a particular flow. With POTs, you have three ways of managing mutual exclusion.

Lock Server

The POTs programming model can use a single microengine to be a lock server to keep track of what critical data is locked and not locked. In this method, threads in the pool that need to take out a lock on critical data request it from the lock server microengine. This microengine manages the locked state for all the critical data. The critical data identifier is loaded into the CAM and the critical data itself is stored in local memory (or in the SRAM Q_Array if the protected data is a linked list or ring). Because most applications need to manage critical sections across hundreds or thousands of flows or connections, the lock server mechanism uses the caching mechanism described in Chapter 5 to extend the maximum number of flows beyond the 16 entries of the ME CAM.

Test_and_set

Using the SRAM or Scratch memory test_and_set instruction solves the problem of the microengine CAM when it needs to manage more than 16 flows (or other critical data) per POTs class. When a large number of flows must be managed, the only way to ensure that the mutex is globally visible to all the threads is to have it stored in SRAM (or scratch memory for smaller amounts), which is a common resource available to all the threads. When using the SRAM test_and_set method, each flow has a descriptor that has one bit assigned as a lock bit. When a thread wants to take out a lock, it sets a lock bit in the flow's descriptor that is stored in SRAM. Figure 7.20 shows a sample data structure.

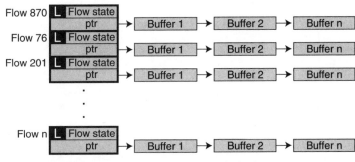

Flow descriptors with a single bit—*L*—representing a locked status.
If a 1 value, data is locked. If 0, the lock is cleared.

Figure 7.20   Example Data Structure for SRAM test_and_set

A requesting thread can take out a lock only if the critical section isn't already locked. A simple way to do so is the SRAM bit test_and_set command. This command atomically sets one or more bits in a particular SRAM location and returns the previous unmodified value to a transfer register in the requesting microengine. To set this lock value, a thread issues this instruction to a particular flow descriptor's lock bit. The command then returns the previous value for the software to test to determine whether the data is already locked. If the thread discovers that the critical section was previously locked, the requesting thread does not own the critical data, and therefore, it must wait until the lock is cleared. While waiting, it is polling that memory location using the same test_and_set instruction, waiting for a 0 value to be returned. When it discovers a 0 value, it knows the lock has been cleared by the previous thread and proceeds with processing the critical data. When finished with the critical section, the thread clears the lock by issuing an SRAM bit clear command to that memory location.

Figure 7.21 provides the pseudocode for this operation.

```
SRAM[cmd, xfer, src_op1, src_op2], opt_tok
Where: cmd = test_and_set, or Clr (to clear bit(s))
   Xfer = bit mask of bits to set to 1 (or clear),
         and previous value of SRAM data
   Src_op1 + Src_op2 = byte address in SRAM
                       to test and set.
   Opt_tok = (see IXP2xxx PRM for detailed
             syntax description.)
```

Figure 7.21   SRAM Bit test_and_set Syntax

The SRAM bit test_and_set method is quite simple to implement. It requires only one bit to be reserved in a flow's descriptor for lock status. While accessing SRAM does consume memory bandwidth, resulting in latency problems, this latency can be hidden using the multithreading techniques described in Chapter 5. Also, if the data structure is designed for it, the SRAM memory location containing the lock bit can also contain flow state information, as Figure 7.20 illustrates. Thus, the test_and_set instruction can also be used to read flow state information, data that would be required anyway. No additional memory bandwidth is consumed in setting the lock. The only additional memory bandwidth consumed would be when the requesting thread polls the descriptor that is waiting for the lock condition to be cleared. However, assuming minimal contention based on the anticipated traffic pattern, these problems should be minimal.

The main problem with the SRAM test_and_set method is that it doesn't ensure the strict ordering of locks. In many situations, critical data needs to be processed in order, such as in ATM AAL5 reassembly or IPv6 header decompression. If several threads are simultaneously accessing the same critical data and the lock is suddenly cleared, a thread could access the critical data before a prior thread gets to do so. The thread that has been waiting the longest doesn't have any guarantee that it will get a fair chance at the critical data. With no fairness mechanism built in, lock starvation could result. A sequential mechanism is needed for situations that depend on ordering of the locking.

Deli Ticket Server

The *deli ticket server* mechanism ensures that threads are granted locks in the order that they are requested. The deli ticket server (DTS) mechanism is very similar to the ones we use at the paint store, ice cream shop, sandwich delicatessen, or other places where we need to wait in line for our turn at being served. In these situations, several consumers are requesting service from a shared resource like the deli sandwich maker. Because the shop wants each person in line to get their turn, the consumer takes a ticket and waits until his or her number is called. The three important numbers in this example are:

- The current service number that the shop attendant is working on

- The token number that a customer holds while waiting to be served

- The service delta number or the difference between the two which indicates how long a consumer has to wait until served

The POTs model uses a method similar to DTS to ensure fairness. With DTS, a lock head pointer and a lock tail pointer is associated with each flow descriptor. The lock head pointer holds the sequence number of the thread being currently serviced. The tail pointer holds the ticket number for new threads wanting service. The actual size of these pointers is application dependent, but eight bits is a reasonable number. Because the test_and_increment instruction works on 32 bits, the actual number of outstanding tokens can be very large. This is illustrated in Figure 7.22.

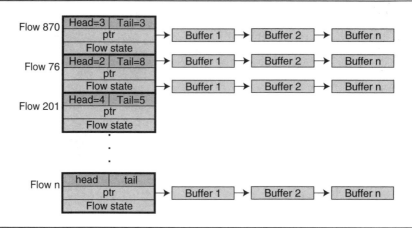

Figure 7.22   POTs Deli Ticket Server Example Data Structure

With DTS, when a thread requests a lock, it issues an SRAM test_and_increment command at the tail location of the relevant flow descriptor. This instruction increments the tail pointer then returns the previous value. Next, it reads the head pointer and compares it to the tail pointer. If they are the same, as in flow 870 in the diagram, the data structure is not currently locked down and the new lock request is granted. When the thread owning the lock is finished with the critical section and wishes to clear the lock, it issues an SRAM increment command on the head pointer, advancing the ticket server. If the tail and head pointers are different, the requestor must wait until they are the same. While waiting, the requestor is polling the head pointer and comparing the head and tail pointer until they match. Because polling consumes memory bandwidth, it is desirable to control the polling frequency. If a large difference exists between the head and tail pointer, as in flow 76 above, the requestor can poll at a lower frequency than if they are close together, as in flow 201.

This method is very similar in real life. For example, when you are waiting to be served at your neighborhood paint store, you may want to go to the hardware department or wall paper section if you have a high ticket number relative to the one currently being served. You can do something else while waiting your turn to get your paint. Alternatively, if your number is only 1 or 2 tickets away, you probably should stay close to the counter so you can get served as soon as your number is called.

The deli ticket server mechanism is the best way of ensuring ordered mutual exclusion. However, what is its cost? For one thing, it uses more memory than the SRAM test_and_set method. It also incurs additional memory reads because the head and tail ticket service numbers need to read individually and that read can't be combined with reading additional data such as state metadata. As in all things, you have tradeoffs. To determine the best locking method, you should analyze your data and traffic patterns.

HTC or POTs? Which Approach Should You Use?

Determining whether to use HTC or POTs depends a lot on the application. Because the IXP2XXX family of network processors is a software programmable architecture, you aren't forced to pick one packet-processing model. In general, POTs should be the first choice unless proven otherwise. In general, POTs is simpler to implement than HTC. The POTs approach also scales a bit more elegantly. As your application moves from an IXP2400 to the IXP2800, which contains more microengines, the additional threads are just added to the pool of the existing application. The overall software functionality doesn't change. With HTC, as additional microengines are added to process higher line rates, the pipeline must be modified. Because the pipeline period is based on packet arrival rate, the number of pipe stages, and hence the number of microengines, will change as well. For more information about performance optimization, see Chapter 9.

The primary difference between the two, however, lies in the way they manage common or disparate network traffic. If the application expects a statistically large percentage of traffic to be processed within the same time period, using the same software tasks, then HTC is likely the best method. In this scenario, the traffic is more likely to be associated with the same connection or flow, and therefore needs the highest performance dependency checking for critical sections. Because HTC brings dependency checking into the microengine using the MEv2 CAM, this process runs much faster than dependence checking when the mutex is in SRAM. Because the processing time is more predictable for a large percentage of packet types, the processing can better fit in the pipeline model that HTC uses. HTC has much greater determinacy that POTs.

When an HTC functional pipeline is designed, the pipe-stage period must be designed for the worst case processing time to be sure that packets don't get dropped. If most of the packets conform to the worst-case scenario, the pipeline is constantly full and working on packets.

However, if only a small percentage of the packets conform to the worst-case processing time scenario, the pipeline won't be used efficiently. Most of the packets are finished before the smaller percentage of worse case ones are. Because of the strict thread ordering, many of the threads are idle, waiting for the thread working on the worse case packet to complete.

Because of this situation, POTs fits the application better than HTC when the application has a wide variety of traffic patterns whose processing time varies considerably from packet to packet. A good example is IPv6 and IPv4 processing, as shown in Figure 7.23:

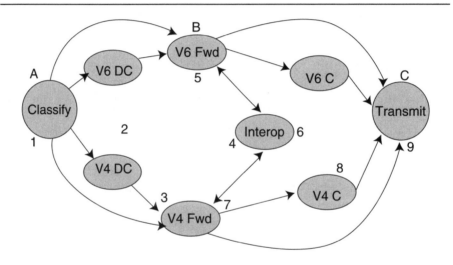

V4, V6 DC = IPv4 & IPv6 Decompression
V4, V6 C = IPv4 & IPv6 Compression

Figure 7.23 IPv6 and IPv4 Inter-working

Consider two possible processing paths that a packet may take. If a packet is classified as a standard IPv6 packet to be forwarded, it would take the path: A > B > C. However, an IPv6 packet that is encapsulated in an IPv4 packet would take the path: 1 > 2 > 3 > 4 > 5 > 6 > 7 > 8 > 9. Thus, depending on the packet type, processing time could vary over a wide range. If HTC is used to process these kinds of traffic patterns, the pipeline is nine stages long to be sure that no packets are dropped. If this nine-stage pipeline processed the shorter path, six stages would be empty. In reality, several stages are repeated in the longer path, resulting in a loop. With software pipelining, each possible loop has to be made linear, causing a very inefficient processing flow.

Because of these loops and packet processing variation times, POTs is the optimal programming model. Threads that complete quicker due to shorter paths can insert their packet into AISR and then pick up another packet. Threads are constantly utilized in the POTs array regardless of the packet processing requirements (although the queue manager may be blocked, as described earlier). However, if packet-processing time is relatively consistent from one packet to another and the highest possible performance is desired, HTC might be the better programming model. HTC by its very nature attacks packet ordering and lock contention head on, using inter-thread signaling hardware and the MEv2 CAM. Significant performance gains can be achieved when using these hardware features.

Determining which model to use implies a statistical understanding of the packet-processing time duration for the various packet types of the incoming traffic stream. This variation is illustrated in Figure 7.24. Assume that the X axis is packet processing time and the Y axis is the number of packets that require this processing time.

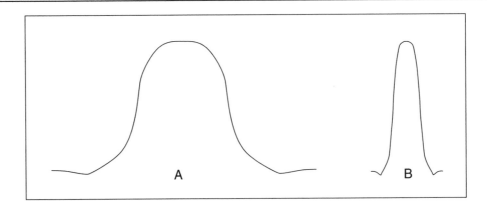

Figure 7.24   Variation in Packet-processing Times

In diagram A of Figure 7.24, you can see wide variation in processing time for the incoming traffic. In diagram B, the variation in packet-processing time is minimal. Figure 7.25 shows the efficiency of the two programming models processing widely distributed traffic. Because the HTC functional pipeline must be tuned to the worst-case anticipated processing path, it finishes at T=n. On the other hand, the average processing time of a thread using POTs is T=m, faster than when using HTC. Threads can be quickly turned around and reused when they are finished with a packet. HTC has a fixed completion time for the packets; the only variation is due to memory latency variation and not to packet-processing variation. With HTC, threads completed early become idle until the pipeline reaches the final stage.

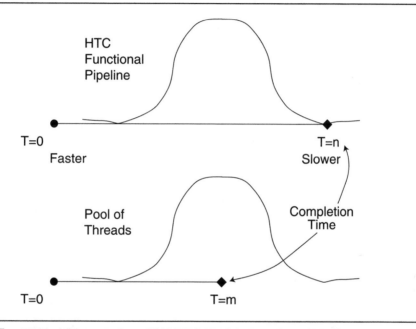

Figure 7.25   POTs Advantage Over HTC With Widely Distributed Traffic

While POTs has an advantage over HTC with widely varying traffic types, what happens when the traffic has a narrow distribution, as shown in Figure 7.26?

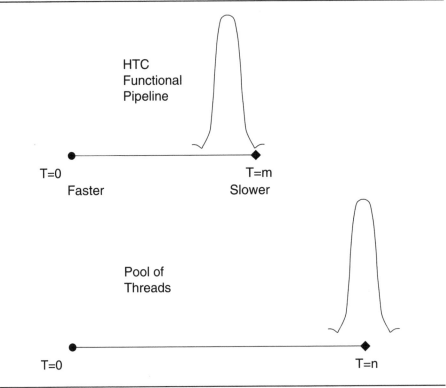

Figure 7.26   HTC Advantage Over POTs with Narrowly Distributed Traffic

When the traffic pattern is narrowly distributed with no processing loops, HTC can be used. The benefits of the MEv2 CAM come into play by accelerating critical sections. Threads are in continuous use and aren't idling. POTs loses its big advantage over HTC with this traffic type because HTC now is fully utilizing packets, just like POTs. Also, HTC has the added advantage that critical section dependency checking uses the very speedy MEv2 CAM while POTs utilizes mutexes in much slower SRAM. With HTC, packet ordering is maintained by way of strict thread assignments to incoming packets. While HTC is faster and gives determinacy with this packet processing behavior, it has a certain complexity that some designers may want to avoid, especially for moderate speed applications.

While the previous analysis is fairly general in addressing the differences between HTC and POTs, some immediate, specific considerations might be raised as well. With HTC, packet headers can be immediately received from the MSF and read into the microengine's transfer registers. With POTs, the packets are buffered into DRAM while waiting to get picked up by free thread. This intermediary buffering consumes DRAM bandwidth in a way that is not experienced with HTC. In the OC-192 POS design for the IXP2800 processor, the DRAM headroom is 46 percent for HTC while it is 20 percent for POTs. Because of no fixed assignment of threads to packets—no strict packet ordering—POTs can't leverage the efficiencies of next neighbor registers to communicate from one microengine to another, as an HTC context pipeline does. Communication mechanisms used with POTs rely on the more generalized ring buffers and reflector bus signaling. While very flexible, they use more bandwidth on the internal command bus and the reflector bus, as well as external SRAM bandwidth via the ring buffers.

Let's summarize the pros and cons. With POTs, lock contention isn't handled as efficiently as it is with the functional pipeline of HTC. Because the model can't guarantee that only one microengine will process a task at any one particular time, the MEv2 CAM is of limited use. A thread can use its local CAM to store critical section identifiers, but threads in other microengines must use test-and-set instructions in SRAM. To ensure packet ordering is maintained with POTs, the programmer must use special mechanisms, such as AISR and the deli ticket server. While HTC offers many performance advantages, POTs actually can be more efficient for widely distributed packet flows, achieving higher performance than HTC, and POTs is easier to program.

Because the IXP2XXX network processors are software-based, any programming model can be used. The systems architect isn't forced to use a programming model that doesn't match the unique characteristics of an application.

Combining POTs with HTC

In applications where POTs is the best choice for the front-end packet processing, a mixture of POTs and HTC is the best programming model to use. When combining them, POTs is used for the heavy lifting of front-end packet processing, and HTC is used for the back end. In this combined application, only HTC context pipelines are used. The front-end functional pipeline is replaced by a pool of threads, as illustrated in Figure 7.27.

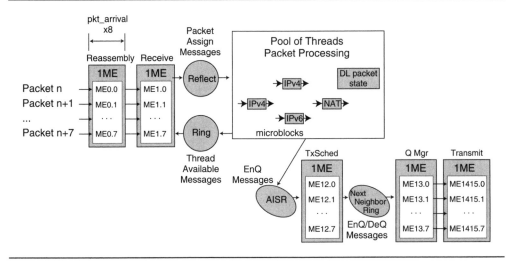

Figure 7.27   HTC and POTs

When POTs and HTC are combined, the front-end reassembly and packet dispatcher are implemented as a two-stage context pipeline. The dispatcher determines which threads are available in the pool from a scratch ring and issues packet assignment messages to the appropriate thread via a reflector write operation. The pool of threads produces entries into the AISR array, which is composed of an SRAM ring. The transmit scheduler consumes these entries. The rest of the flow follows the HTC flow using a context pipeline.

In some applications, a particular processing stage does not need to maintain packet order. One example is performing metering and congestion management functions. These tasks can be included in the pool of threads, as shown in Figure 7.28.

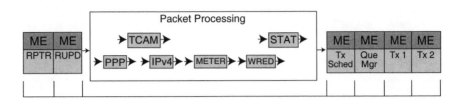

Figure 7.28   Unordered Metering and Statistics

In other applications maintaining packet order might be very important. Similar to the previous example, Figure 7.29 illustrates ordered metering, statistics, and WRED. Because ordering need not be enforced, these functions are included in an HTC context pipeline.

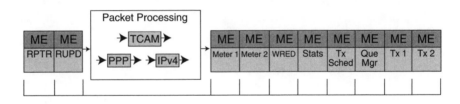

Figure 7.29   Ordered Metering and Statistics in an HTC Context Pipeline

Chapter 8

Performance Considerations

After reading through eight chapters of this book on the Intel Internet Exchange Architecture, you may still be asking yourself whether IXP2XXX network processors are up to the job of performing your application. You may have some questions:

- How many tasks can an IXP2XXX network processor perform?

- Which IXP2XXX network processor should I use?

- What frequency IXP2XXX network processor should I use?

- How much memory does my IXP2XXX based system need?

- How much headroom does my IXP2XXX system have?

Answering these very important questions requires a bit of work, but isn't difficult. All you need to understand is some basic resource budgeting principles to accurately estimate performance. A network processor application is very different from a standard desktop application running on your PC. A word processing or spreadsheet application doesn't have to respond to a continuous stream of data or input stimulus and risk failing. Unlike real-time applications, the input stimuli for the desktop application—that's you typing—can merely slow down to allow the PC to catch up. For any background processing that's needed, you can always wait for your PC to respond, which isn't really catastrophic, although you might find it irritating in the short term and highly unproductive over the long term. The system does not fail due to a choked input stream, and it still can be productive.

The packet-processing work done by a highly sophisticated router is much different. The packets keep coming and coming and the router must keep up with them or risk dropping packets. As such, any performance analysis must look at how fast packets arrive, what resources are consumed in processing them, and what tasks are performed.

The goal of this chapter is to help you understand some general principles of estimating performance on IXP2XXX network processors. You will learn about budgeting techniques and about assigning tasks to microengines. Ultimately, coding an application using the software development tools, then integrating it into your target hardware system is the only sure way to determine performance. However, by properly estimating performance early in the design process, you can make architectural decisions that can save a tremendous amount of time and frustration later on. For a very good paper on a formal performance methodology, see "Network Processor Performance Analysis Methodology" (Lakshmanamurthy et al. 2002).

Three Performance Variables

To estimate performance, you have to understand three primary performance variables:

- *Packet arrival rate* is the frequency, measured in millions of packets per second, at which packets enter the system and are processed. Packet arrival interval, is another way of saying the same thing, but is measured in time (nanoseconds), rather than in frequency. Network equipment makers typically specify their equipment under worst-case, minimum size packet conditions, without dropping packets.

- *IXP2XXX network processor packet processing resources* include the microengines, memory, and I/O resources available to process a packet. These resources are actually measured in bus bandwidth or the number of instructions that are available to process a packet.

- *Packet processing tasks* are the functions the network processor is required to perform. Examples are packet reassembly, IPv4 forwarding, traffic scheduling, and enqueueing and dequeueing tasks. These tasks are then analyzed as to how much IXP2XXX resources they use per packet.

These three variables must be considered when estimating performance. While the packet arrival rate (PAR) might seem constant in a real-time system, this isn't necessarily the case. The system might have a fixed number of Gigabit Ethernet interfaces—for example, an overall bit rate of 2 gigabits per second, full duplex—the type of packets and their relative percentage mix in the data stream can vary tremendously. Some packets require a lot of processing cycles and others need a smaller amount. Not only can this fixed rate link have multiple types of packets, the packets themselves can vary in length. The input stream can contain many more minimum-sized packets than larger packet sizes, or the opposite may occur as well. In fact, the packet size distribution can be "all over the map." In short, the mere fact that the network processor receives a fixed steam of bits doesn't imply that a fixed amount of processing is required for those bits. Both packet type and packet length have a significant impact on the processing requirements of the network processor.

The IXP2XXX network processor's hardware resources appear to be a fixed constant because silicon is what it is; however, this isn't necessarily the case either. Based on the tasks performed, you might choose a lower frequency IXP2XXX network processor or different version of the processor altogether to save costs. Memory speed and quantity can also be lowered to save costs and power. Finally, the packet processing tasks are variable. Using a single IXP2XXX network processor is optimal, but often two or more are needed to insure the proper headroom.

With several factors to consider, one must make assumptions to arrive at a solution. These assumptions depend on assigning two of the variables as constants and using the third as a variable. For example, suppose you want to optimize for functionality, given a PAR and specific IXP2800 processor configuration, as shown in Table 8.1. The PAR in this table is actually the period (in nanoseconds) that the packets arrive at the network processor.

Table 8.1   Optimizing for Functionality

Variable	Description	Value
Packet arrival rate	OC-192 POS with 40-byte IPv4 payload and 9-byte PPP encapsulation (5-byte header and 4 byte CRC).	40.7 ns IPv4 packet arrival interval
IXP2800 processor resources	Model number of IXP2800 processor, frequency, memory, bandwidth	1 IXP2800 @ 1.4 GHz SRAM: 4 channels @ 200 MHz RDR: 3 channels @ 533 MHz
Desired tasks (the variable)	Reassembly, classification, forwarding, IPv4 internetworking, EnQ/DeQ, scheduling, scheduling, transmitting	Question: Which of these tasks can be performed and with what headroom?

Determining the number of desired tasks that can be performed given a PAR and available IXP2XXX net

Packet Arrival Rate

Why isn't this section titled line rate? The IXP2XXX processors process packets and not necessarily raw bits.[1] Thus, given a certain bit rate, large packets have a lower PAR while smaller packets have a higher PAR. Raw bit rate can also be misleading. Certain link layer protocols, such as Ethernet, have an Inter-Packet Gap (IPG) specification that forces a minimum length of dead time between packets. This IPG is a minimum of 12-byte times for Ethernet, which also has an 8-byte preamble. Thus, for a 64-byte packet, there are 20 bytes of overhead. The IPG and preamble is a sizable percentage of the total bandwidth and needs to be incorporated into the packet arrival rate calculations. As you can see, packet arrival rates for different layer 2 protocols at the same bit rates vary, as described in Table 8.2. The IXP1200 is included for comparison purposes.

---

[1] The raw bit rate does have a direct impact on DRAM bus utilization, both internal and external because that is where the packets are stored.

Table 8.2 Packet Arrival Rates for Various Line Rates and Layer 2 Protocols

Network Traffic Type	Line rate available to frames1	40 Byte IP frame size on wire (Bytes)	Arrival Interval (ns)	IXP1200 Arrival Interval clocks @ 232 MHz	IXP2400 Arrival Interval clocks @ 600 MHz	IXP2800 Arrival Interval clocks @ 1.4 GHz
OC-3c ATM	149,760,000	53	2831.00	656	1698	3963
OC-12c ATM	600,768,000	53	705.80	163	423	988
OC-48c ATM	2,404,800,000	53	176.30	40	105	246
OC-192c ATM	9,620,928,000	53	44.07	10	26	61
OC-3c POS	149,760,000	49	2618.00	607	1570	3664
OC-12c POS	600,768,000	49	652.50	151	391	913
OC-48c POS	2,404,800,000	49	163.00	37	97	228
OC-192c POS	9,620,928,000	49	40.74	9	24	57
10 Mb/s Enet	10,000,000	84	67200	15590	40320	94080
100 Fast Enet	100,000,000	84	6720	1559	4032	9408
1 GigE	1,000,000,000	84	672	155	403	940
10 GigE (LAN)	10,000,000,000	84	67.20	15	40	94
10 GigE (WAN)	9,620,928,000	84	69.85	16	41	97

[1] SONET overhead is stripped

Table 8.2 really highlights packet overhead on packet arrival rates. For instance, OC-12c ATM has a packet arrival interval of 705.8 nanoseconds, while POS, with its smaller minimum-packet size has an interval over 50 nanoseconds shorter. Even more interesting is Gigabit Ethernet compared to OC-12c POS. You would expect Ethernet to have a much shorter interval period because it is close to 50 percent faster than OC-12c POS. However, the POS traffic actually has a slightly shorter packet arrival interval, caused by Ethernet's larger packet header, larger minimum-sized packet length, 12-byte inter-packet gap, and 8-byte preamble. All these characteristics add up, increasing the arrival period for Ethernet.

Table 8.2 also shows the packet arrival interval in time (nanoseconds) compared to equivalent clock ticks at various frequencies. These clock ticks correspond to the frequencies of the IXP1200 at 232 megahertz, the IXP2400 at 600 megahertz, and the IXP2800 at 1.4 gigahertz. The ticks represent the number of network processor clocks that elapse during a single packet interval. If you assume a 1:1 ratio between clock cycles and instructions for ideal RISC behavior, you have an estimated number of IXP instructions that can execute during one packet arrival interval. For example, the packet arrival rate of Gigabit Ethernet is 672 nanoseconds, which translates to 940 clock ticks at 1400 megahertz. This estimate implies that an IXP2800 processor can execute 940 instructions during one packet interval.

Finally, this table shows the dramatic increase in processing capabilities at the higher clock rates. For 10 Gigabit Ethernet (LAN), the IXP1200 running at 232 megahertz can only process about 15 instructions before the next packet arrives. The IXP2800 processor running at 1.4 gigahertz, on the other hand, can process 94 instructions during that same packet interval. With increasing semiconductor process technology, faster clock rates will result to help solve these problems. Each decrease in transistor size directly translates to higher processor frequencies and more instructions you can devote to each packet.

IXP2XXX Hardware Resource Budget

For any specific IXP2XXX network processor hardware configuration, the amount of available resources is fixed. Only so much memory bandwidth, command bus bandwidth, and so forth are available for a given application. These resources are called a "budget," the available hardware-given resources within which your application must fit. Tables 8.3 and 8.4 show the available bus bandwidth budgets for 49 byte POS packets for the IXP2800 and IXP2400 processors, respectively, at their maximum operating frequencies.

Table 8.3   IXP2800-1.4GHz Resource Budgeting

Bus	Bus Bandwidth[1] (cycles per second)	Budget[2] (for 24.54 Million packets/sec POS)
Command Bus 0	700 MCmd/s	28 Cmd/pkt
Command Bus 1	700 MCmd/s	28 Cmd/pkt
SRAM Reads	3200 MB/s	130 Bytes/pkt
SRAM Writes	3200 MB/s	130 Bytes/pkt
SRAM Pull 0	2800 MB/s	114 Bytes/pkt

Table 8.3   IXP2800-1.4GHz Resource Budgeting (continued)

Bus	Bus Bandwidth[1] (cycles per second)	Budget[2] (for 24.54 Million packets/sec POS)
SRAM Push 0	2800 MB/s	114 Bytes/pkt
SRAM Pull 1	2800 MB/s	114 Bytes/pkt
SRAM Push 1	2800 MB/s	114 Bytes/pkt
DRAM Total	6396 MB/s	260 Bytes/pkt
DRAM Push	5600 MB/s	228 Bytes/pkt
DRAM Pull	5600 MB/s	228 Bytes/pkt

[1] The budget is per OC-192c POS 40 Byte IP packet with 9-byte header.

[2] Budget = Bus BW/24.54 million packets/sec

Table 8.4   IXP2400-600MHz Resource Budgeting

Bus	Bus Bandwidth[1] (cycles per second)	Budget[2] (for 6.13 Million Packets/sec POS)
Command Bus 0	300 MCmd/s	48 Cmd/pkt
Command Bus 1	300 MCmd/s	48 Cmd/pkt
SRAM Reads	1600 MB/s	261 Bytes/pkt
SRAM Writes	1600 MB/s	261 Bytes/pkt
SRAM Pull 0	1200 MB/s	195 Bytes/pkt
SRAM Push 0	1200 MB/s	195 Bytes/pkt
SRAM Pull 1	1200 MB/s	195 Bytes/pkt
SRAM Push 1	1200 MB/s	195 Bytes/pkt
DRAM Total	2400 MB/s	391 Bytes/pkt
DRAM Push	2400 MB/s	391 Bytes/pkt
DRAM Pull	2400 MB/s	391 Bytes/pkt

[1] The budget is per OC-48c POS 40 Byte IP packet with 9-byte header.

[2] Budget = Bus BW/6.13 million packets/sec

The numbers in the preceding tables give the overall bandwidth of the chip resources referenced to a packet rate rather than to absolute time (e.g., seconds). For example, during one packet time of the IXP2800 based OC-192c application above, 56 total I/O commands can be issued across the command buses, a total of 260 bytes of DRAM can be read or written, and 130 bytes can be read and written to/from SRAM. To determine the total headroom, the resource utilization for each task that is required to process a packet is totaled up and then compared to the overall budget numbers above.

Determining the Resource Budget

The IXP2XXX network processor's bus bandwidth is a fixed constant, varying only on the core frequency. However, determining the resource budget is dependent on the packet arrival rate of the traffic stream being analyzed. Here are the calculations to arrive at this particular budget for the 1.4 GHz IXP2800 processing minimum size 40 byte IP packets over OC-192c SONET:

- Packet size = 40 Byte IP packet + 9 Byte PPP header = 49 byte packet.

- IXP2800 processor clock rate = 1.4 GHz = 0.71 ns period

- Media Frame Bit Rate = 9,620,928,000 bits per second (SONET overhead removed)

- Frame Rate = 49Byte * 8 bits/Byte / 9,620,928,000 bits/sec = 40.74 ns

- Frames per Second = 1000 / 40.74 ns = 24.54 Million packets/sec (pps) (The 1000 number converts nanoseconds to microseconds to give a million packets per second unit.)

- IXP clocks/Frame Rate = 40.74 ns * 1.4 x 10⁹ clocks/sec = 57 clocks per frame. Assuming ideal 1:1 instruction/clock cycle risc behavior, 57 instructions can be applied to process the packet during one packet interval.

Determining SRAM budget per frame interval:

■ SRAM frequency: 200 MHz

■ SRAM read (write) bandwidth per channel:

200 MHz x 2 txfers/clk * 2 Bytes = 800 MB/sec

■ SRAM R/W bandwidth per IXP2800

4 channels x 800 Mbytes/sec = 3200 MB/s

■ SRAM bandwidth per frame interval

3200 MB/s / 24.54 Mpps = 130 bytes/frame interval

Determining DRAM budget per frame interval:

■ RDRAM frequency = 533 MHz

■ RDRAM bandwidth per channel

533 * 2 txfers/clock * 2 Bytes = 2132 MB/s

■ RDRAM bandwidth per IXP2800

3 channels/IXP2800 x 2132 = 6396 MB/sec

■ RDRAM bandwidth per frame interval

6396 MB/s / 24.54 Mpps = 260 bytes/frame interval

So far, you've seen the packet arrival rate and hardware resource variables and how they are normalized to IXP2XXX network processor clock ticks. By normalizing the PAR and resources to IXP2XXX clock ticks, you can do performance calculations using common metrics. IXP2XXX network processor hardware resources, such as "mega-commands per second" or SRAM "megabytes per second", can simply be converted to resources available for a given packet interval rate. Now you need to look at the third and last variable, task performance metrics. Once you have the actual resources consumed for a task, you can compare the actual versus budgeted ratio to determine the resource headroom that you have.

Task Resource Utilization

To determine the utilization of important IXP2XXX hardware resources, each task needs to be examined. Determining the PAR and hardware utilization is straight-forward, but determining the task resource utilization requires a bit more analysis. What you are ultimately going to do is a high-level architectural system design for your IXP2XXX network processor-based system. While this amount of work might seem significant for a performance analysis, you eventually have to do it before you can start implementing any software design. This performance estimation process can also be a forcing function to determine the best software architecture for a particular task. The kinds of questions that you answer during this phase of the design are:

- What do the table and other data structures look like? (helps determine memory size and bandwidth utilization)

- What is the packet-processing algorithm? (helps determine number of instructions)

- Are there critical sections? (helps determine the total task wall time)

In short, by doing a thorough high-level description—something you should do anyway—you are much better prepared to write code, and you get a much better handle on performance early in the design process. The end goal of determining task resource utilization is to determine the actual hardware resources consumed by a task on a single packet. These hardware resources were described in the earlier section. Because you already know what the budget is, you can then determine the headroom available.

When analyzing a task, consider three general groups of resources:

- Memory bandwidth
  - SRAM reads and writes
  - DRAM reads and writes
  - Scratch reads and writes
- Internal bus bandwidth
  - Command bus bandwidth (I/O instructions)
  - DRAM push and pull bus bandwidth
  - SRAM push and pull bus bandwidth

- Total processing time
  - Instruction count time
  - Dependent memory latency time

To determine memory bandwidth, you need to examine several components of your software design and determine how many accesses to/from SRAM, DRAM, and scratch memory for several types of data structures:

- Free buffer lists
- Ring buffers
- Linked lists
- Miscellaneous data structures

Determining the internal bus bandwidth gets a bit more complex. Because the IXP2XXX network processors allow internal data transfers in addition to external memory operations, these internal operations need to be calculated for the highest performance designs.

- MSF - ME
- MSF - Memory
- I/O commands
- Reflector reads and writes
- Hash reads/writes

The total cycle count for a particular task has two components:

- Instruction cycle time
- Dependent memory latency time

Determining the total instruction cycle time is probably the most difficult because the only way to be totally precise is to write the actual code and count cycles. When doing preliminary performance estimates, a reasonable assumption can be made that the overall memory latencies exceed compute cycles, that is, the stall bound case as described in Chapter 5. As such, total instruction count can be roughly estimated or sometimes completed ignored. You must be careful here, as this assumption only holds true if the application requires many memory references, so you need to go through the previous calculations first.

Budgets can be frequency-related (bandwidth) and time-related. An example of a frequency metric is SRAM reads per packet or commands per packet. An example of time-related metric would be the total task wall time. This budget is the total of instruction time plus memory latency time that may meet, but not exceed, the packet arrival interval. Probably the largest single component to total task cycle time is the number of dependent memory operations. As you read in Chapter 5, dependent memory operations are ones for which software must wait until a memory operation is completed before executing more instructions. Code is dependent on the memory operation completing. Considering that the typical latency of an SRAM operation is about 130 nanoseconds for the IXP2800 processor running at 1.4 gigahertz, dependent memory operations usually exceed the total instruction cycle time. Just three dependent memory operations are close to 400 instruction cycle times. These dependent memory operations are much easier to count than actual instructions as they can be included in the high-level software design quite independent of coding, whereas the software has to actually be written to count instruction cycles.

A Real-Life Example

In this real-life example of a performance estimation exercise, we will calculate the total bus bandwidth headroom for the IXP2400 processor running the OC-48 Packet-Over-SONET (POS) ingress application. In this exercise, a pseudo-code analysis is performed to analyze the instruction counts and I/O references and their impact on external SRAM and DRAM memory bandwidth. Calculating the internal bus bandwidths, such as DRAM pull or push, SRAM pull or push, and command bus, is a bit too detailed for this analysis and would be distracting. Internal scratch operations are shown for each task because of the reliance on this memory for many operations. However, the final analysis does not include the scratch bandwidth budget, but is included in the task budgeting to include important pseudocode operations. Pseudocode for the various tasks gives you a basic understanding of the process of performance estimation. For the purposes of this chapter, you need not understand each pseudo code operation in detail. In fact, some operations might seem rather cryptic unless you have a solid understanding of the OC-48 POS example design. The description of this design is adapted from the *Intel Internet Exchange Architecture Software Building Blocks Developers Manual* (Intel October 2002).

This example focuses on the ingress packet-processing path and assumes the ingress/egress configuration described earlier in Chapter 3 and illustrated again in Figure 8.1.

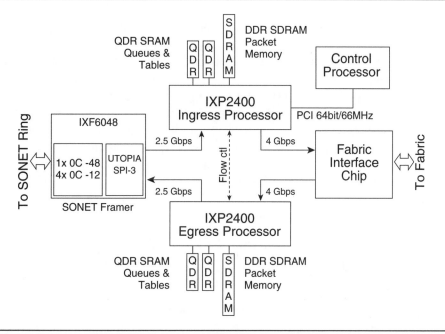

Figure 8.1   IXP2400 Dual Ingress/Egress Architecture

The ingress path takes packets from a SONET framer via the SPI-3 SONET interface, processes them, then transmits those packets to the switch fabric through a fabric interface chip, or FIC. The five basic tasks of egress processing in this particular line card example are:

- *POS Reassembly*—receives frames from the SONET framer via the SPI-3 interface and reassembles them in DRAM.

- *Packet Processing tasks* — perform layer 2 PPP decapsulation and IPv4 forwarding of the IP frames that were received from the network.

- *Queue Manager*—receives enqueue requests from the packet processing stage and dequeue requests from the CSIX scheduler.

- *Transmit CSIX Scheduling*—processes the packets according to the two level, hierarchal CSIX scheduler.

◼ *Transmit Process*—takes packets from the transmit queues and sends them to the available ports.

These tasks were described in detail in Chapter 2 and won't be elaborated here.

This example assumes a worst case minimum-sized packets of a 40 byte IP packet, a 9 byte PPP header, and 1.47 equivalent bytes of SONET overhead, resulting in a 50.47 total packet length. At an OC-48 line rate of 2.48 gigabits per second, the effective line rate after the SONET overhead is stripped off is 2.408 gigabits per second. This equates to a packet arrival rate of 6.14 million packets per second, or an arrival rate of 162.81 ns, which equates to 97.68 core clock cycles for an IXP2400 running at 600 megahertz. Thus, the instruction budget per packet is 97 instructions for one microengine. The example uses all eight microengines of the IXP2400 network processor.

Figure 8.2   OC-48 POS Ingress Processing Task Flow

POS Receive

The Packet receive microblock on the Ingress IXP2400 performs frame-reassembly on the m-packets coming in on the media interface. It reassembles and writes the packet data to a buffer in DRAM and queues the packet buffer handle on a microengine-microengine scratch ring for processing by the next stage in the pipeline. The Packet RX microblock also sets up per packet metadata (offset, size, etc.), which are passed down the pipeline either in a descriptor in SRAM or in the microengine-microengine scratch ring itself. Up to 16 virtual ports are supported and the re-assembly context for all these ports is kept in local memory. To maintain packet sequencing, the threads execute in strict order.

The Packet RX microblock uses eight threads on a single microengine, each of which handles one m-packet at a time.

The pseudocode for this stage follows, and the corresponding commands and bus bandwidth consumed are tabulated in Table 8.5.

Instruction cycles for worst-case execution path: 88 clocks

```
Phase 1
1a: Move Data from RBUF to DRAM (DRAM-Wr: 64B)
1b: Dequeue next buffer handle from SRAM (SRAM-Rd: 4B)

Phase 2
2a: Write metadata to SRAM (SRAM-Wr: 16B)
2b: Return RBUF to free list via fast write to MSF (1
CMD)
2c: Return thread to free list via fast write to MSF (1
CMD)
2d: Write message to scratch (Scratch-Wr: 20B)
```

Table 8.5   POS Receive

Step	Cmd bus	SRAM read	SRAM write	DRAM read	DRAM write	Scratch read	Scratch write
A-1a	1				64		
A-1b	1	4					
A-2a	1		16				
A-2b	1						
A-2c	1						
A-2d	1						20
Total	6	4	16		64		20

The units in this table are bytes of memory bandwidth or number of commands.

Layer 2 PPP Decapsulation/Classify/IPv4

The PPP decapsulation/classify microblock removes the layer-2 PPP header from the packet by updating the offset and size fields in the packet metadata. Based on the PPP header, it also classifies the packet into IPv4, IPv6, PPP control packet (LCP, IPCP, etc.). If the packet is a PPP control packet, it is marked as an exception packet to be sent to the Xscale™ core (IX_EXCEPTION). Otherwise, the packet is sent down the microengine pipeline for further processing.

The IPv4 forwarder microblock validates the IP header per RFC 1812. If the validity checks fail, the packet is set up to be dropped. Otherwise, a Longest Prefix Match (LPM) is performed on the IPv4 header. The result is an IPv4 Next Hop ID, a fabric blade ID (identifying a unique IXP2400 on the fabric) and an output port identifying the output port on the Egress IXP2400. The Next Hop ID is passed over the CSIX fabric to an Egress IXP2400 where it is used to look up information about the Layer-2 header to be pre-pended to the packet buffer. The output port is also passed over the CSIX fabric to the Egress IXP2400 and is used to transmit over the appropriate port. All three fields are stored in the packet metadata. If no match is found, the packet is sent to the Intel XScale core for further processing. Packets are also sent to the core in a number of other cases, for example, when the packet is destined for a local interface or is to be fragmented.

The PPP decapsulation/classify microblock runs in a functional pipeline with the IPv4 microblock on 4 microengines or 32 threads.

Instruction cycles for worst case execution path: 266 clocks

The equivalent processing time per packet is 266/4 = 66.5 clocks because four MEs are operating on this task.

```
1: Get message from scratch memory (Scratch-Rd: 20B)

2: Read packet header from DRAM (DRAM-Rd: 32B)

3: Dbcast check from SRAM (SRAM-Rd: 32B)

4: Longest Prefix Match (LPM) Long (SRAM-Rd: 20B)

5: LPM Short (SRAM-Rd: 12B)

6: Read Next-Hop info (SRAM-Rd: 16B)

7: Write packet header to DRAM (DRAM-Wr: 32B)

8: Write metadata to SRAM (SRAM-Wr: 32B)

9: Write message to scratch for Queue Manager (Scratch-Wr: 12B)

10: Read control block from SRAM (SRAM-Rd: 4B)

11: Statistics update to SRAM (SRAM-Wr: 8B)
```

Table 8.6   PPP Decapsulation/Classification/IPv4

Step	Cmd bus	SRAM read	SRAM write	DRAM read	DRAM write	Scratch read	Scratch write
B-1	1					20	
B-2	1			32			
B-3	1	32					
B-4	5	20					
B-5	3	12					
B-6	1	16					
B-7	1				32		
B-8	1		32				
B-9	1						12
B-10	1	4					
B-11	2		8				
total	18	84	40	32	32	20	12

The units in this table are bytes of memory bandwidth or number of commands.

Queue Manager

The queue manager (QM) is responsible for performing enqueue and de-queue operations on the transmit queues, which are implemented using the hardware SRAM link lists. It accepts enqueue requests from the functional pipeline via a scratch ring. The enqueue requests are on a per-packet basis. The dequeue requests come from the transmit scheduler microengine on a per-cell basis where a cell is a CSIX cframe. Whenever an enqueue results in the queue state going from empty to non-empty or a dequeue operation results in the queue state going from non-empty to empty, the Queue Manager sends a message to the transmit scheduler via a next neighbor ring. Also after every dequeue, the QM passes a transmit request via a scratch ring to the CSIX TX microblock.

The threads on the QM microengine execute in strict order using local inter-thread signaling. SRAM queue array entries are cached in the SRAM controller, and the CAM is used for managing the tags for these. To maintain coherence among threads, folding is used.

The QM is a context pipe-stage that is implemented as a single microblock running on one microengine. Because this is the only code running on the microengine and it does not really process packets, there is no need for a dispatch loop.

Instruction cycles for worst case execution path: 74 clocks

```
Phase 1
1a: Read Dequeue Request from Scratch (Scratch Rd: 4B)

1b: Evict stale queue descriptor from Q_Array to SRAM
(SRAM-Wr: 16B)

1c: Read new queue descriptor from SRAM to Q_Array (SRAM-
Rd: 16B)

1d: Enqueue packet to SRAM linked list (SRAM-Wr: 4B)

1e: Send message of new packet to TX scheduler (Scratch-
Wr: 8B)


Phase 2
2a: Read enqueue request (Scratch Rd: 12B)
2b: Dequeue packet from linked list (SRAM-Rd: 4B)

2c: Evict queue descriptor from Q_Array to SRAM (SRAM-Wr:
16B)

2d: Read new queue descriptor from SRAM to Q_Array (SRAM-
Rd: 16B)
```

Table 8.7   QM Actual Bandwidth

Step	Cmd bus	SRAM read	SRAM write	DRAM read	DRAM write	Scratch read	Scratch write
C-1a	1					4	
C-1b	1		16				
C-1c	1	16					
C-1d	1		4				
C-1e	1						8
C-2a	1				12		
C-2b	1	4					
C-2c	1		16				
C-2d	1	16					
total	9	36	36			16	8

The units in this table are bytes of memory bandwidth or number of commands.

CSIX Transmit Scheduler

The CSIX scheduler schedules packets to be transmitted to the CSIX fabric. The scheduling algorithm implemented is Round Robin among the ports on the fabric and optionally Weighted Round Robin among the queues on a port. Because this application is not QoS and has only one queue per port, the Weighted Round Robin scheduling may either be compiled out or made to degenerate to round robin scheduling. The scheduling and transmit is done one Cframe at a time.

The CSIX scheduler microblock is a context pipe-stage that is implemented as a microblock that runs on 1 microengine. Because only this code is running on the microengine and it does not process packets, no dispatch loop is needed. The following is the pseudocode for the transmit scheduler. It has only one I/O instruction because this is more computationally intensive.

Instruction cycles for worst case execution path: 88 clocks

```
1: Issue deq request to the QM with a message to
     Scratch ring buffer. (Scratch-Wr: 4B)
```

Table 8.8   CSIX Transmit Scheduler Actual Bandwidth

Step	Cmd bus	SRAM read	SRAM write	DRAM read	DRAM write	Scratch read	Scratch write
D-1	1						4
total	1						4

The units in this table are bytes of memory bandwidth or number of commands.

CSIX Transmit Processing

The CSIX transmit microblock is a context pipe-stage that runs on a single microengine. It receives transmit messages from the queue manager. With each transmit request, the microblock moves a cframe into a TBUF, which is then transmitted into the fabric by the MSF Transmit State Machine. Because an entire CSIX frame is segmented into smaller frames prior to transmit, the transmit processing microengine caches the segmentation status locally.

Like in previous stages, the threads use folding and execute in strict order. If an entire buffer for a packet has been transmitted, the buffer is freed.

Instruction cycles for worst case execution path: 71 clocks

```
Phase 1
1a: Read transmit request from message ring (Scratch-Rd:
8B)

1b: Write prepend CSIX traffic manager data to MSF (1
CMD)

1c: Fill TBUF with payload from DRAM (DRAM-Rd: 120B)

1d: Validate TBUF to start transmit (1 CMD)

1e: Free packet buffer with SRAM enqueue operation (SRAM-
Wr: 4B)


Phase 2
2a: Evict LRU CSIX transmit segmentation status(SRAM-Wr:
16B)

2b: Read new CSIX segmentation status data (SRAM-Rd: 16B)

2c: Read Metadata of CSIX frame from SRAM (SRAM-Rd: 24B)
```

Table 8.9   Transmit Processing Actual Bandwidth

Step	Cmd bus	SRAM read	SRAM write	DRAM read	DRAM write	Scratch read	Scratch write
E-1a	1					8	
E-1b	1						
E-1c	1			120			
E-1d	1						
E-1e	1		4				
E-2a	1		16				
E-2b	1	16					
E-2c	1	24					
total	8	40	20	120		8	

The units in this table are bytes of memory bandwidth or number of commands.

OC-48 Performance Summary

Table 8.10 provides a summary of the OC-48 processing tasks. The "Total Budget" column indicates the total number of IXP2400 memory bus accesses and instructions that are available to process a *single* 49 byte POS packet at 2.4048 gigabits per second (with SONET overhead removed). The tasks in the other columns indicate how many bus accesses and instructions they individually use to process a *single* packet during a *single* packet time. The sum of these individual tasks is then compared to the total processing budget available to arrive at the total utilization and headroom. In this example, four of the tasks (POS receive, QM, TX schedule, and TX fill) use a single microengine, and thus their resource utilization is for a *single* packet. The PPP & IPv4 forwarding stage, however, is a four-stage functional pipeline utilizing four microengines, which has a total time duration of *four* packet arrival intervals. This task has a maximum 266 instructions during this four-packet arrival time period. However, because this analysis references each task to a single packet arrival time, the average number of instructions during a packet time is 66 (266 total instructions/ 4 packet arrival times). Because the total budget available is normalized to a *single* packet, this particular column for this task is scaled down for a *single* packet. By showing it this way, the total budget and all the tasks and then referenced to a single packet. A more representative way of illustrating this concept would be to duplicate the PPP and IPv4 column four times, but this would be too cumbersome for the text (and the table would stretch off the end of the page!).

Determining Task Memory Bandwidth Utilization

The task resource utilization is determined by simply taking a percentage of the resources used by a task vs. the total available. This example assumes a 49 byte packet size (40B IP packet with 9B PPP header). This equates to 6.13 million packets per second (Mpps) for an OC-48 bit rate. For example, the resource utilization results for the POS receive task is calculated as follows. See Table 8.3 for budgeted values.

Instructions:

Actual worst case instructions cycle time: 88 instructions
Budgeted instruction time: 97 clocks
% Utilization = 88/97 = 91%

SRAM (Writes):

SRAM writes: 16 Bytes
Total SRAM write budget: 261
% Utilization = 16/ 261 = 6.13 %

DRAM (Total):

DRAM writes: 64 bytes
Total DRAM budget: 391
% Utilization = 64/391 =   16.3 %

Command Bus:

I/O commands: 6
Total command budget: 96
% Utilization = 6 / 96 = 6.25 %

Once the resource utilizations are determined for each task, they are totaled to determine an overall utilization percentage. Determining the % headroom is simply 100 – utilization.

Table 8.10   Total Bandwidth Summary

Total Budget	POS Receive	PPP & IPv4 (Note)	Queue Manager	Transmit Scheduler	Transmit Fill
DRAM RD Utilization 38.9%	0	32 8.2%	0	0	120 30.7%
DRAM WR Utilization 24.6%	64 16.4 %	32 8.2%	0	0	0
Total DRAM (391 bytes/pkt) Headroom 36.5% Utilization 63.5%	64 16.4%	64 16.4%	0	0	120 30.7%
SRAM RD (261 bytes/pkt) Headroom 37.1% Utilization 62.9%	4 1.5%	84 32.2%	36 13.8%	0	40 15.4%
SRAM WR (261 bytes/pkt) Headroom 57.1% Utilization 42.9%	16 6.1%	40 15.3%	36 13.8%	0	20 7.7%
Command Bus (96 CMDs/pkt) Headroom 56.4% Utilization 43.6%	6 6.2%	18 18.7%	9 9.4%	1 1.0%	8 8.3%
Instruction 97/packet	88 90.7%	66 68.5%	74 76.3%	88 90.7%	71 73.2%

The units in this table are bytes of memory bandwidth or number of commands.

So far, this analysis has only focused on bandwidth performance. A time budget memory latency performance analysis is also needed. However, this second analysis is not nearly as elaborate or time-consuming. To help explain this technique, let's look at a simple single-ME task, where each thread processes a single packet. A single-phase task has 97 clocks per packet if the task is processing 49-byte IP over POS frames. With 8 threads per ME, the wall time is 97 x 8 = 776 clocks. In other words, each thread must retire a packet every 776 clocks before another packet arrives. Let's assume that SRAM and scratch operations have 130 cycles of latency and DRAM accesses have 300 clocks of latency. If a particular task has 1 DRAM, 2 scratch, and 1 SRAM operation, the total latency is $300 + 2*130 + 130 = 690$ cycles, which meets the 776 clock budget.

This analysis can be very helpful if you feel comfortable that you already have enough memory and bus bandwidth and those memory latencies are greater than total instruction processing time, which is a good assumption in many cases. By simply adding up your dependent memory references, you can get a very good first approximation if a particular task will fit in the allotted microengine(s).

Glossary

3DES is a more secure standard of DES that runs its algorithm three times with variations on the algorithm. The IXP2850 processor implements this algorithm.

ADT stands for Architecture Development Tool. Intel developed this tool to help system engineers estimate performance of applications and map tasks to microengines.

AES stands for Advanced Encryption Standard. The National Institute of Standards and Technology (NIST) initiated it to replace DES.

Aggregate_ID is an identifier used in the Pool of Threads (POTs) programming model to group similar packets together. By grouping similar packets together, threads won't block waiting for out-of-order packets from dissimilar flows to arrive at ordered processing nodes (OP nodes).

AISR stands for Asynchronous Insert, Synchronous Remove, the data structure and mechanism used in the Pool of Threads (POTs) programming model to ensure end-to-end packet ordering.

Atomic Memory Operation is a multi-access, Read-Modify-Write (RMW) memory operation in which no other memory accesses are interleaved between the separate memory accesses of the RMW. Atomic memory operations are important when updating critical data so software mechanisms aren't needed to lock the data during updates.

Cached Queue Descriptor is a queue descriptor that is cached in an SRAM Q_Array entry. A queue array "qnum" identifier is then stored in the MEv2 CAM.

Cbus is the CSIX flow control bus used to connect an egress IXP2XXX network processor that receives flow control messages to an ingress IXP2XXX network processor that is responsible for scheduling the data to be transmitted.

Cframe is another name for a CSIX frame. The three categories of Cframes are: data, control, flow control.

Chassis refers to the internal buses and arbitration units that form the internal data paths of network processors in the IXP2XXX product line.

Classification is the process of identifying a packet's flow, connection, input port, destination address, etc. The identification can be done by examining an application defined bit field within the packet's header. A bit field can also be examined in the payload for content based routing applications. The bit field is extracted from the packet and various search algorithms applied to compare the bit field to a table in external memory.

Context Pipeline Stage is a software pipeline wherein different functions are performed on different microengines as time progresses and the packet context is passed between the functions or microengines. Each microengine constitutes a context pipe stage and cascading two or more context pipe stages constitutes a context pipeline. The context pipeline gets its name from the fact that it is the context that moves through the pipeline.

Context is oftentimes called a thread. The MEv2 can maintain up to eight contexts (program counters, GPRs, Xfer registers, or local memory address pointers). The term context is also used to describe the current state of a flow or connection.

CP PDK stands for Control Plane Platform Development Kit. These control plane utilities and APIs are defined by the Network Processor Forum (NPF) and they run on the Intel XScale core or optional external control plane processor.

Control Plane is the abstraction for a functional area of an application that controls and configures the data plane and handles exception packets, distinguished from the data processing plane. Typically, control plane activities are performed by code modules within the IXA application. Compare this to "management plane," whose activities are in a host application that is usually outside the Intel IXA-based application.

Core Component is the slow-path counterpart of the microblock running on the XScale core.

Critical Section is a section of code executing one processing thread that requires exclusive access to a data structure so the code can update that data without concern that other threads simultaneously update the same data, causing data corruption errors. Critical sections need to ensure this exclusive access by locking down the data structure. A critical section is composed of three parts: the actual code that updates memory, the critical data that is being updated, and a critical data identifier that is used by the application software to reference the critical data.

CSIX-L1 stands for the Common Switch Interface. CSIX defines an interface between a Traffic Manager (TM) and a Switch Fabric (SF) for ATM, IP, MPLS, Ethernet, and similar data communications applications. The Network Processor Forum (NPF) controls the CSIX-L1 specification. The IXP2XXX network processor implements the TM functions in software.

Data Plane is commonly called the "fast path." The IXP2XXX micro-engines process the bulk of packet data.

Deli-Ticket Server refers to the method that ensures ordered locking in critical sections when using the Pool of Threads programming model.

Dependent Memory Operation is a memory operation that is required to complete before additional processing can take place.

DES stands for Data Encryption Standard. It is a crypto algorithm used in the IXP2850 and a 64-bit block cipher that uses a 56-bit key.

Dispatch Loop combines microblocks on a microengine and implements the data flow between them. The dispatch loop also caches the commonly used variables in registers or in local memory.

Distributed Cache is an Intel IXA mechanism that is used to minimize memory latency when updating critical data occurring during read-modify-write operations. Whereas a traditional cache closely dedicates a tag with its data, this distributed cache separates them, putting the cache tag into the MEv2 local CAM and the data either in the MEv2 local memory or in the SRAM Q_Array for linked list memory operations. Memory latency is reduced significantly because critical section data updates and dependency checking is done locally in the microengine.

DRR stands for Deficit Round Robin, a transmit-scheduling algorithm that allows for variable length packets.

Egress Path. When used in the context of a full-duplex line card for the IXP2XXX product line, the egress path is from the switch fabric to the network.

EOP stands for End of Packet.

Fast Path is also known as the data plane. The microengines of Intel IXA process the bulk of packet data, although the Intel Xscale core does some fast-path processing for some protocol processing. It is called the fast path because processing must keep up with line rate or risk dropping packets.

FIC stands for Fabric Interface Chip. The FIC interfaces IXP2XXX network processors with a switch fabric. Because the IXP2XXX processors implement traffic scheduling algorithms in software, the FIC doesn't require TM functionality.

Flow Control. Generally, the two types of flow control in the context of an Intel IXA system are: 1) link-level flow control, and 2) virtual output queue (VoQ) flow control. Link-level flow control regulates the transmission of data from one chip to another so that the receiving chip's input FIFO doesn't overflow. VoQ flow control ensures that a traffic manager on one blade won't overflow a virtual queue on another blade. While link-level flow control uses simple signals to regulate data flow, VoQ flow control uses message passing between a receiving node and a transmitting node in a system. Ethernet flow control can also be implemented with supported MACs.

Folding is a software technique that is used by threads running on the same microengine to optimize read-modify-writes in a critical section. The technique uses the CAM and strict thread ordering enforced via inter-thread signaling to fold the read/modify/write into a single read, into multiple modifies, and into one or more writes, depending on the cache eviction policy.

Function Pipeline is a software pipeline where the context remains within a microengine while different functions are performed on the packet as time progresses. The microengine execution time is divided into n pipe stages and each pipe stage performs a different function. The function pipeline gets its name from the fact that it is the function that moves through the pipeline.

GTS stands for generalized thread signaling, also known as event signaling. Event signals are used to coordinate a program with completion of external events. For example, when a microengine issues a command to an external unit to read data, which will be written into a Transfer_In register, the program must ensure that the microenine does not try to use the data until the external unit has written it. No hardware mechanism flags that a register write is pending then prevents the program from using it. Instead, the coordination is under software control, with hardware support.

HAL is the Hardware Abstraction Library, which provides operating system-like abstraction of hardware assisted functions. It is composed of two sub-libraries: the instruction simplification library and the OS emulation library.

HMAC stands for Hashed Message Authentication Code.

HTC stands for Hyper Task Chaining, a software pipeline programming model that uses a functional pipeline and context pipeline. HTC is the optimal packet processing model when homogeneous processing tasks are expected over the vast majority of traffic. HTC achieves its high speed due to the folding techniques used in functional and context pipelines.

Ingress Path. When used in the context of a full-duplex line card for the IXP2XXX product line, the ingress path is from the network to the switch fabric.

Intel IXA stands for Intel Internet Exchange Architecture, an architecture that allows for software-reprogrammable silicon and open APIs.

Intel XScale core is a general purpose processor core based on the ARM V5TE instruction set.

Interleaved Threading is a software technique that is used when a large imbalance of memory latencies happens over compute cycles. To offset the imbalance, a thread processes multiple packets so the microengines are busy constantly and not waiting for the completion of dependent memory references.

IXF1010 is an Intel SPI-4.2 MAC that integrates ten Ethernet MACs of 1 Gigabit.

IXF1104 is an Intel SPI-3 MAC integrating four 1 Gigabit Ethernet MACs.

IXF18105 is an Intel SPI-4.2 dual port Gigabit Ethernet MAC with dual XAUI interfaces.

IXF6048 is an Intel SPI-3 framer that integrates one OC-48 SONET framer or four OC-12 framers.

IXF810X is an Intel framer that performs section/line and high-order path termination for STS-192C. It implements PPP mapping and 10 Gigabit Ethernet MAC. This framer supports Generic Framing Procedure for RPR, DPT, Ethernet and SONET.

Linked List refers to an ordered list of data buffers stored at discontiguous addresses. The first buffer added to the queue is the first buffer removed from the queue. Queue entries are joined by creating links from one data buffer to the next. Packets are enqueued (added) to the tail of the list and dequeued (removed) from the head. A linked list descriptor contains the head address, tail address, and other relevant parameters to manage the queue.

Long Word refers to a 32-bit word, 4 bytes long.

MAC stands for Medium Access Control, a protocol layer responsible for providing access to a shared communications medium. It also stands for Medium Access Controller, the device used to interface with the physical layer medium.

MSF stands for Media and Switch Fabric Interface. The MSF is the primary packet interface between network processors in the IXP2XXX product line and the network (via MACs and framers) or switch fabrics (via FICs).

Microblock is a discrete unit of microcode or MicroC that is written according to the guidelines specified in the Intel IXA Portability Framework. Microblocks conform to one of three types: source, transform, or sink. Typically, a microblock has an Intel XScale core component that is used to configure and manage the microblock.

Microblock Group refers to one or more microblocks that have been combined into a thread that is executable on a microengine. Typically, all threads on the microengine execute the same microblock group, but they are not required to do so.

MEv2 refers to the microengines used in network processors in the IXP2XXX product line.

M-packet is a media bus interface data transfer unit that can be configured to be 64, 128, or 256 bytes in length.

MPHY is a term used to describe SPI and UTOPIA PHYs that have multiple ports.

MUTEX, for MUtual EXclusion, is a data structure used to protect critical data during a read-modify-write operation. A thread that is about to perform an RMW sets a MUTEX to a lock state so other threads can determine that the data is currently being updated and is unavailable. Context and functional pipelines use a MUTEX in the CAM that is local in the microengine. The Pool of Threads programming model has a MUTEX in external SRAM.

NPF stands for Network Processor Forum, a standards body that standardizes software and hardware interfaces for network processors.

Next Neighbor Registers are MEv2 registers for processors in the IXP2XXX product line that receive data from the previous neighbor via a direct, low latency data path. The register set allows for efficient message and data passing from one microengine to its nearest downstream neighbor.

OP stands for ordered processing node. An OP node is used in the Pool of Threads programming model to identify a node in a flow graph that requires packets to be processed in order.

OSSL stands for Operating System Services Library, an operating system abstraction API used within the Intel IXA SDK to achieve portability.

Partial Packet Ordering requires packets to be processed in order at OP nodes within a flow graph. This method is opposed to end-to-end packet order which is resolved by the AISR data structure and Sequence_ID numbers.

POS stands for Packet over SONET.

PHY is the physical layer, the first layer in the seven-layer OSI reference model.

Policing is a mechanism to force traffic to comply with certain quality of service metrics, such as constant bit rate and maximum burst size.

POTs stands for Pool of Threads, a packet-processing model optimized for heterogeneous packet processing where processing time can vary widely from packet to packet. POTs uses a familiar programming model in which the packets run to completion from beginning to end, by one program that is written in either microcode or microC.

Q_Array Controller is a data structure and any associated control logic integrated within each channel of the network processor's SRAM unit. The Q_Array controller allows for automated linked list and ring buffer operations.

QoS stands for Quality-of-Service, a networking term that specifies a guaranteed throughput level.

Queue is a linked list of packets.

Queue Manager is an context pipeline for the IXP2XXX product line that receives enqueue messages from a packet processing stage and dequeue messages from a traffic scheduler. The enqueue messages request a packet to be put on the tail of a queue while dequeue messages request a packet to be removed from the head of a queue.

Quadword is a 64-bit word, 8 bytes long.

RBUF is the receive buffer in the IXP2XXX network processor's MSF.

Reflector Reads and Writes refers to a SHaC function that supports reading the data from a device on the pull bus and writing the data to a device on the push bus, thereby reflecting the data from one bus to the other. A typical implementation of this mode is to allow a microengine to read or write the transfer registers or CSRs in another microengine.

Resident Queue Descriptor is a non-cached, linked list descriptor that resides in a Q_Array entry, and it is used for frequently used data structures such as free buffer lists.

Resource Manager is a programming interface between Intel XScale core applications and the microcode running on the microengines for IXP2XXX network processors.

Ring Buffer is a circular queue consisting of a base address, length, head address, and tail address.

Scratchpad Memory is a third memory resource for applications to use in addition to SRAM and DRAM. Scratch memory is used for frequently used data to minimize SRAM bandwidth and for situations where the lowest latency access is required.

SDK 3.0 is the product name for the Intel IXA Software Development Kit for assembling, compiling, linking, and simulating MEv2 microengine code for IXP2XXX network processors.

Sequence _ID# is used with the Pool of Threads programming model. The packet receiver assigns a sequence_ID to a newly received packet so AISR can properly maintain end-to-end packet ordering. The sequence number is assigned based on the order in which a packet was received. Multiple sequence_IDs are within a single aggregate_ID.

SHA-1 refers to the Secure Hash Algorithm, which is used in the IXP2850's crypto unit.

SHaC is a functional unit in IXP2XXX network processors that contains the scratch memory, hash unit, and chip wide CSR registers. The SHaC also controls reflector read and writes.

Sink Microblocks refers to a function or macro that disposes of a packet, that is, either enqueues it within the processor or sends it to an external interface.

SLA stands for Service Level Agreement.

Slow Path is the execution path of packets that require exception handling. This group can be error packets or packets that need to be handled differently than the normal case. In this case, these packets take longer to process because they are handled by a general-purpose processor (the Intel XScale core in systems based on Intel IXA).

SOP is start of packet.

Source Microblocks refers to a function or macro that obtains a packet, that is, either dequeues it within the network processor or gets it from an external interface.

SPI stands for System Packet Interface.

SrTCM is Single Rate Tri-Color Market metering algorithm.

TBUF is the transmit buffer in the MSF unit.

TCAM stands for Ternary Content Addressable Memory. This specialized co-processor memory chip searches for an address when given the data. A TCAM can search on data patterns that use bits 0, 1, or X (called "don't care"bits) for range matching.

Threads. One physical processor can behave as multiple logical processors or threads. A single MEv2 microengine supports up to eight threads.

Transform Microblocks is a function or macro that parses, analyzes, classifies, or modifies a packet.

Transmit Queue is an ordered list of scheduled packets that are waiting to be transmitted.

UTOPIA stands for Universal Test and Operations Interface for ATM, which is the standard chip-to-chip interface for ATM traffic shapers, SARs, and framers.

VoQ stands for Virtual Output Queue.

VPN stands for Virtual Private Network.

Wall Time refers to the total time for a thread or a group of threads—for example, eight threads for one MEv2 microengine—to complete a task before picking up another packet for processing or risk dropping the packet. The total processing time is a sum of all the compute cycles and memory references.

WRR stands for Weighted Round Robin, a transmit scheduling algorithm that ensures fairness to all queues by assigning a weighted priority to each.

WRED stands for Weighted Random Early Detection, a congestion avoidance algorithm that randomly discards packets based on current queue depth for the packet. WRED discards a packet based on its relative priority.

Xfer registers are I/O registers in the microengine allow data to be transferred between a microengine and other microengine or functional units of the network processor. Transfer registers attach to the internal S and D push and pull buses of the chassis.

References

Adiletta, Matthew, Mark Rosenbluth, Debra Bernstein, and Hugh Wilkinson, "The Next Generation of Intel IXP Network Processors," *Intel Technology Journal*, Volume 06, Issue 03 (August 15, 2002). www.intel.com/technology/itj/2002/volume06issue03/index.htm.

CSIX_L1 Specification. The document is available from the Network Processor Forum (NPF) at www.npforum.org.

Durham, David and Raj Yavatkar. *Inside the Internet's Resource ReSerVation Protocol: Foundations for Quality of Service*. New York: John Wiley and Sons, 1999.

Feghali, Wajdi, Brad Burres, Gilbert Wolrich, and Douglas Carrigan, "Security: Adding Protection to the Network via the Network Processor," *Intel Technology Journal*, Volume 06, Issue 03 (August 15, 2002). www.intel.com/technology/itj/2002/volume06issue03/index.htm

Intel® Internet Exchange Architecture (IXA) Portability Framework Developer's Manual, Intel Corporation, October 2002.

Intel® IXP2800 Hardware Reference Manual, Intel Corporation, January 2003.

Intel® IXP2400 Hardware Reference Manual, Intel Corporation, October 2002.

Intel® IXP2400/IXP2800 Network Processor Programmer's Reference Manual, Intel Corporation, 2003.

Johnson, Erik J and Aaron Kunze. *IXP2400/2800 Programming: The Complete Microengine Coding Guide*. Hillsboro: Intel Press, 2003.

Lakshmanamurthy, Sridhar, Kin-Yip Liu, Yim Pun, Larry Huston, and Uday Naik, "Network Processor Performance Analysis Methodology," *Intel Technology Journal*, Volume 06, Issue 03 (August 15, 2002). www.intel.com/technology/itj/2002/volume06issue03/index.htm

PCI Local Bus Specification Revision 2.2, PCI Special Interest Group, December 18, 1998. www.pcisig.com.

Index

C

" *As the pace of technology introduction increases it's difficult to keep up. Intel Press has established an impressive portfolio. The breadth of topics is a reflection of both Intel's diversity as well as our commitment to serve a broad technical community.*

I hope you will take advantage of these products to further your technical education. "

Patrick Gelsinger
Senior Vice President and Chief Technology Officer
Intel Corporation

**Turn the page to learn about titles
from Intel Press for system developers**

Get Up to Speed on the Latest Intel Network Processor Family

IXP2400/2800 Programming
The Complete Microengine Coding Guide
Erik J. Johnson and Aaron R. Kunze
ISBN 0-9717861-6-X

Intel Senior Network Software Engineers Erik Johnson and Aaron Kunze bring their key insights to programming for the Intel® IXP2XXX Network Processor family. Software and firmware engineers developing products based on the IXP2400, IXP2800, or IXP2850 network processors will find this guide to be an invaluable resource. Whether you are new to programming Intel® network processors or already familiar with the IXP1200, this book is designed to help you come up to speed quickly on the IXP2XXX architecture.

IXP2400/2800 Programming progresses through a set of tasks typically faced by network software engineers, from basic receive and transmit operations to more complex packet processing. Each task is decomposed, through working example code in both microengine C and microengine assembly, into what the appropriate parts of the software and hardware can do, and explains why it is important to the design and implementation. The various tradeoffs that are possible within the software and hardware are fully analyzed as well. The book progresses in steps from simple, single-threaded programs to a complete multithreaded reference application using the microblock programming paradigm. Application and programming notes are used throughout the book to accelerate the pace for readers already familiar with IXP1200 programming. Complete and working code examples from the book are included on the accompanying CD-ROM, as well as the Intel® IXA Software Developer's Kit.

> **66** *Every developer who wants to program the IXP2XXX should read this book.* **99**
>
> Steve Yates, President & Chief Technology Office, ADI Engineering

IXP1200 Programming

The Microengine Coding Guide for the Intel® IXP1200 Network Processor Family
By Erik J. Johnson and Aaron Kunze
ISBN 0-9712887-8-X

As very deep submicron ASIC design gets both more costly and time-consuming, the communications industry seeks alternatives providing rich services with higher capability. The key to increased flexibility and performance is the innovation incorporated in the IXP1200 family of network processors. From engineers who were there at the beginning, you can learn how to program the microengines of Intel's IXP12xx network processors through a series of expanding examples, covering such key topics as receiving, processing, and transmitting packets; synchronizing between hardware threads; debugging; optimizing; and tuning your program for the highest performance.

Increase performance with this hands-on coding guide

Introduction to PCI Express†

A Hardware and Software Developer's Guide
By Adam Wilen, Justin Schade, and Ron Thornburg
ISBN 0-9702846-9-1

Written by key Intel insiders who have worked to implement Intel's first generation of PCI Express chipsets and who work directly with customers who want to take advantage of PCI Express, this introduction to the new I/O technology explains how PCI Express is designed to increase computer system performance. The book explains in technical detail how designers can use PCI Express technology to overcome the practical performance limits of existing multi-drop, parallel bus technology. The authors draw from years of leading-edge experience to explain how to apply these new capabilities to a broad range of computing and communications platforms.

❝This book helps software and hardware developers get a jumpstart on their development cycle that can decrease their time to market.❞

Ajay Kwatra, Engineer Strategist, Dell Computer Corporation

● InfiniBand† Architecture Development and Deployment
A Strategic Guide to Server I/O Solutions
By William T. Futral
ISBN 0-9702846-6-7

InfiniBand, a contemporary switched fabric I/O architecture for system I/O and inter-process communication, offers new and exciting benefits to architects, designers, and engineers. Intel I/O Architect William Futral was a major contributor to InfiniBand architecture from its inception. Currently, he serves as Co-Chair of the InfiniBand Application Working Group. His comprehensive guide details the InfiniBand architecture, and offers sound, practical expert tips to fully implement and deploy InfiniBand-based products, including deployment strategies, InfiniBand-based applications, and management.

Develop leading edge server I/O solutions

● Serial ATA Storage Architecture and Applications
Designing High-Performance, Low-Cost I/O Solutions
By Knut Grimsrud and Hubbert Smith
ISBN 0-9717861-8-6

Serial ATA, a new hard disk interconnect standard for PCs, laptops, and more is fast becoming a serious contender to Parallel ATA and SCSI. Computer engineers and architects worldwide must answer important questions for their companies: "Why make the change to Serial ATA? What problems does Serial ATA solve for me? How do I transition from parallel ATA to Serial ATA and from SCSI to Serial ATA?" The authors of this essential book, both Intel Serial ATA specialists, have the combined expertise to help you answer these questions. Systems engineers, product architects, and product line managers who want to affect the right decisions for their products undoubtedly will benefit from the straight talk offered by these authors. The book delivers reliable information with sufficient technical depth on issues such as Phy signaling and interface states, protocol encoding, programming model, flow control, performance, compatibility with legacy systems, enclosure management, signal routing, hot-plug, presence detection, activity indication, power management, and cable/connector standards.

❝This book provides explanations and insights into the underlying technology to help ease design and implementation.❞

Rhonda Gass, Vice President, Storage Systems Development
Dell Computer Corporation

About Intel Press

Intel Press is the authoritative source of timely, highly relevant, and innovative books to help software and hardware developers speed up their development process. We collaborate only with leading industry experts to deliver reliable, first-to-market information about the latest technologies, processes and strategies.

Our products are planned with the help of many people in the developer community and we encourage you to consider becoming a customer advisor. If you would like to help us and gain additional advance insight to the latest technologies, we encourage you to consider the Intel Press Customer Advisor Program. You can **register** here:

www.intel.com/intelpress/register.htm

For information about bulk orders or corporate sales, please send email to **bulkbooksales@intel.com**.

Other Developer Resources from Intel

At these Web sites you can also find valuable technical information and resources for developers:

developer.intel.com	general information for developers
www.intel.com/IDS	content, tools, training, and the Early Access Program for software developers
www.intel.com/software/products	programming tools to help you develop high-performance applications
www.intel.com/idf	world-wide technical conference, the Intel Developer Forum